Migration, Education and Change

Migration has become increasingly important in Europe with far-reaching consequences in the political, economic and social spheres, and particularly regarding education. This book discusses educational responses to immigration in six European countries – France, Germany, Great Britain, Greece, the Netherlands and Sweden – as well as in Australia from different viewpoints.

The multifaceted contributions in this book deal with both the classical and the more recent forms of migration and investigate their divergent educational implications regarding key questions such as integration and cohesion, language education, and multicultural education. An examination of Australia's experiences as a 'classical country of immigration' contributes to a better understanding of some of the processes experienced in European countries due to migration.

Another focal point of this collection is the challenges yet to be met. The following aspects in particular are examined closely: the underachievement of students with a migration background in comparison to the educational norm; the situation of children whose parents are undocumented migrants and the role of changing patterns in transnational migration as regards future developments in education.

The detailed discussion of the history of migration and its impacts on education in nation states make *Migration, Education and Change* essential reading for advanced students and researchers in the fields of education and migration and those interested in the current discourse on multicultural education.

Sigrid Luchtenberg is Professor in the Faculty of Education at Duisburg-Essen University, Germany. Her research interests and publications deal with many aspects of multicultural education including questions of comparative, media, bilingual and citizenship education.

Routledge research in education

Migration, Education and Change

Edited by Sigrid Luchtenberg

Routledge
Taylor & Francis Group

LONDON AND NEW YORK

First published 2004
by Routledge
2 Park Square, Milton Park, Abingdon, Oxfordshire OX14 4RN

Simultaneously published in the USA and Canada
by Routledge
29 West 35th Street, New York, NY 10001

Routledge is an imprint of the Taylor & Francis Group

© 2004 Editorial matter and selection, Sigrid Luchtenberg;
individual chapters, the contributors

Typeset in Baskerville by Wearset Ltd, Boldon, Tyne and Wear
Printed and bound in Great Britain by MPG Books Ltd, Bodmin

British Library Cataloguing in Publication Data
A catalogue record for this book is available from the British Library

Library of Congress Cataloging in Publication Data
Migration, education, and change / edited by Sigrid Luchtenberg.
    p. cm.
  Includes bibliographical references and index.
  1. Immigrants–Education. 2. Multicultural education. 3. Emigration
and immigration–Social aspects. I. Luchtenberg, Sigrid, 1946–
    LC3715.M54 2004
    371.9′086′912–dc22

                                                              2004000326

ISBN 0-415-32203-0

Contents

Illustrations

Figures

Tables

Contributors

James A. Banks is Russell F. Stark University Professor and Director of the Center for Multicultural Education at the University of Washington, Seattle. His books include *Teaching Strategies for Ethnic Studies*, *Educating Citizens in a Multicultural Society*, the *Handbook of Research on Multicultural Education*, and *Diversity and Citizenship Education: Global Perspectives*. Professor Banks is a past president of the National Council for the Social Studies (NCSS) and of the American Educational Research Association (AERA). He is a member of the Board on Children, Youth and Families of the National Research Council and the Institute of Medicine of the National Academy of Sciences. He is also a member of the National Academy of Education.

Guus Extra studied Applied Linguistics at the University of Nijmegen in the Netherlands from 1964 to 1970. From 1970 until 1981, he was a Senior Lecturer at the same university, in the Department of Dutch Studies and Applied Linguistics. After defending his dissertation on second language acquisition at Nijmegen University (1978), he was a postdoctoral fellow at Stanford University (Department of Linguistics) and at Berkeley (School of Education) in 1978–1979. Since 1981 he has held the Chair of Language and Minorities in the Faculty of Arts at Tilburg University. In 1999, he was appointed Director of Babylon, Center for Studies of Multilingualism in the Multicultural Society, at Tilburg University. Recent publications include: Extra, G. and Gorter, D. (eds) (2001) *The Other Languages of Europe*, Clevedon: Multilingual Matters and Extra, G., Aarts, R., Avoird, T., Broeder, P. and Yağmur, K. (2002) *De Andere Talen van Nederland*, Bussum: Coutinho.

Christine Inglis is Honorary Associate Professor and Director of the Multicultural and Migration Research Centre, University of Sydney. She obtained her Ph.D. from the London School of Economics. Her research interests involve migration and ethnic relations. Current research projects include a study of transnationalism among Turkish, Hong Kong and Chinese born in Australia, a study of second generation mobility in Australia. Among her books are *Multiculturalism: New Policy*

Responses to Diversity (1996); *Teachers in the Sun: The Impact of Immigrant Teachers on the Labour Force* (1995); '*Making Something of Myself . . .*' *Educational Attainment and Social and Economic Mobility of Turkish Young People in Australia* (1992).

Françoise Lorcerie is a graduate of the Paris Institute of Political Studies and of the Paris University of Arts (with the 'agrégation', the highest teaching diploma in France). She has been teaching at various universities (Paris, Algiers, Aix-en-Provence), and is now a CNRS researcher at the Institute for Research and Studies in the Arab and Muslim World – IREMAM (L'Institut de recherches et d'études sur le Monde arabe et musulman) in Aix-en-Provence. Her main working topic is public action in European states as challenged by ethnicity and immigrants' integration, particularly in the educational field. Recently, she has carried out empirical studies on the connection between French educational policies and urban policies, and on the dialectics between modernizing Islam and politicizing Islam in French public debates (notably the question of changing secularism). She has also redefined interculturalism in this environment and, parallel to this, has concentrated on elaborating the theory of ethnicity and ethnicization in social sciences while clarifying the major conceptual connections in the paradigm that was founded by Max Weber. She is the author of numerous articles and chapters (in French) in this field of work. Her book *L'Ecole et le défi ethnique* (ed. INRP & ESF, Paris, 2003, with coll.) provides an integrated presentation of the theory of ethnicity, and various sociological and normative perspectives on school(s) in France.

Sigrid Luchtenberg has a Ph.D. in German Linguistics and Literature and habilitated in Multicultural Education. She is Professor in the Faculty of Education at Duisburg-Essen University, Germany. Her research interests and publications have always been closely related to German as a first, second or foreign language, but over the last years multicultural education, multicultural communication, the multiculturalism discourse in the media, and citizenship education in a multicultural society have become her dominant areas of research. Multicultural education is closely connected with her interests in comparative education (with a focus on Australia, where she has stayed several times as a Visiting Professor at the University of Sydney). Recent publications include *Interkulturelle Kommunikative Kompetenz. Kommunikationsfelder in Schule und Gesellschaft (Intercultural Communicative Competence)*, (1999) Wiesbaden: Westdeutscher Verlag; 'Bilingualism and bilingual education and its relationship to citizenship from a comparative German–Australian viewpoint', *Intercultural Education* 13: 1, 2002, 49–61; 'Ethnic diversity and citizenship education in Germany', in J. A. Banks (ed.) *Diversity and Citizenship Education: Global Perspectives* (2003). San Francisco: Jossey-Bass/Wiley, 245–271.

Sabine Mannitz (born 1965) is a researcher at the Peace Research Institute in Frankfurt on Main. She studied ethnology, social anthropology and political science at the University of Hamburg and the Goethe University of Frankfurt on Main. She specialized in urban anthropology, migration, and the social construction of identities, and was research officer at the European University Viadrina of Frankfurt on the Oder and at the University of Essex, UK. She is author of several articles on education and migration and the strategies of identification among post-migration youths in Germany. Her most recent article is to be found in: *Civil Enculturation: Nation-State, School and Ethnic Difference in Four European Countries*, Schiffauer, W., Baumann, G., Kastoryano, R. and Vertovec, S. (eds) (2004) Oxford and New York: Berghahn Books.

Soula Mitakidou is an Assistant Professor in the Department of Primary Education at Aristotle University of Thessaloniki, Greece. She received her BA from the English Department at Aristotle University, her MA in American Literature from McGill University in Montreal and her Ph.D. in Education from Aristotle University. She teaches anti-racist education, second language acquisition among non-native speakers and literature-based approaches to language learning. Her teaching experience covers a wide age range from preschool to graduate school students, and she has worked extensively with teachers in in-service workshops. Her recent publications and presentations focus on many aspects of diversity including integrated instructional strategies and marginalized learners. She is the co-author of the books *Mr. Semolina-Semolinus: A Greek Folktale* (New York: Atheneum Books for Young Readers, 1997) and the book *Folktales from Greece: A Treasury of Delights* (Greenwood, Colorado: Libraries Unlimited, 2002), both in English. She also co-authored the book *Teaching Language and Mathematics Through Literature* (Thessaloniki: Paratiritis, 2002), in Greek.

Tore Otterup is a university teacher and researcher at the Institute for Swedish as a Second Language, Department of Swedish Language, Göteborg University, Sweden. His special field of interest is second language acquisition in school and bilingualism among youths. He teaches subjects in connection with this within teacher training programmes and other university programmes as well as advanced training courses for practicing teachers. In addition to this he is a participant in the (Swedish) national research project 'Language and Language Use among Youths in Multilingual Settings' and also a member of the EU–ERASMUS CDA – project CANE (Cultural Awareness in Europe). He has published articles mainly about language acquisition, language development and identity-forming among adolescents in multicultural and multilingual settings, e.g. 'From monolingualism to multilingualism – The Swedish example', in Furch, E. (ed.) (2003) *Cultural Awareness in Europe*, Wien: Lernen mit Pfiff, 160–188.

Ludger Pries teaches in the Department of Social Science, Ruhr-Universität (Ruhr University) Bochum, Germany where he holds a Chair in the Sociology of Organizations and Participation Studies (SOAPS). His research fields are Comparative Sociology of Work, Organizations and Migration. Recent publications include 'Labour migration, social incorporation and transmigration in the New Europe. The case of Germany in a comparative perspective', *Transfer* (Brussels), Vol. 9, 2003; 'Emerging production systems in the transnationalization of German carmakers: Adaptation, application or innovation?', *New Technology, Work and Employment*, Vol. 18: 2, 2003, 82–100; *New Transnational Social Spaces. International Migration and Transnational Companies* (ed.), London: Routledge, 2001; 'The disruption of social and geographic space. US–Mexican migration and the emergence of transnational social spaces', *International Sociology*, Volume 16: 1/201, 55–74; *Soziologie Internationaler Migration. Einführung in Klassische Theorien und neue Ansätze (Sociology of International Migration. An Introduction to Classical Theories and New Approaches)*, Bielefeld: Transcript, 2000; *Auf dem Weg zu Global Operierenden Konzernen? BMW, Daimler-Benz und Volkswagen – Die Drei Großen der deutschen Automobilindustrie (Towards Globally Operating Companies? BMW, Daimler-Benz and Volkswagen – The Big Three of the German Automobile Industry)*, München/Mering: Rainer Hampp Verlag, 1999.

Sally Tomlinson is Emeritus Professor of Education at Goldsmiths College, London University, and a Research Associate in the Department of Educational Studies, Oxford University. She has researched, written and taught in the area of race, ethnicity and education for some 30 years. Her book *Education in a Post-Welfare Society* won a British Education Studies prize for the best education book published in 2002 (McGraw-Hill/Open University Press). An article on 'Globalization, race and education' is published in the *Journal of Education Change*, 2003 (Kluwer).

Georgios Tsiakalos is a Professor at Aristotle University of Thessaloniki, Greece where he is currently the Dean of the Faculty of Education. He received a Ph.D. (Dr.rer.nat.) from the University of Kiel (Germany) in Biology and Geology/Palaeontology, and a Ph.D. (D.Phil.) from the University of Bremen (Germany) in Education and Social Sciences. He taught in numerous universities in Germany before he was appointed as Professor of Education at Aristotle University of Thessaloniki in 1984. He has done research in the following areas: population genetics; racism and sociobiology; social exclusion and poverty; education of migrants and minorities; educational praxis; educational reforms. His recent main publications are the books (all in Greek): *Handbook of Antiracist Education* (Athens: Ellinika Grammata, 2000), *The Promise of Pedagogy* (Thessaloniki: Paratiritis, 2002), *Reflections of Human Society* (Thessaloniki: Paratiritis, 2004). He is an activist in many initiatives in support of immigrants, minorities and socially excluded people.

Kutlay Yağmur received his BA degree in English Language Teaching from the Middle East Technical University, Ankara. He pursued his postgraduate degrees in Australia. He received his MA in Applied Linguistics from Macquarie University, Sydney in 1991 and a postgraduate diploma in Education from Charles Stuart University, Australia in 1992. He investigated first language attrition and ethnolinguistic vitality of Turkish in Australia as part of his Ph.D. dissertation. He defended his dissertation at Nijmegen University, the Netherlands in 1997. He worked at Middle East Technical University from 1993 until 1996. Since 1996 he has worked as Assistant Professor of Applied Linguistics at Babylon, Tilburg University. Recent publications include Yağmur, K. and Akinci, M. A. (2003) 'Language use, choice, maintenance and ethnolinguistic vitality of Turkish speakers in France: Intergenerational differences', *International Journal of the Sociology of Language*, 164: 107–128; Fürstenau, S., Gogolin, I. and Yağmur, K. (eds) (2003) *Mehrsprachigkeit in Hamburg: Ergebnisse einer Sprachenerhebung an den Grundschulen in Hamburg* (*Multilingualism in Hamburg: The Status of Immigrant Minority Languages at Home and at School*), Münster and Berlin: Waxmann.

Foreword

James A. Banks

Migration within and across nation states is a worldwide phenomenon. The movement of peoples across national boundaries is as old as the nation state itself – as the chapters in this book make clear. However, never before in the history of world migration has the movement of diverse racial, cultural, ethnic, religious and language groups within and across nation states been as numerous and rapid or raised such complex and difficult questions about citizenship, human rights, democracy and education. Many worldwide trends and developments are challenging the notion of educating students to function in one nation state. They include the ways in which people are moving back and forth across national borders, the rights of movement permitted by the European Union, and the rights codified in the Universal Declaration of Human Rights.

Prior to the ethnic revitalization movements of the 1960s and 1970s, the aim of schools in most nation states was to develop citizens who internalized their national values, venerated their national heroes, and accepted glorified versions of their national histories. These goals of citizenship education are obsolete today because many people have multiple national commitments and live in multiple nation states. However, the development of citizens who have global and cosmopolitan identities and commitments is contested in nation states throughout the world because nationalism remains strong. Nationalism and globalization coexist in tension worldwide.

The chapters in this book describe the complex educational issues with which nation states in Europe must deal when trying to respond to the problems wrought by international migration in ways consistent with their democratic ideologies and declarations. As Tomlinson points out (Chapter 5) when discussing the schooling of non-White ethnic groups in Britain – and other authors note when describing the education of minority groups in other European nations – there is a wide gap between the democratic ideals in European nations and the daily educational experiences of minority groups in their schools. Ethnic minority students in Europe, as in other nations throughout the world, often experience discrimination because of their cultural, language and value differences. Both students and teachers often perceive these students as the 'Other'. When they are marginalized within school and treated as the 'Other', ethnic minority students, such as the Turkish students described by Mannitz in Chapter 4, tend to emphasize their ethnic identity and to have a weak attachment to their nation state. Mannitz also points out that Turkish students in Germany are also ambivalent about a German identity because of the Nazi period in Germany's history.

The chapters in this book examine a number of salient issues, paradigms and ideologies that democratic nation states and their schools must grapple with as their populations become more culturally, racially, ethnically and linguistically diverse. The extent to which nation states make multicultural citizenship possible, the achievement gap between minority and majority groups, and the language rights of immigrant and minority groups are among the unresolved and contentious issues examined in this informative book.

Nation states throughout the world are trying to determine whether they will perceive themselves as multicultural and allow immigrants to experience multicultural citizenship (Kymlicka 1995) or continue to embrace an assimilationist ideology. In nation states that embrace Kymlicka's idea of multicultural citizenship, immigrant and minority groups can retain important aspects of their languages and cultures as well as have full citizenship rights. Nation states in various parts of the world have responded to the citizenship and cultural rights of immigrant and minority groups in significantly different ways. Since the ethnic revitalization movements of the 1960s and 1970s, many of the national leaders and citizens in the United States, Canada and Australia have viewed these nation states as multicultural democracies (Banks and Lynch 1986). An ideal exists within these nation states that minority groups can maintain important elements of their community cultures and become full citizens of the nation state. However, there is a wide gap between the ideals within these nation states and the experiences of ethnic groups. Ethnic minority groups in the United States, Canada and Australia experience discrimination in both the schools and in the wider society.

Other nation states, such as Japan and Germany, have been reluctant to view themselves as multicultural societies. Citizenship has been closely linked to biological heritage and characteristics in these nation states. Although the biological conception of citizenship in both Japan and Germany has eroded within the last decade, it left a tenacious legacy in both nation states. As Mannitz writes in Chapter 4, 'the distinction of foreigners vis-à-vis Germans was a matter of routine in most teachers' daily practice and discourse, and it was connected to culturalist interpretations'. Castles refers to Germany's response to immigrants as 'differential exclusion', which is 'partial and temporary integration of immigrant workers into society – that is, they are included in those subsystems of society necessary for their economic role: the labor market, basic accommodation, work-related health care, and welfare' (2004: 32).

Since the 1960s and 1970s, the French have dealt with immigrant groups in ways distinct from the immigrant nations of the United States, Canada and Australia. In France the explicit goal is assimilation (now called integration) and inclusion (Castles 2004). Immigrant groups can become full citizens in France but the price is cultural assimilation. Immigrants are required to surrender their languages and cultures in order to become full citizens.

The academic achievement gap between ethnic minority and majority group students is another salient issue examined by several of the chapters in this book. African-Caribbean, Pakistani, and Bangladeshi students in Britain and Turkish students in Germany are not achieving on a level equal to that of the majority groups in their nation states. There is also a significant achievement gap between African-American students and White students in the United States (Banks and Banks 2004). However, the underachievement of minority students is a complex issue worldwide that defies facile solutions and responses. Tomlinson (in Chapter 5) points out that Indian and Chinese students are the highest achieving students in Britain. In Chapter 6 Lorcerie reports a study by Vallet and Caille (1996) which found 'a statistically strong advantage in favour of the immigrants' children on entering secondary schools' in France. In the United States, Chinese, Japanese and Asian-Indian students often exceed White students in academic achievement.

Throughout his career the anthropologist John U. Ogbu (Gibson and Ogbu 1991) tried to uncover some of the complex issues related to the differential achievement of ethnic minority groups in various nations. He believed that researchers needed to identify the important difference among ethnic minority groups in order to understand why some were highly successful academically and others were not. His classification of ethnic groups into three types (*autonomous, immigrant* or *voluntary*, and *castelike* or *involuntary*) provides a useful way to conceptualize differences among ethnic groups. However, it can lead to harmful generalizations about the characteristics of specific groups and divert attention from structural factors that cause minority underachievement. The issue of minority underachievement is undertheorized and requires more complex and nuanced explanations and theories than those that currently exist. The examples of the differential achievement of minority groups in the various European nations in this book provides important information that needs to be considered in the construction of theories about minority underachievement.

Global migration has increased the number of languages within the nation states and schools in Europe as it has within the United States, Canada, Australia and Japan. One of the most significant issues discussed in this book is the increasing language diversity in European nation states and how schools in various nations are responding to it. Constructing a thoughtful and equitable national language policy related to the languages of immigrant and ethnic groups is a complex and divisive issue in European nation states as it is in other nations throughout the world. In Chapter 8, Extra and Yağmur provide a rich description of the language diversity in European nations and propose that all children be taught three languages. Experiences in various nations since the 1960s teach us that an exclusive language approach to the educational problems of ethnic and immigrant groups is insufficient because languages are integral parts of cultures, and that cultures have differential status and capital within societies and nation states. In order for the language of an ethnic group to attain legitimacy and status within a society, the group that speaks the language must have power and high status. The power of the United States within the international community is probably related to the recommendation by Extra and Yağmur that English should become the lingua franca for international communication.

The chapters in the book raise other important issues and problems – often in thoughtful and probing ways – that require deliberation, thoughtful research, theorizing and action before ethnic minority groups will experience social justice and democracy in their societies and nation states. These issues include reforming teacher education so that it can more effectively prepare teachers to work with students from diverse cultural and language groups and transforming the curriculum so that it reflects the increasing diversity within European nation states. This book will stimulate educators to rethink the purpose of schools in multicultural democratic societies and to conceptualize ways in which schools can actualize human rights and social justice. I hope it will attain the wide readership it deserves.

References

Banks, J. A. and Banks, C. A. M. (eds) (2004) *Handbook of Research on Multicultural Education* (Second Edition), San Francisco: Jossey-Bass/Wiley.

Banks, J. A. and Lynch, J. (eds) (1986) *Multicultural Education in Western Societies*, London: Holt, Rhinehart and Winston.

Castles, S. (2004) 'Migration, citizenship, and education', in J. A. Banks (ed.) *Diversity and Citizenship Education: Global Perspectives*, San Francisco: Jossey-Bass/Wiley.

Gibson, M. and Ogbu, J. (1991) *Minority Status and Schooling: A Comparative Study of Immigrant and Involuntary Minorities*, New York: Garland.

Kymlicka, W. (1995) *Multicultural Citizenship: A Liberal Theory of Minority Rights*, New York: Oxford University Press.

Acknowledgements

Editing a book with international contributions – on questions, topics and challenges of international relevance – requires a lot of support, which I received, and for which I would like to express my gratitude here.

First of all, I would like to thank the contributors to this book for the pleasant cooperation, exchange of ideas and mutual learning. In addition to this, I also have to thank them for their patient cooperation as regards answering my many questions and thus constantly improving the chapters.

Let me also thank the anonymous referees who have given many helpful ideas to improve the book.

I am most grateful to James Banks who graciously agreed to write the foreword for this book.

Moreover, I would like to thank Siegfried Gasparaitis, Vanessa Dhar and Andreas Lauf, University of Duisburg-Essen, for help in the early stages of the book. I also want to give my warmest thanks to Simone Höfer and Monika Irber, University of Munich, for their support in the final stages of the book: they have typed many versions of the book, checked quotations and references for the chapters most carefully and have helped to meet the editorial demands in all stages of the book's development.

I am very grateful to Judith A. Lightfoot, Oldenburg, who has corrected my contributions – and those of many colleagues – with the care and thoroughness that I have always known since we first started working together. Furthermore, she has helped with all the questions that occurred regarding English – always very quickly and, if necessary, even at weekends.

I am indebted to the interdisciplinary Graduate Programme 'European Societies' (financed by the DFG, the German Research Council) at Essen University (now the University of Duisburg-Essen) for providing financial support for the contributors' meetings. It should be stressed that the interdisciplinary focus on European topics of this Graduate Programme has also influenced the development of this book. This also applies to the IMAZ (Institute for Migration Research, Multicultural Education and Second Language Teaching) at Essen University (now the University of Duisburg-Essen). We jointly felt the need to discuss educational responses to immigration in the light of more complex forms of immigration than those discussed in the 1980s and 1990s. This seemed to be of special interest for education when – after long debates and restrictions – multicultural education had finally developed in most European countries as a response to permanent immigration. Now education and educational policies are confronted with the fact of rather new forms of migration, which are described by sociologists as transnational migration. The result of many discussions was to seek approaches to such newer forms of migration and examine their impact on education in a European context. Since we were aware of the importance of the developments in the traditional countries of immigration, we also sought an exchange with colleagues from classical countries of immigration, such as Australia, to give us an impression of their more recent developments in migration.

A book such as this needs all kinds of support and help, including critical discussions with colleagues, and it has been most enriching to experience that support.

1 Introduction

Sigrid Luchtenberg

This book discusses educational responses to immigration in six European countries – France, Germany, Great Britain, Greece, the Netherlands and Sweden – as well as in Australia from different viewpoints. While reflecting upon the history of migration, there is also a focus on the challenges to be met at present and in future. Migration has become more and more important in Europe, but the contributions in this book show not only different reactions in politics and education, but also the shift from emigration to immigration in some countries. Changes with regard to migrant groups are also revealed. Therefore, it is of great relevance to include a contribution from Australia as one of the 'classical countries of immigration'. This helps us to understand some of the processes European countries are experiencing due to migration, though there are, of course, significant differences between a country like Australia, which is based on immigration, and the European states, which have taken and are still taking a long time to acknowledge their status as countries of immigration – with all the consequences this has for education.

Migration has become one of the great challenges worldwide. This is due to the increasing numbers of migrants in all parts in the world, though migration is by no means a new phenomenon. Nevertheless, Castles and Miller (1993) call this era the 'age of migration'. The challenges posed by migration affect many fields, from politics to education, with different answers found in different countries and under different circumstances. In this introductory chapter, we will discuss aspects of migration that are especially important with regard to Europe, but also in comparison to the situation in classical countries of immigration such as Australia. Such comparative studies have proved to be the best way not only to explain phenomena that occur in several countries, but also to clarify questions regarding a single country by comparing these to similar ones in other countries (cf., e.g. Bommes *et al.* 1999; Castles and Miller 1993; Müller-Schneider 2000; Pitkänen *et al.* 2002).

It will be stressed that integration is one of the key words in the political as well as in the educational discourse in most countries of immigration (cf. Pitkänen *et al.* 2002: 3ff.). This applies to all seven countries dealt with in this volume. Yet, even if integration is a common response in most European and classical countries of immigration, its meaning can still differ since this common approach does not neglect the fact that there are also differences between these countries due to their varying national and cultural developments. There have been periods in world history as well as in European history where mass emigration was part of daily life – generally amongst the poorest social classes of a country. In Europe, the Irish emigration during the great famine is an example as well as emigration from Germany during and after the Industrial Revolution in the nineteenth century. In European history, there has, however, not only been work migration or migration due to poor economic conditions, but also migration due to political or religious persecution, e.g. the emigration of the Huguenots from France into Prussia. This example also illuminates the pull-and-push effects of migration, since Prussia was very much interested in the migrants because of their craftsmanship. We also find examples of work and settler immigration that were welcomed by the countries of immigration, such as migration into Russia at the time of Empress Catherine the Great. Here, the pull effect is stronger than the push effect. While migration is no new theme to mankind, neither worldwide nor in Europe, we find new developments in the ways in which migration challenges societies today. Migration has become part of the daily life of many, if not most people in Europe since migrants are present in most neighbourhoods or work places. Migrants and their families have also become a topic in the media – though often with negative connotations. This contributes to the fact that most people are aware of migration, migrants, and especially of the changes in their societies due to migration. These changes are experienced in different – positive and negative – ways. While the richer variety of cuisine is generally well accepted, a shortage in housing, which is thought to be a result of migration, is not. Migration has also become an option for more people in European countries and this holds true especially for the middle classes. This kind of migration is often due to studies or work in another country for a limited time and is therefore not always regarded as migration. Thus, emigration is nowadays less reflected on than immigration. Furthermore, immigration is often discussed critically due to its impact on the labour markets, the socio-economic structure and on the educational system of the receiving country.

Although migration is no new phenomenon in Europe, it has challenged European nation states since the post-war period in many aspects despite differences amongst states as to when it took place, the migration groups themselves and the political reactions to it. This is also applicable to a certain extent to the classical countries of immigration, as, for example, when Australia was in urgent need of new immigrants after the Second World War and the experience of being in danger of foreign occupation. Worldwide, countries of development have experienced immigration as well as emigration due to natural catastrophes and wars of different kinds such as civil wars or wars of liberation. The European development is of special interest as these migration processes fall in the time of the growth of European unity. Therefore, the impact of the European developments on migration is one important aspect, but the other one is that of studying differences and similarities of immigration and the handling of its influence on politics, economics and especially education within Europe (cf. The Council 1988).

While, worldwide, most war refugees migrate into a neighbouring country and thus, in the developing countries in Asia, Africa and South America, pose the greatest problem, migration into Europe is more complex. This is due to a combination of reasons for migration, such as war or civil war, undemocratic or unstable political conditions, or poor economic conditions in the country of origin. In most European countries this is dealt with as refugee migration. There is also work migration into Europe, which is due to labour force shortage in different periods and different branches. It has also to be taken into consideration that all forms of legal immigration are followed by family immigration, thus adding to the number of people immigrating. Illegal immigration has become a further challenge within European countries, but also in the classical countries of immigration, among which Australia in particular has been shocked by the experience that illegal immigration is possible. This has led to political overreactions and deep confusion within the population. Illegal immigration – recently also referred to as 'sans-papier immigration' or undocumented immigration – is fought against since it is related to criminal gangs bringing migrants without documents into the countries (cf. Lindemann 2001). While these gangs are the real 'criminals', the persons without documents are often treated as criminals. Illegal immigration is also a challenge to be dealt with from a political, socio-economic and educational viewpoint since there are no rules about how to deal with these people (cf. Mitakidou and Tsiakalos, Chapter 7 in this volume).

While the main reasons for migration, like political insecurity or poverty, are to be found in the countries of origin, there is also often a connection to the country chosen, such as a political closeness. This is often the case in former colonial states, so that we find immigrants from Northern Africa in France. A migration into the country of the forefathers describes the situation of the 'Aussiedler' (resettlers or ethnic Germans) in Germany. Another possibility is the existence of a large group that had already migrated earlier, which applies, for example, to the Italians in Victoria, Australia, or the Germans in Southern Australia, but also for the Turkish communities in Berlin or Frankfurt.

Migration into the three main immigration countries – the USA, Canada and Australia – was and is needed by these countries. Here migration took and takes place in a regulated procedure and immigration has thus always been understood in these countries as a permanent process leading to citizenship fairly quickly. Migration into Europe was largely different and only seldom planned by the European countries as permanent immigration. Immigration regulations are therefore less elaborate and often not very stringent. Again, there are differences due to the historical background, because the former colonial states – here England, France and the Netherlands – took different approaches to members of their former colonies than, e.g. Germany or Sweden did to migrants who were invited into the countries to overcome labour shortage.

Germany is a good example of a mixed form of partly planned, partly unplanned migration: the country needed a high amount of workers in the late 1950s and early 1960s and therefore work migration was initiated with the help of bilateral contracts with southern European countries. This was the 'Gastarbeiter' model which was supposed to solve the labour market problem without permanent immigration by limiting each worker's stay to a maximum of two to five years. This rotation model did not function as planned so that immigration became more and more permanent, mainly due to family members joining their working partners and parents. This happened even more after work migration came to a stop in 1973 due to an economic recession. Thus, families received the status of residents, but no citizenship under the conditions of the legal regulations of the foreigner law. Germany belongs to the western European countries which only recently began a political discussion about an immigration law without even daring to call it such. Instead, the possibilities of the German language were used to create an expression that is thought to be less emotive ('Zuwanderung' instead of 'Einwanderung' i.e. more a case of 'joining' than 'coming into' the country and therefore not such a great threat). A lot of damage has resulted from the recent failure of this law in the political arena as regards the relationship both of migrants and Germans and migrants and Germany respectively, because the failure can be understood as a lack of political will to accept migration and migrants after nearly 50 years of immigration.

All European countries have their own, varying immigration experiences, though now at least the members of the European Union live under newly related conditions: Europeans have the possibility to move within Europe and find new places to live and work. Thus, countries like Italy or Spain who have sent 'guest workers' to Germany and other western European countries, are now member states of the European Union. This, in turn, allows for different, rather flexible forms of migration as short term migration.

The phenomenon of 'guest workers' is one of the ways in which migration is occurring in Europe and which is of relevance within Europe, but of less importance within the classical countries of immigration where permanent immigration is dominant. While work migration takes place in most European countries, there are other forms of migration that can be found, though not in all European countries to the same extent:

- In Scandinavia there are special rules which allow for movement and work within the Scandinavian countries. This explains the high amount of Finnish immigrants in Sweden.
- Former colonies face the immigration of inhabitants from their former colonies. These people often had citizenship or could claim citizenship and thus had or still have full rights in their country of immigration. This holds true for Great Britain, France, Belgium and the Netherlands, but also for Spain and Portugal.
- Only in Germany do we find the immigration of ethnic Germans whose ancestors emigrated from Germany into the former Russian Empire and other East European countries (cf. Bade and Oltmer 1999; Dietz and Hilkes 1994). These emigrants and their descendents continued to cultivate their German heritage there. This led to discrimination and worse in the communist realm and therefore they were granted immigration into Germany as German citizens.
- In all European countries immigration of refugees takes place, though the rules applied to them differ, even if a general European regulation may be expected. There are already European rules existing like the Schengen agreement, which allows non-controlled travelling within the European states involved due to stricter controls at their outer borders. Yet, a more stringent and all inclusive regulation is still to come.

While immigration was well known, though not always accepted in the northern and western countries of Europe, the countries in the south experienced mainly emigration. They now encounter immigration in very different forms: immigration from former colonies can be found especially in Spain and Portugal, undocumented (illegal) immigration has become a phenomenon especially in Italy and Greece. East European countries have faced special challenges since the fall of the Iron Curtain, especially those about to become member states of the European Union since they have to comply with the existing rules of the European Union with regard to protection against illegal immigration and to refugee policies, according to which they are often regarded as the first 'safe' country entered by refugees. Then they are the receiving country into which refugees could be sent back by Germany or Austria.

Immigration is often divided into work migration, refugee migration and family migration. Nearly all European countries face these different forms of immigration, though to a different measure and in varying intensity. These various forms of migration can also be divided into voluntary migration (of workers and their families) and involuntary migration of refugees. The situation of people who leave their countries due to insufficient living conditions could be characterized as being between the poles voluntary – involuntary. In general, these forms of migration occur simultaneously. Different frameworks have been developed in order to explain different migration patterns (cf. Brettell and Hollifield 2000; Castles and Miller 1993; Castles and Davidson 2000; Müller-Schneider 2000; Pries, Chapter 2 in this volume).

The reactions to migration have been rather different in the European states and their societies. It is no secret that in most European countries right wing parties have gained success by condemning immigration. Even in countries where immigrants have gained citizenship at no great delay and have thereafter actively engaged in the further development of the country, discrimination and even violent acts have happened (Cohen 1999; Institut für Sozialpädagogische Forschung 1997; Vasta and Castles 1996; Chapters 5, 9 and 10 in this volume). These, in turn, have led to different measures of combating discrimination and racism.

Migration is a political and economic phenomenon and most relevant decisions are now made on the political level. Yet, migration is also a very important topic both within education and educational policy as well as educational programmes and practice, though educational issues are not generally independent from political decisions and, only with great difficulties, if at all, can they be realized against political doctrines. Thus education has played an important role in all immigration processes, though normally in an interdependent relationship with political and societal reactions towards migration.

Which are the main questions education has to respond to?

- Which education has to be offered to migrant children? Are there differences between the different migrant groups such as work migrants and refugees? How can the children of undocumented (illegal) migrants be dealt with?
- What is the aim of the education of children with a migration background? Should they be integrated into the mainstream educational system? Which measures are necessary to attain such integration?
- What is the role of the countries of origin? To what extent should they be involved in the education of children with migration background? Which forms of involvement are possible?
- Can remigration play a significant role in the discussion of the education of children with migration background?
- Which effects have to be considered with regard to the school system and the children of the majority?
- In what way has society changed due to migration and the diversity resulting from migration? Which impacts can be seen on the educational system?

It emerges that the main dichotomy to be found is between reactions to integrate migrants versus those of separation with the final aim of remigration. Integration plays a very dominant role in the discussion of migrant education and is, in a first approach, strongly connected with language education, i.e. the acquisition of the majority language of the country of immigration. The languages of origin were originally mainly regarded as a tool of remigration, but never completely neglected in the education of migrant children. There are three different approaches to the education in the languages of origin to be found in Europe (cf. Reich 1997):

1 Education in the language of origin is regarded as a duty of the countries of origin who are supported in organizing this education by the country of immigration.
2 Education in the language of origin is regarded as a duty of the local ethnic communities who are supported in organizing this education by the country of immigration.
3 Education in the language of origin is regarded as a duty of the new country.

In all three approaches, minority languages are only regarded as being of relevance for children of these minority groups, whereas a possible value for the majority is not taken into consideration. This is different for example in Australia, where minority languages are considered as a national resource (cf. Clyne 1991). Yet, this general approach does not guarantee good practice (Luchtenberg 1997).

The second big issue in education has been the question of whether there is only a need for the education of migrant children or whether there is a need to change the educational system as a whole due to the new diversity. This matter has been decided since the 1980s when models of multicultural education (intercultural education in the terminology of the Council of Europe) became more and more acknowledged and were introduced into the national educational systems within the immigration countries – though at different speeds and levels of intensity. This acknowledgement of multicultural education is also to be found within the European institutions – especially the Council of Europe and the EC, as it was called then.

Though there are different definitions of multicultural education there are some issues upon which agreement exists: multicultural education can thus be described as an education within a plural society with the aim of making all students aware of its diversity and to enable them to cope with this diversity by accepting it as enriching, though often difficult. Thus, multicultural education is an inclusive education (cf. Gundara 2000). Furthermore, there is a common agreement upon the fact that migrant students need special care and support to succeed in the educational systems of the countries of immigration. This is particularly applicable to those countries where the recent OECD study on literacy (OECD 2001) has revealed that migrant students are not coping sufficiently, so that one can only assume that they do not gain enough support (cf. Chapters 2, 3 and 9 in this volume). While language education especially, but by no means merely in the majority languages, is regarded as a dominant sector, other 'branches', such as citizenship education, gain in importance and relevance (cf. Banks 2003; Castles and Davidson 2000; Hahn 1998). Difference within the concept of multicultural education exists, e.g. with regard to the extension to European or even global aspects, cultural relativism versus universalism or the role of ethnocentrism (cf. e.g. Inglis 1996; Nieke 2000; Steiner-Khamsi 1992). The question of extending to European aspects is closely related to the European Dimension in Education (cf. The Council 1988).

While Sweden and the Netherlands included aims of multiculturalism and multicultural education in their different national policies in the 1980s and 1990s, Germany did not receive a positive signal until 1996 from the 'Kultusministerkonferenz' i.e. the Ministers of Education from the various German state, who then launched a recommendation for multicultural education (cf. Sekretariat der Ständigen Konferenz der Kultusminister der Länder in der Bundesrepublik Deutschland 1996).

In general, we can see that most national educational systems have come to the conclusion that there is a kind of permanent immigration which has to be dealt with for the welfare of the immigrants and their integration, as well as for the welfare of the whole society who has to accept its increasing multilingual and multicultural structure. Thus, education – though not on all levels of educational policy in all European countries – has fully acknowledged the fact of a permanent immigration which demands measures of integration and the preparation of all inhabitants – majority as well as immigrants – for a multilingual and multicultural society (cf. Inglis 1996).

Migration is still an important issue in European countries, the EU, in the classical countries of immigration, but also in many states, especially in Asia, as indeed worldwide. Due to the close relationship between European countries there are many similar questions with regard to migration and the political, societal and educational reactions, though responses may differ or occur in different sequences. Australia has experienced very similar reactions to migration as many European countries in spite of her different migration history. Integration – including linguistic aspects – turns out to be a key issue in nearly all countries where migration is of relevance. Integration is always part of the underlying question of societal cohesion, which is regarded as threatened without integration. Therefore, integration is the main connecting question of this book, where it is discussed in its relevance for the states from economic, political, but especially from educational or linguistic viewpoints. It has to be kept in mind that, the more permanent migration turned out to be, the more important integration became.

The acknowledgement of permanent migration – and the search for integrative measures as a response – is certainly a big issue and could be called a success in the approach towards immigration. However, there are also new developments in the forms of migration that have to be taken into consideration as they pose new challenges for education and educational policies (cf. Cohen 1997 for the diaspora approach).

Again, this is a common challenge in most European countries as well as in Australia, as can be seen in the contributions in this book, and it proves to be a further cohesive aspect without neglecting the differences to be discussed.

The authors of this book agree on the necessity of heightening the awareness as regards the international parallel aspects of migration, i.e. it is vital that the national researchers in the field of migration, including the political, societal and educational responses to it, are conscious of similar processes taking place in other European countries. In addition to this, the fruitful discussion that an international exchange inspires, especially when including a classical country of immigration, must be shared with all working in this field. Education belongs to the disciplines at the centre of interest because – after long debates and restrictions – multicultural education as a response to permanent migration has gained acceptance in most European countries and beyond.

Now education and educational policies are confronted with the phenomenon of rather new forms of migration, which are described by sociologists as transnational migration. A main objective of this book is to discuss such newer forms of migration and their impact on education in a European context.

It is both enriching and rewarding in such a challenging situation to also gain an impression of the Australian view on more recent developments in migration and educational responses since Australia was often quicker in finding answers than Europe. Most contributions in this book not only present results of recent research and the present discussion within the different states but also give an overview of the path that led to this present status. This enables a consideration of the obstacles on the road to an inclusive multicultural society with an appropriate education which may even appear when integration has already been accepted and multicultural concepts have been developed (cf., e.g. Chapters 5 and 9 in this volume). Thus, change with regard to education in countries of immigration not only refers to new challenges but also indicates that results and achievements in multicultural education can be reduced or even reverted which is, of course, also a new challenge. This recent reappearance of rejection makes an international discussion of the common question even more important. This book wants to contribute to this debate to meet the challenges.

Ludger Pries' chapter on 'Transnationalism and migration: new challenges for the social sciences and education' deals with newer developments of transnational migration which are discussed within a theoretical framework that includes different types of migration. The relevance for education is discussed by referring to the recent OECD study on literacy.

Here, the theoretical foundation is laid with regard to understanding the recent and the future challenges that education faces when it meets migration. Examples from the USA and Mexico show the international relevance of the phenomenon which is not yet sufficiently acknowledged in Europe.

The challenges in education are discussed in more detail by Sigrid Luchtenberg in her chapter on '(New forms of) migration: challenges for education' with a focus on Germany. A main point is the question whether the model of integration in the concept of multiculturalism is compatible with transmigration where migrants live in more than one social and spatial context, either at the same time, in consecutive periods or in a way where social and geographical spaces are split or overlap. Language education for children of migrated parents has to be reflected in the light of these developments as well as citizenship education, which has only recently gained attention in multicultural education. The European development is a further issue here because the European Union not only supports transmigration in the described sense by its legislation but also adds further aspects by pushing the development of European identity, which means that a new social and geographical space emerges.

The Turkish community is at the centre of the chapter by Sabine Mannitz which is entitled 'Collective solidarity and the construction of social identities in school'. The author shows how the German unification has changed the social as well as the geographical space, especially in Berlin from the viewpoint of young people with Turkish background. The focus in her chapter is on identity discourses as developed among this group since the new historical challenge of inner unity as discussed in Germany renders its particular effects on the viable identification strategies of ethnic minority youths. Sabine Mannitz analyses the statements of the immigrant children in order to learn about their feelings of where they belong socially after the experience of the unification. Her findings show that these young people shift the border of supposedly self-evident unities. Her results are highly relevant for education since her analysis questions civil enculturation and thus integration in nation state schooling.

While in Germany multicultural education and the acceptance of a diverse society slowly wins ground in spite of all problems, the situation in Great Britain turns in a different direction, as Sally Tomlinson points out in her chapter on 'The education of migrants and minorities in Britain'. This is all the more surprising as Britain was early in developing affirmative approaches to migration and multiculturalism, becoming a role model for multicultural education for quite a while in Europe. The author traces the different steps in both directions very carefully and can thus point out where the educational discourse and the underlying political decisions have changed.

Françoise Lorcerie deals with the French development of the 'ethicized schools' which are discussed from the viewpoint of minority students – most of them North Africans – and their parents, but also from the viewpoint of 'French' students and their parents. The analysis reveals a high amount of institutional discrimination, but also the relationship between ethnicity, socio-economic class and school career. A further point is the way in which minority students may achieve good results. The author applies Goffman's framework (1963) to the way in which minority students behave in school. In this chapter, integrative processes are implicitly part of all questions about how minority students fit into the French school system, in how far their presence has changed this school system and the effects on the majority.

Greece is an excellent example for changing migration patterns in Europe since the country from which emigrants migrated into all classical immigration countries and also into European countries in search of a place of work has now become a host country of immigrants, many of whom are undocumented or illegal immigrants. Soula Mitakidou and Georgios Tsiakalos explain in their chapter that this latter form of immigration is always a great challenge to an educational system since it has to be clarified whether the illegal status of a family should effect the education of their children. A factual overview on the implication of recent migration to Greece is given and then analysed with regard to its impact on integration and education. Here the authors consider the measures taken by the Greek state and compare them with the official statements given by the Greek government. This is finally contrasted with the educational reality in practice. Here, as in all chapters, language is of high relevance.

Languages – i.e. migrant languages – in diverse societies are at the centre of the chapter written by Kutlay Yağmur and Guus Extra who present findings of a cross-national home language database with a focus mainly on primary schools. The focus of their contribution is on the linguistic situation in The Hague. All kinds of migration have an impact on the linguistic situation in the countries of immigration. The new multilingualism in multicultural European schools is highly relevant for education and integration. This new study reveals facts about the actual size and variety of student groups and the languages spoken and thus will serve policy-making. It has also to be studied in the light of more complex migration patterns which no longer allow the assumption that migrants in the third generation will give up their original languages since in transnational migration it is nearly impossible to define immigrant generations. In this article, linguistic results and their impact on language policy on immigrant languages are discussed, but the authors also deal with the methods of such linguistic data collections since there are different approaches to be found worldwide.

Sweden has a long experience with migration and, furthermore, is considered worldwide to be the most advanced European country with regard to the development of multiculturalism where integrative measures are highly relevant. This is discussed by Tore Otterup with a focus on languages (policy). Here we find a similar development to that of Britain when it is stressed that the excellent achievements have been questioned politically in the late 1990s. A further similarity in the approach to the minority languages, which is also to be found in Germany, can be observed. Swedish as a second language has been developed – and partly established – in a more reflected way than most second language approaches in other countries but again, reality does not meet the guidelines.

Though the focus of this book is on European developments and the challenge Europe faces with migration and especially with its complex patterns, it is extremely desirable for the discourse on migration and its educational impacts not to lose contact with the development in the classical countries of immigration, among which Australia has achieved the highest degree in acknowledging multiculturalism. Australia has always regarded immigration as permanent, though the country has also learnt that not all immigrants stay there. Integration, but also the cohesion within a very diverse society have been very relevant in the Australian migration discourse. It was only in recent years that official programmes were initiated which included temporary migration. In this pattern middle class and highly-skilled migrants, who will probably work in several countries during their life, are also to be found. Christine Inglis analyses the impact of these immigrants' expectations on the linguistic education of their children and compares this new development with the former approaches to mother tongue teaching in Australia under the assumption of permanent immigration. Thus, in her article, language education is a main issue, which is dealt with under two completely different immigration patterns: permanent immigration versus transnational part time immigration. The recent relevance that anti-racist education has gained is also discussed.

The contributions in this book all deal with the phenomenon of migration in its classical and more recent forms in a complex and diverse way since they illustrate the developments in different countries. They tackle different forms of migration and they examine educational implications with regard to identity education, citizenship education and language education. Integration and integrative measures on the political as well as on the educational arena are at the centre of discussions in research and politics in many states, even if the focus within which integration is debated may change. For our joint work it has been very rewarding to include European countries with different migration experiences as well as Australia as a classical immigration country with a long experience of multiculturalism and integration. Though a wide spectrum of questions is dealt with, our book is far from able to analyse all aspects. Therefore, we also understand our book as an invitation to further international discussion on the questions which are asked here. In this sense, we hope that later books will continue our discussion by integrating more countries and thus broadening the focus of this one.

References

Bade, K. and Oltmer, J. (eds) (1999) *Aussiedler: deutsche Einwanderer aus Osteuropa*, Osnabrück: Universitätsverlag Rasch.

Banks, J. (ed.) (2003) *Diversity and Citizenship Education: Global Perspectives*, San Francisco: Jossey-Bass/Wiley.

Bommes, M., Castles, St. and Wihtol de Wenden, C. (eds) (1999) *Migration and Social Change in Australia, France and Germany*, Osnabrück: IMIS.

Brettell, C. B. and Hollifield, J. F. (eds) (2000) *Migration Theory. Talking Across Disciplines*, London: Routledge.

Castles, St. and Davidson, A. (2000) *Citizenship and Migration. Globalization and the Politics of Belonging*, Houndsmill and New York: Palgrave.

Castles, St. and Miller, M. J. (1993) *The Age of Migration. International Population Movements in the Modern World*, London: The Macmillan Press.

Clyne, M. (1991) *Community Languages: The Australian Experience*, Cambridge: Cambridge University Press.

Cohen, P. (1999) *New Ethnicities, Old Racisms*, London: Zed Books.

Cohen, R. (1997) *Global Diasporas. An Introduction*, London: University College London.

The Council and the Ministers of Education Meeting with the Council (1988) Resolution on the European dimension in education of 24 May 1988, *Official Journal of the European Communities* No. C 177/5.

Dietz, B. and Hilkes, P. (1994) *Integriert oder isoliert? Zur Situation rußlanddeutscher Aussiedler in der Bundesrepublik Deutschland*, München: Olzog.

Goffman, E. (1963) *Stigma, Notes on the Management of Spoiled Identity*, Englewood Cliffs: Prentice-Hall.

Gundara, J. S. (2000) *Interculturalism, Education and Inclusion*, London: Paul Chapman.

Hahn, C. L. (1998) *Becoming Political: Comparative Perspectives on Citizenship Education*, Albany: State University of New York Press.

Inglis, C. (1996) *Multiculturalism: New Policy Responses to Diversity*, Paris: Unesco.

Institut für Sozialpädagogische Forschung Mainz (IMS) (ed.) (1997) *Rassismus und Fremdenfeindlichkeit in Europa*, Neuwied: Luchterhand.

Lindemann, U. (2001) *Sans-papiers–Proteste und Einwanderungspolitik in Frankreich*, Leverkusen: Leske und Budrich.

Luchtenberg, S. (1997) 'Sprachunterricht in Australien: Aspekte der Heterogenität und Mehrsprachigkeit', *Zeitschrift für Fremdsprachenforschung* 8, 1: 65–78.

Müller-Schneider, Th. (2000) *Zuwanderung in westliche Gesellschaften. Ein integratives Erklärungsmodell*, Leverkusen: Leske und Budrich.

Nieke, W. (2000) *Interkulturelle Erziehung und Bildung – Wertorientierungen im Alltag*, Leverkusen: Leske und Budrich, 2nd edn.

OECD (eds) (2001) *Knowledge and Skills for Life. First Results from PISA 2000*, Paris.

Pitkänen, P., Kalekin-Fishman, D. and Verma, G. K. (eds) (2002) *Education and Immigration. Settlement Policies and Current Challenges*, London and New York: Routledge.

Reich, H. H. (1997) 'Wie geht das Bildungswesen mit der (auch migrationsbedingten) Vielsprachigkeit um? Verschiedene Ansätze in Europa', *Deutsch Lernen* 1: 48–59.

Sekretariat der Ständigen Konferenz der Kultusminister der Länder in der Bundesrepublik Deutschland (1996) Empfehlung 'Interkulturelle Bildung und Erziehung in der Schule'. Beschluß der Kultusministerkonferenz vom 25.10.1996, Bonn.

Steiner-Khamsi, G. (1992) *Multikulturelle Bildungspolitik in der Postmoderne*, Opladen: Leske and Budrich.

Vasta, E. and Castles, St. (eds) (1996) *The Teeth Are Smiling. The Persistence of Racism in Multicultural Australia*, St. Leonards: Allen & Unwin.

2 Transnationalism and migration

New challenges for the social sciences and education

Ludger Pries

When the results of the PISA (Programme for International Student Assessment) survey were published in 2000, German politicians and the general public were deeply shocked (PISA 2003). Among the 43 OECD countries surveyed, Germany, the 'land of poets and thinkers', was placed in the bottom third with regard to reading, mathematics and other skills.[1] Besides other structural factors – some of which will be mentioned later – migrants' language capabilities became the focus of a public debate that attempted to justify the low average results attained by 15-year-old German pupils. But it would be an oversimplification not to recognize that migrants' language skills, and those of their children, are related to their pattern of incorporation in their 'host society'. Many scholars have argued that socio-cultural integration, in terms of language skills and educational attainment, is a prerequisite for successful economic or 'structural' integration. However, one could also argue that economic integration facilitates language learning and the acquisition or upgrading of other skills. Educational attainment, for instance, correlates strongly with marriage and reproduction patterns, as well as with labour market positioning. After introducing a typology of migrant incorporation patterns and suggesting how they could influence educational attainment, closer attention will be given to transnationalism as an increasingly significant addition to other well-established incorporation patterns and forms of internationalization.

Obviously there is a complex interplay between migrants' educational attainment, their overall assimilation, integration or incorporation dynamics and the 'politics of belonging' in the host and sending countries. Given these complex and dynamic interrelations, some debates seem to be caught up in a 'chicken-or-the-egg' mode of argumentation. On one level, for instance, the economic and educational incorporation dynamics of migrants are interrelated. But on another level, the overall incorporation dynamics of migrants also vary according to their status and position in and 'between' their corresponding countries of origin and destination. For instance, if Turkish migrants in Germany or Mexican migrants in the United States perceive themselves (and are perceived by others) as temporary or transitory workers who will return to their countries of origin within a few years, the integration strategies of the migrants themselves and those of the corresponding societies will be limited. In comparison, those who designate themselves, or are designated as, immigrants will normally develop long term strategies of assimilation and/or integration.

In general, it is possible to distinguish amongst four ideal types of migrants according to their specific relationships to their regions of origin and of destination and the timeline along which migration takes place (see Table 2.1 and Pries 2001). The emigrant/immigrant ideal type is exemplified by the millions of Europeans who left their countries for the United States at the start of the twentieth century. In search of better economic and socio-cultural conditions, they integrated themselves into life there, adopting the United States as their new homeland. They maintained manifold ties to their regions of origin, the social and geographic space in which their ancestors were rooted, but were aware that these ties were increasingly of a nostalgic nature and relatively removed from their new everyday lives. In contrast to this, the ideal-typical return migrant is exemplified by the European guest workers of the 1960s and 1970s and a large number of Mexican migrants in the United States. Their duration of stay is short, limited to a period of a few years in which they try to earn a sufficient amount of money to invest in personal undertakings (like establishing a business) in their region of origin. Thus, for return migrants, the region of destination is just a 'host country' in which they have no problems with maintaining social differences.

The ideal-typical diaspora migrant is exemplified by the Jewish people and communities distributed throughout the world. Often driven to

Table 2.1 Four ideal types of international migrants

	Relationship to region of origin	Relationship to region of destination	Main impulse for moving	Timeline for migration
Emigrant/ immigrant	roots/ancestry/ permanent departure	integration/ new homeland	economic/ socio-cultural	long term/ unlimited
Return migrant	continuous point of reference	maintenance of difference/ 'host country'	economic/ political	short term/ limited
Diaspora migrant	(at least symbolic) reference to the 'homeland'	maintenance of difference/ space of suffering or of mission	religious/ political/ organizational	medium term/ limited
Transmigrant	ambiguous mixture	ambiguous mixture	economic/ organizational	indeterminate/ sequential

migrate for religious or political reasons, or by virtue of attachment to a particular organization (such as a diplomatic corps or a business organization), diaspora migrants maintain strong symbolic ties to their region of origin, which is sometimes referred to as the 'homeland' or 'promised land'. The region of destination is experienced as a space in which the suffering caused by departure or expulsion must be endured, or in which a particular mission is to be carried out. Finally, ideal-typical transmigrants do not tend to distinguish in this way between region of origin and of arrival, but develop instead an ambiguous strategy of simultaneously striving for inclusion while maintaining differences. With the aid of modern communication and transportation technologies, transmigrants often move – physically and mentally – between countries and cultures. Decisions related to migration are taken in the medium term and in a sequential manner.

One important assumption underlying the following is that problems related to migrants' educational attainment and behaviour, and to their general incorporation patterns, have to be situated within a more general typology of internationalization processes. It is important to recognize that, in the era of globalization, social spaces of belonging and of inclusion and exclusion are becoming increasingly 'de-territorialized': multi-dimensional and pluri-local belonging to various groups that are bound to particular places or territories is an increasingly decisive feature of contemporary socialization. The link between migration and education will vary according to how one perceives the specific dynamics of internationalization in which migration processes are embedded. The (often too global) globalization discourse has to be more closely differentiated, and transnationalism has to be taken into account as an important ideal type within a general typology of internationalization patterns.

Migrants' educational attainment and incorporation: the need for a transnational perspective

Findings like those of the aforementioned PISA study invite discussion of migrants' educational attainment in the broader context of general patterns of assimilation, integration and incorporation.[2] Any discussion of the German situation must take into account at least three particular aspects of the German education system. First, in Germany children enter kindergarten relatively late, normally at the age of four or five years. Moreover, the integration of migrant children into the education system is incomplete: only about one-quarter of all migrants' children attend kindergarten (Esser 2000: 50), while almost all children of German natives do. While in other countries, like France, a secular public preschool system begins compensating for language and basic value differences at the age of three or four years, in Germany many children from migrant households have their first intensive encounter with the majority population at the age of six or seven, when they enter primary school (Hettlage 1999). The lack of language acquisition (both the native and German languages) and subsequent difficulties in coming to terms with German as the language of public discourse are the major results of these preschool and primary school deficits (Weidacher 2000; EC Report 2001).

A second particularity of the German education system is the segmentation of secondary schooling into three different streams (Hauptschule, Realschule and Gymnasium), and the practice of assigning pupils to a particular stream at the very early age of ten years. Movement between the various streams after the initial placement is made difficult by various institutional barriers. The deficits in language and other relevant skills that the children of migrants acquire in the primary phase of schooling are cemented and accentuated at the secondary level, as most are relegated to the lowest stream (Hauptschule), where often the majority of pupils come from migrant households. Riphahn (2001) and Hunger and Thränhardt (2001) have shown that the average education level of second generation migrants is significantly below that of Germans of the same age. Whether or not the relative educational disadvantages of migrants' children have declined in recent decades is still the subject of debate. In 1970 only 3.7 per cent of all Germans had a higher level of secondary education; in 1996 the share rose to 14.9 per cent, nearly four times as many as in 1970. During the same period the group of migrants increased its level of secondary education attainment only threefold, from 1.8 per cent to 5.5 per cent (Kalter and Granato 2001: 19). Based on GSOEP data and controlling the overall migrant population for immigration cohorts, Frick and Wagner (2001: 309) found that after parents had lived for a period of 20 years in Germany their children had the same chances of being assigned to the higher secondary stream as their native counterparts.

A third characteristic of the German education system – and one that factors significantly into any discussion of the relationship between education and employment opportunities – is its strong vocational training system. As good training opportunities in this apprenticeship system depend on the trainee having a qualified school degree, the disadvantages acquired by children of migrant households during the preschool and primary school years become even more tangible. Bender and Seifert (1996) found that only half of all 'foreigners' aged 20 to 30 acquire a diploma (vocational or academic), as compared to more than three-quarters of their German counterparts. Seifert (2000) showed that 29 per cent of all migrants leave the education system without any valid diploma whatsoever. Concerning the attendance of Gymnasium (the completion of which is the prerequisite for admission to university), Frick and Wagner (2001) noted that only one out of five children born to migrants, compared to one-third of native Germans and one-quarter of children born to migrants with German citizenship, are allotted to this stream.

Comparative studies have reflected on the above-mentioned hindrances to migrants' educational incorporation in Germany as they relate to more general theories and concepts of migrant incorporation patterns. In one such study carried out by the European Commission (EC Report 2001) the integration dynamics and patterns of CIM (children of international migrants) in France, Great Britain and Germany were analysed. The term 'integration' was subdivided into structural, cultural, social and 'identificational' integration, and the research sought to identify individual and institutional factors that could explain the outcome of migrants' integration dynamics. The report stated that the 'national context systematically explains much more variance than individual variables' in all three countries (EC Report 2001: 16). France was characterized as employing a universalistic and republican 'assimilation approach' of incorporation, which resulted in relatively strong cultural integration, to the detriment of structural integration, for example in the areas of training and employment. The United Kingdom was said to have an approach that recognizes and promotes the building of multi-ethnic and multicultural communities, and which encourages migrants to identify with Great Britain, but which failed to prevent the segmentation of training and employment along ethnic lines. As to Germany, the report offered the following judgment: 'Germany has comparative strengths in training and employment of CIM, but weaknesses in legal and identificational integration. An ambiguous policy seems to have produced ambiguous results' (EC Report 2001: 16f.).

Based on ethnographical case studies in Berlin, London, Paris and Rotterdam, Schiffauer *et al.* (2002) studied the process of political incorporation of migrants as mediated by the school system. They underlined the specific function of school in the different societies, as well as the ideas and concepts that schooling conveys to students about their society. According to the authors, the French and British cases represent two ideal types of incorporation approaches, with France representing the idea of a homogenous Republican nation and Great Britain representing the liberal concept of a multi-ethnic, community-based society. Germany and the Netherlands were described as embodying mixtures of these concepts of incorporation. One significant conclusion to be drawn from these comparative European studies on incorporation is that migrants' educational attainment and behaviour is profoundly linked to the overall integration strategies of the migrants themselves and of the host society. A second conclusion to be drawn is that there is neither a single best approach nor convergence towards a unique European model of incorporation.

Though decreasing in number, the variety of incorporation strategies and patterns seems to be becoming highly differentiated, and transnationalism is one driving force behind this. The subjective and declared desire or intention either to return to the country of origin or stay indefinitely in the host country could be considered an important indicator of transnational life orientations and biographical projects, and is thus useful for differentiating between immigrants, return migrants and transnational migrants. Generally speaking, the return to the (family's) country of origin constitutes a dominant theme in everyday migrant discourses, especially amongst Turkish migrants (Çağlar 1989). Wolbert (1997) analysed the symbolic character of the trope of return: according to him, it functions as a *wild card* that is played, at least mentally, when migrants are confronted with experiences of exclusion. Hettlage (1999) found out that 60 per cent of migrants surveyed were satisfied living in Germany, but that only 25 per cent felt rooted in German society. Sackmann *et al.* (2000) found that 47 per cent of all migrants wished to stay in Germany, 20 per cent were undecided, 17 per cent wanted to return and 17 per cent preferred commuting. Seifert (1998) analysed migrants' subjective self-positioning and noted that half of them wished to stay in Germany but lacked a sense of 'being German'. These results are interesting, as they convey the limits of possible incorporation and reflect the restrictive integration and naturalization policy in place in Germany. They also indicate that there is a considerable socio-cultural space in which transnational strategies of belonging can be developed. In sum, migrants in Germany are more or less satisfied with their way of life, but they do not feel that they are a part of an integrating and inclusive national project (as, for instance, in the case of France), nor do they perceive themselves as being integrated in an ethnic community that is recognized as being part of a project to build a multicultural society (as, for instance, in the case of Great Britain).

Perhaps the space for developing transnational strategies of identification and incorporation is opened up by these ambivalent experiences and feelings. Whereas identities are normally believed to rely on a binary classification scheme ('the self' and 'the other'), transnationalism entails a multifaceted contradictory belonging. As two of the first scholars studying new transnational phenomena, Kearney and Nagengast (1989) pointed to new identity formations in pluri-local, as opposed to unidirectional, transnational migration. Kearney (1995) defined transnational belonging as more than just the combination of socio-cultural elements of the countries of origin and of destination. According to him, transnational belonging refers to a condition 'in which the subject shares partial, overlapping identities, with other similarly constituted decentred subjects that inhibit reticular social forms' (Kearney 1995: 558).

Having touched on the significance of transnationalism for educational attainment and the incorporation strategies of migrants in general, the focus of this chapter will now turn to illustrating the characteristics of transnationalism that set it apart from other forms of migration. Transnational migration clearly differs from immigration and return migration, which are characterized by one-time moves between countries. It also differs from the diaspora migration of political refugees, members of diplomatic corps or managerial expatriates, for whom the home country or 'promised land' remains the dominant point of reference during their limited stays 'abroad'. Instead, transnational migration consists of frequent shifting across borders that is unconnected to seasonal job opportunities, but rather serves to span individual and household lives between places in different countries. The transmigrants' corresponding sense of identity and socio-cultural positioning are characterized by ambiguity and multiple frames of reference, and their life strategies are based on pluri-local landscapes of transnational social spaces.[3]

Varieties of internationalization: a typology for the twenty-first century

The container approach to viewing national societies as a coincidence of social and geographical space represents an important historical trend in the way social reality is perceived and conceptualized. The concept of 'national container societies' as the most important units of reference and analysis, and the corresponding notion of international migration as being a singular shift between such national container societies, are part of that tradition. At the beginning of the twenty-first century, the relationship between 'space' and the 'social' is being reconceived. The conditions, forms and outcomes of these new conceptions, as they relate to the geospatial reach and span of the 'social', represent an important aspect of social change itself. Some scholars argue that the old (one-dimensional) frame of reference tied to national container societies should be replaced by another (one-dimensional) frame of reference that supposedly signifies the end of the nation state paradigm and denies the significance of physical space in society: globalization (see Urry 2001; Castells 1996, 1998). But it seems that the current experience of internationalization could better be understood by *combining* the various geographic frames of reference – the local, the regional, the national, the supra-national and the global – with basic units of social analysis like families/households, organizations and governance structures.

The term internationalization stands for two different forms of rearrangements of geographic–social spaces beyond, alongside and above the formerly dominant national society paradigm. On the one hand, the double exclusiveness of social and geographic space could be maintained, assuring the continuity of an absolutist combination of geography and social space. This could be accomplished as follows:

1   interconnections between the containers could be intensified (*internationalization*);
2   the containers themselves could be widened to include various (former) nation states (*supra-nationalization*);
3   one container could be reduced or divided into various new ones (*renationalization*);

4   the national containers could be extended in their spatial/social scope to encompass the world as a whole (*globalization*).

On the other hand, the double exclusiveness of social and geographic space could be uncoupled, leading to a pluri-local combination of 'space' and the 'social'. This could lead to:

5   the global being conceived as a combination of one place and local social spaces (*glocalization*);
6   a combination of motherland as imagined nation and diasporas as satellites (*diaspora building*);
7   a framework of transnational local places building coherent social spaces (*transnationalization*).

In the following, these seven ideal types of ongoing processes of border shifting and border spanning will be sketched out (see Table 2.2).

The first ideal type of internationalization is *internationalization*, in the form of bi- and multi-nationalization. It refers to relations and interactions *between* nations, i.e. nation states and national societies. Examples of such internationalization include: the Franco–German war (1870–1871); the labour migration treaties and resulting movements between, for example, Italy and Germany (1955) or Turkey and Germany (1961); the Friendship Treaty of 1927 between Italy and Hungary; the founding of the European Community for Coal and Steel by France, Germany, Italy and the Benelux countries in 1951; and the work of the European Council of Ministers. The main characteristic of this type of internationalization is the predominance of nation state activities and the perception of international relations as being based on national container societies. The example of the Franco–German war indicates that this ideal type of internationalization is not limited to the activities of political leaders. On the contrary, it is always based on, reproduces or leads to mass activities, or at least it is perceived as doing so. Economic exchanges between important national trading companies, ideological national movements and mobilizations, as well as cross-border relations between national associations of artists or scientists could all be the basis or outcome of this type of internationalization. In any case, the point of reference is the interchange between spatially coherent, nationally bounded units of action. This type of increasingly significant international contact and societal exchange developed historically in conjunction with the nation-building process itself. But its weighting in current internationalization dynamics is obviously not diminishing. The ongoing conflict between India and Pakistan is a contemporary example of risky and highly dangerous international relations.

The second type of internationalization could be coined *supra–nationalization*. It stands for the tendency to 'upgrade' nation states or national container societies to supra-national – but not totally global – units. Some aspects of the European Community, such as the European Parliament in Strasbourg, could be considered an outcome of supra-nationalization. In this case, the legitimate sovereignty for regulating and representing certain (but until now relatively unimportant) issues lies not with the nation state but with a kind of 'supra-national state'. Supra-nationalization creates supra-national units, which are more than the sum of national units. Supra-national units and actors have their own legal, financial and material basis and develop a new supra-national logic of their own, which goes beyond international relations *between* national units. For example, international organizations (like trade unions or professional associations like the International Sociological Association) are organized on the basis of national delegations. They are international organizations, but if they are organized (financially and in terms of voting systems, etc.) on the basis of individual membership and international structures, then they could also be considered supra-national organizations. The European Union could – but must not – become more and more of a supra-national unit. The process of passing a European directive for the compulsory national development of laws regarding the construction of European workers' councils is an example of the complex mix of supra-nationalization, maintenance of national sovereignty and trans-nationalization occurring at the level of the European Union.

The third type of internationalization could be coined *re-nationalization* and refers to a certain kind of counter tendency to the aforementioned supra-nationalization and globalization processes. Re-nationalization thus refers to:

1   a strengthening of existing national container boundaries;
2   the process of dividing formerly more-or-less homogeneous socio-geographic container spaces into various new social entities or spaces claiming their own geographic space and territories (regionalization).

In striving for autonomy, the Basques and Bretons are calling for new regional 'frontiers'; the dissolution of the former Soviet Union and the former state of Yugoslavia led to a multiplicity of nationalisms and regional movements and, ultimately, to the formation of new political entities (or at least competences) at an intra-national level. The European Community's common agricultural policy and the USA's (newly and unilaterally declared) protective steel tariffs are examples of strong nation states' emerging or ongoing process of 'social closure' (Weber 1972) *against* globalization and 'neo-liberalization'. Nation states have certainly not relinquished control over flows of goods and services: in many cases these have merely changed form (e.g. the conversion of tariff barriers into non-tariff barriers).

Table 2.2 Seven figures of internationalization

	Description	Geographical configuration	Example
Internationalization (bi- or multi-nationalization)	relations and interactions *between* nations (perception of) predominance of the inter-national relations as based on states and national container societies		Franco-German war 1870–1871; 'European Community for Coal and Steel' 1951
Supra-nationalization	'upgrading' the nation state and national container society towards supra-national – but not totally global – units		EU Parliament Strasbourg; individual-based international organization
Re-nationalization	strengthening of existing territorial boundaries or dividing formerly more or less homogeneous social-geographic container spaces into various new social entities or spaces		disintegration of the Soviet Union or Yugoslavia; old and new protectionism of the USA or the EU
Globalization	(perception of the) worldwide spanning and extension of international transactions, communications, social practices, symbols, events, risks and rights		global risks of nuclear energy and of global warming; McDonalds franchising all over the world

Glocalization	interrelation between globalized, more or less de-localized phenomena and processes and the very localized concentration of preconditions and/or effects of the former		local reasons and effects of global warming; Bangalore/India
Diaspora-Internationalization	shared social space spreading over different geographic spaces and boundaries of civilizations or nations integrated or constituted mainly by reference to a common 'motherland'		Jewish and other religious diasporas; Diplomatic corps; global companies
Transnationalization	pluri-local and trans-national social relations, networks and practices spanning above and between the traditional container spaces of national societies		transnational companies; Haitian transnational social spaces; Chinese Huanxi's

Note
Rectangles with N_1 etc. mean 'nation state 1' etc.; triangles indicate (local) places.

The fourth and oft-cited type of internationalization is the *globalization process* and its outcome; *globality*. The term refers, on the one hand, to the worldwide spanning and extension of international transactions, communications, social practices, symbols and impacts of some processes and events; on the other hand, it also refers to the worldwide perception and awareness of problems, risks, rights, tendencies and incidents. As Giddens (1990) stated: 'Globalization can thus be defined as the intensification of worldwide social relations which link distant localities in such a way that local happenings are shaped by events occurring many miles away and vice versa' (Giddens 1990: 64). Obviously there are a lot of real tendencies, like nuclear risks and global warming, which have some specific local, national or international origins, but which carry consequences from which no country or individual on the planet can escape completely. People and countries with a lot of economic power, knowledge and other resources will be better able to respond to such global challenges, but they will also definitely be affected by them. Therefore, globalization refers to (at least partially and in the long run) worldwide and omnipresent phenomena. With respect to the relation between geographic and social space, globalization is often conceptualized either as the geographic *widening* of social relations and spaces (as indicated in the above-cited words of Anthony Giddens) or as the annihilation of space and the '*compression* of our spatial and temporal worlds' (Harvey 1989).[4] The aforementioned ideal types of internationalization have in common that the double exclusiveness of geographic and social space is not questioned or uncoupled substantially but rather reinforced and spatially reduced or widened. Even in the globalization approach geographic space is thought of as a coherent mono-place.[5] In this context, some scholars argue that as the spatial broadening of the 'social' reaches the frontiers of the globe as a whole the spatial dimension of the 'social' is losing its general significance. For them, in 'cyberspace' geographical space as physical place loses its significance and everything dissolves in a borderless 'space of flows' (Urry 2001). In contrast to approaches based on one coherent *geographic* space, the following three ideal types are based on the concept of one *social* space that spans transnationally several places. Whereas in the aforementioned concepts internationalization is thought of as an intensifying of relations between geographic container spaces and a widening or reducing of these, in the following, internationalization consists of coherent social spaces covering multi-layered geographic spaces.[6]

The fifth type of internationalization is a product of critics of the globalization concept. Whereas the globalization discourse has emphasized the disappearance or annihilation of geographical space, the 'de-territorialization' of the 'social' or the 'recession of the constraints of geography' (Waters 1995), the term *glocalization* (Robertson 1994) focuses on the dialectics between globalization and localization. Global tendencies and processes are related to and interconnected with local concentrations of power, technology, knowledge, money and other resources and occurrences. Also, the tendency to sweep away borders goes hand in hand with the drawing of new borders. To perceive globalization as a process aimed solely at increasingly *reducing* the significance of geographic space and boundaries is to ignore the mounting efforts to establish new mechanisms of inclusion and exclusion at various territorial levels or to deny the very locally tangible effects of globalization processes. For instance, global warming has both dramatic local effects as well as quite specific local and territorially bounded origins (such as the energy consumption patterns of some OECD countries). The same is true for the global diffusion of fashions and nutrition habits and the corresponding dissolution of local economies and increase in so-called diseases of civilization. On the other hand, the expansion of local software economies like Bengalore in India has to do with the emergence of a relatively globalized market for special software services. In sum, globalization as a special type of internationalization consists of the interrelation between globalized, more or less de-localized phenomena and processes, on the one hand, and the very localized concentration of preconditions and/or effects of the former, on the other. The focus of globalization is on the twofold geographic spaces of 'the global' and 'the local' that provide the territorial scenery for relevant social spaces and mechanisms.

The sixth model describing spatial borders spanning coherent social frameworks is the *diaspora*. Even if the term is used in many different ways, the common factor to be stressed here is the existence of a shared social space that encompasses different geographic spaces and boundaries of civilizations or nations. The common social space is integrated or constituted mainly with reference to a common 'homeland'. The most important historical example of a diasporic social space is the Jewish experience of dispersion and persecution in many places and nations, whereby the reference to and imagination of a common homeland is the nexus. In a more general sense, the social spaces created by diplomatic corps or international business organizations could also be considered diasporas insofar as people in the 'peripheries' (embassies, settlements etc.), driven by religious, political or economic reasons, maintain strong loyalty to the sending centre (homeland, headquarters etc.). Steven Vertovec (2000) distinguishes between three different meanings of the term diaspora (as a social form, as a type of consciousness and as a mode of cultural production), and he defines diasporas as:

> practically any population which is considered 'de-territorialized' or 'transnational' – that is, whose cultural origins are said to have arisen in a land other than that in which they currently reside, and whose social, economic and political networks cross borders of nation states or, indeed, span the globe.
>
> (Vertovec 2000: 141)

This is a very broad concept of diaspora. As mentioned above, the concept of the 'de-territorialization' of the 'social' is very questionable. Of course it is very interesting and important to distinguish among different notions of diasporas according to the quality of the corresponding social spaces themselves. However, the intention here is to differentiate between ideal types of internationalization according to their specific combinations of social spaces and geographic places. It is thus useful to differentiate between globalization, glocalization, diasporic internationalization and transnationalization.

Finally, the seventh type of internationalization to be addressed here is *transnationalization*. This term refers to the growing quantitative and qualitative importance of pluri-local and transnational social relations, networks and practices. Transnationalization denotes the emergence of new trans- and pluri-local configurations which encompass and span traditional container spaces, and which are comprised of concentric circles of local, regional, national, supra-national and global phenomena. Transnationalization is based on a relational socio-geographic space and not on a container space with its double and exclusive embeddedness of social space and geographic space. *Transnational social spaces* can be understood as pluri-local frames of reference which structure everyday practices, social positions, biographical employment projects and human identities, and which simultaneously exist above and beyond the social contexts of national societies. Transnationalization as a *process* could lead to explicit transnational *orders*, such as:

1   habitual and accountable *patterns* of action and behaviour;
2   new transnational values, norms and *rules*;
3   complex frameworks of regulation and institutions.

The emerging significance of transnational migration

This careful delineation of specific types of internationalization is intended to help provide a better understanding of forms of international migration as well. In the context of the old 'national container society' paradigm, international migration was mainly perceived, not as a relatively normal and enduring way of life, but as an exceptional crossing from one place or 'nation container' to another at a specific and limited moment in time. As industrial capitalism developed and nation states emerged, migration mainly took place within nation states and took the form of unidirectional movement from the countryside into the growing cities. Cities were seen as the culmination of civilization and progress (Durkheim 1988; Cohen 1996). Many scholars have maintained that internal and international migration, defined as the movement of people between geographic (and, thus, automatically social) spaces, would – if it did not stop entirely – cease to be a force behind change and challenge in modern, 'established' societies and in a global order based on nation states. In any case, it was assumed that the nomadic way of life, in which movement between places itself represented a *form of social being*, and not only a geographical shift between two *places of social being*, would disappear (Simmel 1903).

At the beginning of the twenty-first century, less than 1 per cent of the world's population lives under nomadic conditions, i.e. without a fixed place of residence. Less than 10 per cent of the world's population do not live in their countries of birth or citizenship. This could lead to the conclusion that international migration is a transitory phenomenon that accompanies the development of modern, territorially fixed states and societies. However, the economic, cultural, political and social aspects of globalization, and the related spread of new communication technologies (the unrestricted availability of telephone services, music and video cassettes, fax and Internet), awareness of marked international differences in risks and opportunities in life, and strong political, ethnic, economic conflicts between and within nation states seem to have changed this view fundamentally. A new 'age of migration' (Castles and Miller 1993) and 'world in motion' (Massey *et al.* 1998) are said to have emerged, whereby not only the quantity, but also the quality of international migration is changing. The social sciences are faced with the challenge of developing a conceptual framework with which to analyse and understand new forms of international migration that cannot be adequately understood using the established concepts of immigration, return migration and diaspora migration.

Recent innovative approaches in international migration theory, like the concepts of migration networks, cumulative causation and migration systems (Portes 1995; Massey *et al.* 1998; Zolberg and Smith 1996) can aid in understanding and explaining the quantity and 'perpetuation' of traditional forms of international migration, as well as the quality of new forms of migration like recurrent or repeat migration. But as far as the underlying notion of the social and the spatial is concerned, migration is often perceived in the traditional way as a demarcated and exceptional shift of residence from one socio-geographic container space to another. One could label this international migration *container hopping* to denote a *shifting between places* in different 'national society containers' in search of a new way of life. The predominant question in this line of study is: why do people migrate and how do they adapt?

In contrast to this, transmigration can be conceptualized as a way of living in a transnational and pluri-local social space, characterized by movement between different geographic spaces. Transmigration is a transitory way of life lived between places in different national society containers. This commuting does not always take the form of frequent and continuous physical shifting, but could to a considerable extent consist of commuting, multiple identities and pluri-local concepts of life and biographies. According to William I. Thomas (1965), the perception, interpretation and communication of social reality forms an inseparable part of the 'social' itself: 'If men define situations as real, they are real in their social consequences'.[7] A guest worker who perceives himself as a return migrant will probably act like a return migrant (i.e. not focus on social, political and cultural integration in the 'host country', but save money and build a nice house in his 'homeland') even if he does not actually physically return except for holidays and family events.

In sum, mental and physical crossings of national society boundaries are two mutually reinforcing elements in a transmigrant's life. The main question to be addressed is: why do people not stop migrating and how do they create new social worlds of living that span different places and nation states? Transmigration is a new ideal type of international migration that integrates different theoretical approaches (Pries 2001). Compared to immigration, return migration and diaspora migration, the crossing of nation state boundaries changes its character: it is neither the one- or two-time movement between different places (that characterizes immigrants, long term return migrants or diaspora migrants), nor the frequent boundary crossing of daily or weekly commuters or recurrent seasonal or short term migrants (that characterizes short term return migrants). Transmigration as a new *ideal type* of migration that describes a modern variant of the nomadic way of life, whereby the crossing of boundaries and shifting between different places is not the exception in an otherwise settled life in one place but a basic way of life, of organizing life trajectories and constructing biographies (see Table 2.1).

Transmigration is structured by and at the same time structures *transnational social spaces* as compacted, condensed and institutionalized frameworks of social practices, artefacts and symbolic representations. It spans pluri-locally over different places in more than one nation state and is stable over time (Pries 1999). Insofar as these new social spaces span different geographic spaces, the traditional assumption of a coincidence and mutual embeddedness of the 'social' and the 'spatial' is no longer valid. The vast majority of social life is structured in uni-local places where the scope of the 'social' coincides with the spread of the 'spatial'. Therefore, the classic ideal types of migration (immigration, return migration and diaspora migration) are not disappearing; rather, the new ideal type of transmigration is replenishing them. This lends some importance to the study of transmigration, even if its significance in quantitative terms is low and hard to measure: like yeast or baking powder, even small quantities of transmigrants could alter the overall dynamics of migration in general.

The transnationalism and transnational migration concepts have already been applied to research in different international contexts. Concerning the notion of transnationalism and transnational migration, Basch *et al.* (1997) presented conceptual considerations and empirical findings for the Caribbean and Haitian situation and the corresponding social relations with the USA. Ong and Nonini (1997) have focused on Chinese transnationalism in its different aspects. Kearney and Nagengast (1989), Smith (1995, 1997), Goldring (1996, 1997, 2001) and Portes (1995) have analysed aspects of transnational migration between Mexico and the USA from an essentially anthropological perspective. Based on the data set of 19 Mexican communities in the *Mexican Migration Project*, Massey *et al.* (1994) stressed the time and community factors that stabilize transnational migration flows. These findings explain the dynamics, self perpetuation and cumulative causation circles of transnational migration streams at a community and country level.

The results of interviews made during a life-history oriented survey of about 800 Mexican migrants, who had been to the metropolitan area of New York City at least once, allow a classification into the four categories of migrants mentioned earlier (Pries *et al.* 1998). One group of Mexicans surveyed had already stayed for a longer period in the USA and had settled permanently in the metropolitan area of New York City: they can be labelled immigrants. Another group of those interviewed had stayed in Mexico for a longer period and said that they did not wish to cross the border to the USA again for work: they come close to the ideal type of return migrants. A third group of persons (about one-quarter to one-sixth of those interviewed) had undertaken a higher number of trips between the two countries. But these movements were neither the typical seasonal migration nor the typical short distance border commuting: this form of migration spans thousands of miles between the sending areas and the New York region and comes close to the ideal type of transmigration.

These typical transmigrants had undertaken five or more trips during their work and migration trajectory. Each of their jobs normally lasted several years and was therefore not seasonal work. The reasons for changing from one job to another (and often thereby moving from one country to the other) were characterized as 'voluntary'. It is remarkable that problems with legal status, dismissals or bankruptcy represented only about one-tenth of all reasons for changing jobs. This is surprising because the vast majority of employment activities (86 per cent) occurred without formal permission to work and reside in the USA, i.e. those interviewed had worked as *indocumentados.*

Other data analyses (Pries 1996, 1998, 2000) suggested that those persons surveyed who moved frequently back and forth between Mexico and the USA cannot be considered 'failed immigrants'. They are also neither traditional commuters nor recurrent migrants like those living in the US–Mexican border region. So the question remained: why do they move for so long and so often at high risk and expense back and forth between Mexico and the USA? One possible answer takes into account the migration trajectories of the spouses, parents and children of the persons surveyed, as well as the qualitative material derived from biographical interviews and field work observations: a significant number of labour migrants between the Puebla region and the metropolitan area of New York City should be considered transmigrants who are moving in pluri-local *transnational social spaces* spanning different places in Mexico and the USA. The individual and collective biographical life projects, everyday life as well as the life trajectory as a sequence of places of residence span different geographic spaces.

A good example of the existence of transnational social spaces and life structures is the family of Doña Rosa, who is over 70 years old and the head of a complicated and transnational clan structure, from which five persons belonging to different generations were interviewed (see Herrera 2002 and Figure 2.1, which was elaborated on by Fernando Herrera and adapted by the author). One part of the family network lives in the USA (mainly in the New York City region), another part lives in Mexico (mainly in the Mixteca Poblana region), and many family members move back and forth between the two sides during the course of their lives. For instance, one woman, Maria Luisa, crossed the border from Mexico once because she was *soltera con hija* – an unmarried mother. She left her daughter with her parents and went to New York City to earn money, but then returned to live and work in Mexico for a while. When asked which region or place she considered her homeland she will reply, 'My home-land is where my family is' and she will refuse to predict precisely where she will and would like to grow old. Being outside a formal social welfare and security system, the wider family clan is the functional equivalent of a

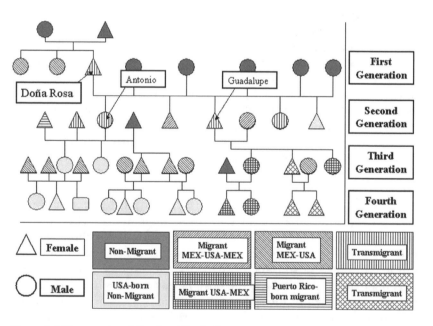

Figure 2.1 Transnational family of Doña Rosa.

social security system – and it spans from Puebla, Mexico, up to New York City.

Knowing both sides of the border, Maria Luisa – as well as the majority of her family network – will admit to experiencing advantages and conveniences as well as shortcomings and negative aspects of life in Mexico *and* the USA. Some of her brothers or sisters will probably become good US citizens and integrate themselves into New York City as immigrants. Others will feel more like Mexicans and return (or try to return) to their region of origin in Puebla. But Maria Luisa will not be able to decide. If her relatives argue that she has to decide and develop a clear strategy, that she 'should know where she belongs', Maria Luisa will answer: 'none of us is forced to choose between his or her father and mother – why should I be forced to decide between Mexico and the United States?' This standpoint could be interpreted as the outcome of a cautious life strategy just not to force things – perhaps because Maria Luisa tried to become a good US citizen and felt that her internalized Mexican history and culture were stronger, or because she failed to integrate herself for several reasons. In sum, frequent border crossing could be an indicator of intended but failed *immigration*, but it also could be an indicator of transnational life strategies and the organization of life within pluri-local transnational social spaces.

To speak of transmigrants is not to idealize the often precarious situation of international migrants. Transmigrants are not the new sovereign cosmopolitans who move freely and voluntarily between different locales, places and opportunities without problems. Transmigrants adapt themselves to uncertain and unpredictable situations, learn to manage risks and to live with them, accumulate cultural and social capital (Espinosa and Massey 1997; Palloni *et al.* 2001) and pay high transaction costs in and between two or more countries. As far as residency and work are concerned, their life planning is not fixed and long term, but sequential and focused on 'exploiting opportunities'. The transmigrants are not free to define the conditions in which they act. The horizon of realizable actions and expectations is limited neither to the region of origin nor the region of destination, it *spans between and over* them.

Conclusions: transnational migration and a new Europe?

That transnational migration or transmigration was becoming an increasingly important frame of reference for studying migration phenomena became clear in the context of Caribbean and Mexican migration to the USA (Kearney and Nagengast 1989; Grasmuck and Pessar 1991). These concepts were then applied to some aspects of Chinese migration in Asia and to the USA (Ong and Nonini 1997), analyses of Muslim transnational networks and politics, as well as to the European context (Morokvasic 1994; Pries 1996, 1997; Faist 1997, 2000a, b). Its usefulness derives from the fact that transmigration as a concept allows for a more differentiated understanding of the patterns of migrants' simultaneous integration into several places and societies, like their 'host' and 'home' societies. Immigrants (like most of the 'Spätaussiedler' in Germany) typically incorporate themselves (gradually) into the economic, social, political and cultural dimensions of life in the newly adopted host society, even if the process takes place over several generations. Ideal-typical return migrants (like Germany's guest workers) go back to their home country after a period of working and living abroad and reincorporate themselves into all dimensions of life there. Diaspora migrants (like diplomats or managers in international companies) incorporate themselves into some dimensions of life in the host country, mainly at a local level (like the economic or political activities they were sent for), but they continue to centre their lives and biographies in their home countries. This is especially true in the case of their cultural and social networks, though it can also apply to economic ties like employment contracts and real estate. Finally, ideal-typical transmigrants maintain ties and network relations in all four dimensions of incorporation, as well as at the local and national levels of the host and home countries. They not only move physically trans-nationally between places but also span their biographical orientations and projects between different places and countries.

Distinguishing between the seven ideal types of internationalization patterns and the four ideal types of migrants and their corresponding integration patterns leads to a more appropriate understanding of the dynamics of *incorporation,* which is a *complex, open-ended and dialectical social process* of self perception and perception by others among different groups. It requires the successful interaction of those to be incorporated with the rest of the society. If the interaction is blocked by one of the interacting sides, then incorporation is minimal, or does not take place at all (a case in point are the Turkish migrants in Germany who perceived themselves and were perceived as guest workers). Incorporation is also a *multidimensional process* involving the economic, political, social and cultural dimensions of a given society. There exists a variety of patterns and outcomes concerning the intensity and sequences of incorporation within these distinctive dimensions. Just as immigrants may belong to a variety of different reference groups, their incorporation also takes place on *different spatial scales* simultaneously. Therefore, it is necessary to differentiate between local, national and transnational scales of incorporation, and to focus on their points of intersection, as processes taking place on one level can induce or inhibit incorporation on another level.

As indicated in this chapter, the specific treatment of migrants by the receiving state and society has significant impacts on their incorporation patterns and dynamics. The very fact that German politicians and the society in general were perceiving and labelling migrants as 'Gastarbeiter' (guest workers) influenced the willingness and the strategies of many migrants to learn the German language, to send their children to a kindergarten (and not only to the compulsory school) and to integrate themselves at least to a certain extent socially and culturally. The educational attainment of migrants' children differs significantly, and migrants' children are disadvantaged when looking for a place in the vocational training system, the most important gateway into the labour market. Besides other deficiencies, the German PISA results have their origins in the decades spent ignoring the fact that Germany was and is an immigration country. Education, migrants' incorporation and transnationalism have to be analysed and treated as deeply interrelated issues.

Notes

1 The results are documented under http://www.pisa.oecd.org/, 31 May 2003, where the results of the 2003 study are presented also. I wish to thank Jennifer Elrick for her critical reading and suggestions.
2 Due to the primacy of the *ius sanguinis* principle until 2004 migrants' children, even those born in Germany (perhaps already in the second generation!) were normally registered and counted as foreigners. Conversely Spätaussiedler were registered as Germans, even if they (and their parents) were born in Russia. The methodological problems of treating and counting 'foreigners' and migrants in Germany cannot be expanded here.
3 In such societies, the population and its processes of socialization are closely tied, in reciprocal exclusiveness, to a more or less clearly definable and known physical/geographic sphere. In other words, a defined space encompassing a geographic area (a 'territory' or 'locale') corresponds to one and only one socially compressed space (for example, a community or a national society). Conversely, every social space 'occupied' precisely one geographically specific space: physical and social space were embedded exclusively in each other. Because of the coincidence of social and geographic space, the well-known *container-concept* of space and of nation state bound national societies was satisfactory and sufficient for treating the 'social' and 'space' (Pries 2001).
4 Malcolm Waters, referring to the work of Roland Robertson, stresses the latter aspect: 'We can therefore define globalization as: A social process in which the constraints of geography on social and cultural arrangements recede and in which people become increasingly aware that they are receding' (Waters 1995: 3).
5 This is also the general spatial connotation of the term civilization as stated, for example, by Braudel: 'Civilizations, vast or otherwise, can always be located on a map. An essential part of their character depends on the constraints or advantages of their geographical situation' (Braudel 1993: 9).
6 Referring to cultural practices spanning the geographic terrains of 'civilizations' Lewis and Wigen distinguish between four space-spanning cultural practices which are useful for our consideration of ideal-typical internationalization patterns:

   1 the 'middle ground' as a type of 'contested terrain' where no cultural hegemony has been established, 'a temporary, fragile, and essentially abstract cultural space ... where cultures continue to negotiate on unevenly shared terrain' (1997: 151) and where diasporas serve as important ties which facilitate economic and cultural exchange;

2 the diaspora constituted by 'maintaining a common identity over daunting distances, such transnational communities served as important conduits for cross-cultural trade' (1997: 152; see also Cohen 1996);

3 archipelagos '"enclaves" of a given culture group [like] the millions of Arabic-speaking Christians scattered through the Middle East or Mandarin-speaking Muslims in the heart of China' (1997: 153);

4 the cultural matrix type of boundary-crossing, akin to cultural syncretism, hybridity or a patchwork identity. Thus, 'in a matrix model, identity is a matter of one's position in a multidimensional lattice' (1997: 152).

7 (Thomas and Thomas 1928, cited in Thomas, W. 1965: 114).

References

Basch, L., Glick Schiller, N. and Szanton Blanc, C. (1997) *Nations Unbound: Transnational Projetcs, Postcolonial Predicaments, and Deterritorialized Nation-States*, Amsterdam: Gordon and Breach (4th edn., first published 1994).

Bender, S. and Seifert, W. (1996) 'Zuwanderer auf dem Arbeitsmarkt: Nationalitäten- und Geschlechts-spezifische Unterschiede', *Zeitschrift für Soziologie* 25, 6: 473–495.

Braudel, F. (1993) *A History of Civilizations*, New York: Penguin Books.

Castells, M. (1996) *The Rise of the Network Society*, Volume 1, Malden and Oxford, Blackwell.

—— (1998) *The Information Age: Economy, Society and Culture*, Volume III: End of Millennium, Malden and Oxford: Blackwell.

Castles, S. and Miller, M. J. (1993) *The Age of Migration: International Population Movements in the Modern World*, Hampshire and London: Macmillan.

Cohen, R. (ed.) (1996) *Theories of Migration*, (The International Library of Studies on Migration 1) Cheltenham/Brookfield: Elgar.

Durkheim, E. (1988) *Über soziale Arbeitsteilung*, Frankfurt/M.: Suhrkamp.

EC Report (2001) *EU Socio-Economic-Research: Effectiveness of National Integration Strategies Towards Second Generation Migrant Youth in a Comparative European Perspective*, Final Report of project ERB-SOE2-CT97-3055 (coord. F. Heckmann), Brussels: EC.

Espinosa, K. and Massey, D. (1997) 'Undocumented migration and the quantity and quality of social capital', in L. Pries (ed.) *Transnationale Migration, Sonderband 12 der Zeitschrift Soziale Welt*, Baden-Baden: Nomos: 141–162.

Esser, H. (2000) *Integration und ethnische Schichtung*, (Manuscript – Report commissioned by the Federal Ministry of the Interior).

Çağlar, A. (1989) *The Myth of Return: Pragmatism and the Turkish Culture in Germany*, Lecture at the symposium 'Muslims, Migrants, Metropolis' (of the Berlin Institute for Comparative Social Research) Berlin: 13–18 June 1989.

Faist, T. (1997) 'Migration und der Transfer sozialen Kapitals oder: Warum gibt es relativ wenige internationale Migranten?', in L. Pries (ed.) *Transnationale Migration, Sonderband 12 der Zeitschrift Soziale Welt*, Baden-Baden: Nomos: 63–83.

—— (2000a) *The Volume and Dynamics of International Migration and Transnational Social Spaces*, Oxford: Oxford University Press.

—— (ed.) (2000b) *Transstaatliche Räume: Politik, Wirtschaft und Kultur in und zwischen Deutschland und der Türkei*, Bielefeld: transcript.

Frick, J. and Wagner, G. G. (2001) 'Economic and social perspectives of immigrant children in Germany', in E. Currle and T. Wunderlich (eds) *Deutschland – ein Einwanderungsland?: Rückblick, Bilanz und neue Fragen*, Efms, Stuttgart: Lucius & Lucius.

Giddens, A. (1990) *The Consequences of Modernity*, Cambridge: Polity Press.

Goldring, L. (1996) 'Blurring the border: Transnational community and social transformation in Mexico? U.S. migration', in D. A. Chekki (ed.) *Research in Community Sociology*, Volume VI, London: JAI Press: 69–104.

—— (1997) 'Power and status in transnational social spaces', in L. Pries (ed.) *Transnationale Migration, Sonderband 12 der Zeitschrift Soziale Welt*, Baden-Baden: Nomos: 179–196.

—— (2001) 'Disaggregating transnational social spaces: gender, place and citizenship in Mexico–U.S, transnational spaces', in L. Pries (ed.) *New Transnational Social Spaces: International Migration and Transnational Companies*, London: Routledge: 59–76.

Grasmuck, S. and Pessar, P. B. (1991) *Between Two Islands: Dominican International Migration*, Berkeley: University of California Press.

Harvey, D. (1989) *The Condition of Postmodernity*, Oxford: Basil Blackwell.

Herrera Lima, F. (2002) *Trayectorias y Biografias Laborales en la Migracion de Puebla y tlaxcala y la Zona Metropolitana de la Ciudad de Nueva York*, Ph.D. Thesis, Department of Anthropology, Universidad Autónoma Metropolitana: Mexico.

Hettlage, R. (1999) 'Von deutscher Wanderlust', *Soziologische Revue* 22, 2: 159–170.

Hunger, U. and Thränhardt, D. (2001) 'Zu den neuen Disparitäten im deutschen Bildungssystem', in Rat für Migration e.V. and K. Bade (eds) *Integration und Illegalität in Deutschland*, Osnabrück: IMIS: 51–61.

Kalter, F. and Granato, N. (2001) *Recent Trends of Assimilation in Germany*, ZUMA – Working Report 2001/02.

Kearney, M. (1995) 'The global and the local: The anthropology of globalization and transnationalism', *Annual Review of Anthropology* 25: 547–565.

Kearney, M. and Nagengast, C. (1989) *Anthropological Perspectives on Transnational Communities in Rural California*, Davis/California: Institute for Rural Studies, Working Group on Farm Labor and Rural Poverty (Working Paper 3).

Lewis, M. W. and Wigen, K. E. (1997) *The Myth of Continents. A Critique of Metageography*, Berkeley, Los Angeles and London: University of California Press.

Massey, D., Arango, J., Hugo, G., Kouaouci, A., Pellegrino, A. and Taylor, J. E. (1994) 'An evaluation of international migration theory: The North American case', *Population and Development Review* 20: 699–751.

Massey, D. S., Arango, J., Hugo, G., Kouaouci, A., Pellegrino, A. and Taylor, E. P. (1998) *Worlds in Motion: Understanding International Migration at the End of the Millennium*, Oxford: Clarendon Press.

Morokvasic, M. (1994) 'Pendeln statt auswandern: Das Beispiel der Polen', in M. Morokvasic and H. Rudolph (eds) *Wanderungsraum Europa. Menschen und Grenzen in Bewegung*, Berlin: edition sigma: 166–187.

Ong, A. and Nonini, D. (eds) (1997) *Ungrounded Empires: The Cultural Politics of Modern Chinese Transnationalism*, London and New York: Routledge.

Palloni, A., Massey, D. S., Ceballos, M., Espinosa, K. and Spittel, M. (2001) 'Social capital and international migration: a test using information on family networks', *American Journal of Sociology* 106, 5: 1262–1298.

PISA (2003) http://www.pisa.oecd.org/, 31 May 2003.

Portes, A. (1995) 'Economic sociology and the sociology of immigration: A conceptual overview', in *The Economic Sociology of Immigration. Essays on Networks, Ethnicity, and Entrepreneurship*, New York: Russel Sage Foundation: 1–41.

Pries, L. (1996) 'Transnationale Soziale Räume: Theoretisch-empirische Skizze am Beispiel der Arbeitswanderungen Mexiko–USA', *Zeitschrift für Soziologie* 25: 437–453.

—— (ed.) (1997) *Transnationale Migration, Sonderband 12 der Zeitschrift Soziale Welt*, Baden-Baden: Nomos.

—— (1998) ' "Transmigranten" als ein Typ von Arbeitswanderern in pluri-lokalen sozialen Räumen. Das Beispiel der Arbeitswanderungen zwischen Puebla/Mexiko und New York', *Soziale Welt* 49: 135–150.

—— (1999) 'Die Neuschneidung des Verhältnisses von Sozialraum und Flächenraum: Das Beispiel transnationaler Migrationsräume', in C. Honegger, S. Hradil and F. Traxler, (eds) *Grenzenlose Gesellschaft? Verhandlungen des 29. Kongresses der Deutschen Gesellschaft für Soziologie, des 16. Kongresses der Österreichischen Gesellschaft für Soziologie, des 11. Kongresses der Schweizerischen Gesellschaft für Soziologie in Freiburg i.Br. 1998*, Opladen: Leske and Budrich: part 2, 437–452.

—— (2000) 'Transnationalisierung der Migrationsforschung und Entnationalisierung der Migrationspolitik: Das Entstehen transnationaler Sozialräume durch Arbeitswanderung am Beispiel Mexiko–USA', *IMIS- Schriftenreihe Beiträge* No. 15, Osnabrück: Universität Osnabrück: 55–77.

—— (ed.) (2001) *New Transnational Social Spaces: International Migration and Transnational Companies*, London: Routledge.

Pries, L., Herrera Limas, F. and Saúl Macías, G. (1998) *Las migraciones laborales internacionales y el surgimiento de Espacios Sociales Transnacionales. El ejemplo de la migración del Estado de Puebla hacia la región metropolitana de Nueva York. Informe de investigación proyecto 'Migración laboral de la Mixteca Poblana hacia Nueva York'* (Convenio No. 400200-5-0234PS, clave 0234P-59506, CONACYT).

Riphahn, R. (2001) 'Cohort effects in the educational attainment of second generation immigrants in Germany: an analysis of census data', *IZA Discussion Paper* No. 291.

Robertson, R. (1994) 'Globalization or glocalization', *Journal of International Communication* 1: 33–52.

Sackmann, R., Prümm, K. and Schultz, T. (2000) *Kollektive Identität türkischer Migranten in Deutschland. Institut für Interkulturelle und Internationale Studien*, Arbeitspapier No. 20: Universität Bremen.

Schiffauer, W., Baumann, G., Kastoryano, R. and Vertovec, S. (eds) (2002) *Staat – Schule – Ethnizität: Politische Sozialisation von Immigrantenkindern in vier europäischen Ländern*, Münster: Waxmann Verlag.

Seifert, W. (1998) 'Social and economic integration of foreigners in Germany', in P. Schuck and R. Münz (eds) *Paths to Inclusion – The Integration in the United States and Germany*, New York: Berghahn Books.

—— (2000) 'Ausländer in Deutschland', *Datenreport 1999*, Bonn: 569–580.

Simmel, G. (1903) 'Soziologie des Raumes', reprinted in H. J. Dahme and O. Rammstedt (eds) (1983) *Simmel: Schriften zur Soziologie*, Frankfurt/M: Suhrkamp: 221–242.

Smith, R. (1995) *'Los ausentes siempre presentes': The imagining, making and politics of a transnational community betwen Ticuani, Puebla, Mexico, and New York City*, Ph.D. dissertation, New York: Columbia University.

—— (1997) 'Reflections on migration, the state and the construction, durability and newness of transnational life', in L. Pries (ed.) *Transnationale Migration, Sonderband 12 der Zeitschrift Soziale Welt*, Baden-Baden: Nomos: 197–220.

Thomas, W. I. (1965) *Person und Sozialverhalten* (ed. E. H. Volkart), Berlin: Luchterhand (American Original 1951).

Urry, J. (2001) *Sociology Beyond Societies. Mobilities for the Twenty-First Century*, London: Routledge.

Vertovec, S. (2000) *The Hindu Diaspora: Comparative Patterns*, London and New York: Routledge.

Waters, M. (1995) *Globalization*, London and New York: Routledge.

Weber, M. (1972) *Wirtschaft und Gesellschaft*, Tübingen: Mohr (1st edn. 1922).

Weidacher, A. (ed.) (2000) *In Deutschland zu Hause: Politische Orientierungen griechischer, italienischer, türkischer und deutscher junger Erwachsener im Vergleich*, DJI Ausländersurvey, Opladen: Leske and Budrich.

Wolbert, B. (1997) 'Paß und Passagen: Zur Dynamik und Symbolik von Migrationsprozessen am Beispiel der Rückkehr türkischer Arbeitsmigranten', *Kea: Zeitschrift für Kulturwissenschaft*, 10: Ethnologie der Migration, Bremen: 49–69.

Zolberg, A. R. and Smith, R. C. (1996) *Migration Systems in Comparative Perspective: An Analysis of the InterAmerican Migration System with Comparative Reference to the Mediterranean-European System*, New York: The New School for Social Research.

3 (New forms of) migration

Challenges for education

Sigrid Luchtenberg

Post-war immigration into Germany did not challenge education for a long time due to the fact that work migration was regarded as temporary in the 1950s and 1960s. When workers began to settle – mainly as a result of the enforced stop of recruitment in 1973 – education had to deal with the situation of migrant children attending German schools in large numbers. The first answer to this new challenge was the concept of migrant education (Ausländerpädagogik). Multicultural education ('intercultural education' in the German diction) was developed in Germany rather reluctantly in the 1980s as a second answer to this challenge when the concept of migrant education was no longer regarded as an adequate one by many educationalists in practice and research. Multicultural education finally got some recognition in the 1990s, when it was partly connected with international education like European aspects or global learning. Europe, but also further developments in migration, led to a new type of short term migration and further newer forms of migration, which have not fully been taken into consideration in education.

In this chapter, we will first discuss the development in Germany since the Second World War with regard to immigration into Germany and its impacts on education. The keywords of this time were integration as well as remigration, and educational concepts were hopelessly torn between both ends of the arguments. In general, education was supposed to be regular education for German students plus additional help for migrant students, if necessary. Migrant education became part of the German educational system as a separate educational task with regard to migrant children. At that time, nearly no thought was given to the fact that the presence of migrant students might, or indeed should have an effect on or should be taken into consideration with regards to the German curricula, German students and German teachers. A general assumption was that the migrants were temporary, so that no need for permanent educational programmes was felt at that time.

While education has mainly acknowledged the fact of a permanent immigration, which demands measures of integration and the preparation of all inhabitants – majority as well as immigrants – for a multilingual and multicultural society, there are also new developments in forms of migration to be taken into consideration. These questions will be discussed in the latter part of this chapter, where we regard the impact of recent forms of migration on education. Throughout the chapter we will deal with the fact that multicultural education is now sometimes regarded as a concept of international education dealing with the cultures of the world. Although this is a necessary approach in our world of global relationships, it tends to neglect local diversity. Future challenges to multicultural education concern the combination of local and global aspects within this concept. There is a further challenge to be considered with regard to a multicultural education that deals mainly with global relationships: the needs of children from migrant families. The recent PISA study (OECD 2001) has clearly pointed out that the German school system has failed so far to give them access to a good school career. It is a great challenge to improve this situation without falling back into concepts of migrant education. This will be discussed on p. 50.

Throughout, we will refer to language education, political education, multicultural education, intercultural communication, media education and the European dimension in these aspects, though with different intensity.

Migration and education in Germany: development and present state

According to the Federal Agency of Statistics (Statistisches Bundesamt 2003) 7,318,528 migrants (foreigners) – about 8.9 per cent of the population – were living in Germany at the beginning of 2003, a high amount of them of Turkish origin. Ethnic groups and individuals have different status with regard to residential rights, citizenship status and cultural independence. Migrants or foreigners are persons who do not have a German passport, but live in Germany, i.e. work migrants, foreign students and refugees. Of these more than 20 per cent were born in Germany, with even more than 70 per cent of the under-18's born in Germany. Thus, a majority of the migrants and foreigners are persons with a migration background, but are not migrants themselves. Yet, many migrants are not 'foreigners' since among migrants there are many ethnic German emigrants (resettlers), who have German nationality (cf. Beauftragte 2001: 79). Resettlers are the descendents of German settlers who migrated into the former Russia and other East European countries about 200 years ago. They are allowed to come to Germany because they were persecuted for being German during the Second World War. It is difficult to extract valid information from statistics that only differentiate between foreigners and Germans, thereby neglecting all persons with migration background who have gained German citizenship. There is a recent trend to replace the differentiation in Germans and non-Germans by a differentiation according to birthplace. This will show that the migrant population is far higher than 9 per cent.

Due to a booming economy, West Germany had to recruit workers from abroad, especially after the GDR closed the frontier in 1961 so that workers from there could no longer come to West Germany. Workers – who were called guest workers at that time – came mainly from the southern and south-eastern European countries, including Turkey – and later on from Morocco as well – due to bilateral contracts. They were supposed to stay for two years (up to a maximum of five years) and then be replaced by others. Most of them did not intend permanent migration themselves but intended to earn enough money to improve their life in the country of origin. The 'rotation model' turned out to be unacceptable for industry so that workers stayed longer and began to settle by bringing their families to Germany. They had also learnt that it was impossible to earn enough money for a better life at home. Family reunion increased when, in 1973, a general recruitment stop was declared by the government due to a recession (cf. Hoff 1995). It should be mentioned that there was also work migration into the former GDR, mainly from socialist countries, especially from developing countries such as Mozambique or Vietnam.

Work migrants got a rather limited work and residential permission in the beginning but could apply for less limited permissions step by step. Most of them have an unlimited residential status nowadays (if not citizenship) and full work permission.

Nowadays not even half of the migrants belong to the workforce, while the others are family members. Officially, no work migrants have been recruited since 1973 but there are exceptions for some professions like nurses, seasonal work in agricultural areas and IT professions. 'New migrants' thus belong mainly to a family already living in Germany: children up to 16 and the husband or wife were allowed to join the family in Germany. It is known that many Turks in their second or even third generation marry a husband or wife from the country of origin though in slightly decreasing numbers (cf. Beauftragte 2001: 25). There is also a small but increasing number of Germans who marry a foreign husband or – more often – wife who has lived in the country of origin so far.

Work migrants do not comprise one homogenous ethnic group but form a group only due to their common reason for immigration. Besides this, they are different with regard to language, religious and cultural backgrounds.

Refugees or asylum seekers make the most heterogeneous group of ethnic minorities in Germany to whom different laws are applied. They differ with regard to the countries of origin, the languages spoken, the education and the personal biography of migration, which often includes war memories and worse (cf. Hoff 1995). According to press information by the German ministry of home affairs, only 71,127 persons asked for asylum in 2002 – in contrast to more than 400,000 in 1992, which is due to changes in the law in 1993. Most refugees in 2002 came from Iraq, followed in number by the former Yugoslavia and Turkey, most of them Kurds (Bundesministerium des Inneren 2003). In the first half of 2003, numbers dropped again (Schmidt-Fink 2003). In the public debate, a difference is made between political and economic asylum seekers, who are often called false (make-believe) or pseudo-asylum seekers and against whom right wing parties campaign.

More than two million resettlers, who are not officially regarded as migrants, came into Germany between 1990 and 2003. In recent years, regulations have become stricter as regards numbers accepted and with tests in the German language, which has reduced their numbers to less than 100,000 per year, e.g. 83,812 in 2001 and only 66,833 in 2002 (cf. Isoplan 2003). Most of those who apply for their acceptance are now non-German family members. This gives the recently demanded test in German new relevance. In contrast to 1990, in 2000 only a few resettlers came from Poland – most of them came from the former Soviet Union, especially from Kazakhstan. There are some resettlers who return to their country of origin. Besides migrants, we find three groups of ethnic minorities who live in a defined territory: Dens at the border to Denmark, Frisians in northern Germany partly close to the Dutch border, partly further north, and Sorbs south of Berlin on the territory of the former GDR. All three groups have special rights with regard to teaching their language in schools and producing media in their languages. They also enjoy full acceptance in the German population. This is different regarding the group of Sinte and Roma, as gypsies have been called in Germany for a few years. Their group is heterogeneous, not only because of the two groups, but also with regard to their status in Germany. Many stem from families that have lived in Germany for a long time, while others came more recently as refugees from eastern and south-eastern European countries. Many of them belong to families that have suffered enormously during the Hitler regime, a fact that has only reluctantly been recognized in Germany. Sinte and Roma were acknowledged as an ethnic minority when Germany ratified the European agreement on national minorities (Bundesgesetzblatt 1998: 57). Furthermore, the European Charter for Regional or Minority Languages has been accepted since 1999 (Council 2004). Thus, Romany could be taught as a minority language (cf. Jonen and Boele 2001: 19).

The present irreversible situation of a heterogeneous or plural society in Germany is mainly due to the development after the Second World War, especially because of the economic challenges connected with the 'Wirtschaftswunder' ('economic miracle') and the lack of workers in West Germany after the erection of the Berlin Wall. Yet, it should not be forgotten that there has long been migration into Germany (as well as out of Germany). The immigration of French Huguenots into Prussia in the eighteenth century and the immigration of Polish miners in the nineteenth and twentieth centuries belong to the better-known examples of earlier immigration (cf. Bade 2002 for further examples).

Since migration was originally mainly regarded as a short term economical necessity, neither politics nor education reacted very much to immigration in the 1960s with the very problematic effect that the German population did not reflect upon the impact of immigration on their own life. Instead, they thought of immigration as an event that would be finished soon. Remigration was supposed to be the natural end of migration, though integration soon became a key concept.

Integration as a key factor in policy and education

While remigration was mainly intended, it had to be reflected on how to fit those migrants – always called foreigners – who were present in Germany into German society, and, later, their children into the educational system. From the very beginning, language was at the centre of all discussions, i.e. the acquisition of German. Thus, all references to language in the integration discourse were always limited to the German language. Adult work migrants were supposed to learn that minimum of German that would enable them to cope in their place of work and with a limited daily life in their neighbourhood. Thus, the early concept of integration mainly concerned the workplace situation. The group of resettlers has been so far the only group of migrants that has received integration support, since they are entitled to courses in German, though now to a reduced extent. The instigation of integration courses is now being discussed – with a main focus on German – at least for (work) migrants who have recently arrived. There were, of course, many possibilities to join classes or courses, which even looked at the different needs of women, young adults or older workers, but no financial support or reduced working hours was given in order to attend them. Integration was – and still is – discussed with regard to the living conditions of migrants, since migrant quarters, where mainly Turks live together, are often regarded as disintegrative ghettos since there is no need to speak German and often even no need to leave these quarters except for work.

When, at the end of the 1960s, it became necessary to deal with children because more and more work migrants began to settle and to bring their families into Germany, education had to reflect the new situation. It was soon made clear that students with a migrant background were obliged to attend school. This is no right in itself since the children of asylum seekers are not obliged to attend school in Germany – like all other children up to the age of 16 – though most states in the Federal Republic allow or even encourage them to go to school. As soon as the family – or the child – has got a status as refugee, the children are obliged to go to school.

In the 1960s and 1970s the situation in school bureaucracy can be characterized as swinging between a concept of integration and a concept of remigration. Schools were even asked to prepare migrant children for both, which proved impossible. Since education in Germany is strictly regulated by the states, different states practiced different concepts.

We find the discussion with regard to schools similar to that of the living areas: it is regarded as being disintegrative when there are too many non-German students in a class. Though the main argument used here is the 'lack of German', the statement itself is made with regard to ethnicity since no language tests are recommended. Several concepts were introduced and later given up, like busing migrant children to schools in districts with fewer migrants. While in the 1970s and early 1980s migrant-only classes were formed in order to give migrant students time to learn German, such classes were rejected in the early times of multicultural education because of their non-integrative, separating approach. Meanwhile, such classes have again been called into being in many states, but with slightly different programmes. These classes are time-limited since integration remains the dominant aim.

Integration is only seldom discussed with regard to social, political or economic participation but mainly reduced to language (German), which holds true both with regard to adults and students.

Language education

While integration concepts always focused on the acquisition of German as a second language, those with regard to remigration favoured the instruction of the mother tongue. This attitude changed when multicultural concepts developed in the 1980s and became dominant in the 1990s. Mother tongue instruction soon became a value independent of remigration but it was regarded as necessary in order to support bilingualism, to facilitate second language learning and to allow family communication not only with those remaining in the countries of origin but also with those who had migrated into other countries.

In many states mother tongue courses are now offered in more languages, but the general economic difficulties in Germany have also led to a reduction of mother tongue instruction which was generally offered up to five hours per week in many schools, though not always during the school morning. Sometimes children had to join other children in a school that they did not go to in the morning and mother tongue teachers complain of very limited contact with their German colleagues. Mother tongue tuition is only seldom connected with the main curriculum, especially German, and is mostly taught independently. Thus it cannot be regarded as part of a bilingual education. To attend a mother tongue class is not compulsory for the students. There are some secondary schools where students can choose their mother tongue as a regular second language – this applies mainly to Turkish.

In spite of the fact that teachers, educational bureaucrats and politicians demand improvements in migrant students' German proficiency, the situation of German as a second language has not improved much since its development in the late 1960s – development being the appropriate word, as this subject did not exist before then. Its main sources – German as a foreign language and German as a mother tongue – have not always been helpful in finding the special needs and requirements of second language teaching. When the above-mentioned special classes were introduced, curricula of German as a second language were developed. In general, they were inadequate for the very heterogeneous groups of migrant students. This likewise applies to teaching materials, which are often oriented to German as a foreign language – even today. At present, German as a second language is mostly taught as support classes in addition to regular classes. It is no subject in its own right and – like mother tongue tuition – not very highly acknowledged in schools.

Political education

Political education in schools aims at critical reflection of political structures, at the establishment of a democratic system of values and the socialization as a democratic citizen. It has been developed for German students after the experiences of the Hitler regime with no special focus on migration and multiculturalism. Political education is not only a task for schools but also other organizations like the Unions or Parties, and special institutions like the 'Bundeszentrale für Politische Bildung' contribute a lot. Besides school education they address mainly adults or juveniles (cf. Luchtenberg 2003).

Political education within school education is integrated in many subjects, which are sometimes integrated into new subjects themselves. Main subjects are history, geography, social science and social education, but also politics and economy. Political education begins early in primary school where is it taught within science (Sachunterricht). Most states in Germany stress the importance of political education, which is underpinned by detailed curricula and teaching proposals. The contents are rather broad and include classical topics such as the constitution and political life in Germany, historical developments, human rights, but also media or economic aspects of life. Migration and multiculturalism also play a role in the curricula of political education: the impact of immigration in Germany; the European integration; globalization and world problems; human rights. Curricula and teaching proposals show that the importance of immigration and multiculturalism is taken into consideration, yet in many cases the focus is still on the question of what immigration and multiculturalism does to 'us' and not yet on the question of how 'we all' cope in a diverse society. In the new states of Saxony, Brandenburg, Mecklenburg–Western Pomerania, Saxony–Anhalt and Thuringia – former GDR – there is only a small percentage of non-German popu- lation. Here, we find a danger of denying the necessity of dealing with migration and a diverse society only because it does not (yet) occur in the neighbourhood. The new states have a special responsibility to develop programmes for this specific situation (cf. Luchtenberg 2003).

Compared with the international discussion on citizenship education in ethnic diverse societies, Germany still lacks the self-understanding as a nation composed of diverse groups and cultures (cf. Banks 2003). This is mainly a failure of politics and politicians but influences the society as a whole and school education as well. In none of the 16 states in Germany is the question tackled whether students with a migrant background require special care in political education or whether they could attribute in a special way. Certainly, some of them have experienced non-democratic regimes and violence against human rights that need careful and sensible help. The experience of different political systems, the challenge of dual citizenship or loss of a former citizenship are experiences that could enrich the discussion in all subjects of political education. Yet the concern shown towards students with a migrant background does not go beyond that of their attendance in these subjects. While the topic of migration is at the centre of political education as far as multicultural aspects are dis- cussed, little attention is paid to the development of a multicultural society. Yet, it has to be taken into consideration that some of the curric- ula in political education are older than ten years and that evaluated cur- ricula can be expected in the near future.

We can conclude that political education is slowly opening up to ques- tions of migration and multiculturalism.

Multicultural education for all

Multicultural education in Germany developed as a counter-concept to migrant education, when it became clear that migrant education could not solve the problems that schools and students have been facing since the 1970s (cf. Hoff 1995; Luchtenberg 1997).

The main differences are:

- All students as the target group instead of an education that addresses migrant students only;
- Orientation towards differences instead of deficits;
- Integration – not assimilation – as a main goal.

Thus, local diversity was the main reason for the development of multicul- tural education in Germany. 'Encountering' soon became a keyword in the sense that students with different backgrounds should meet each other, learn from each other and enrich one another. From the beginning, multicultural education laid great emphasis on culture and mutual cultural exchange. In the beginnings of multicultural education, relativism of cultures was taken for granted whereas the current view is that the reflection on cultures is more complex. There are two implications to be found in the importance of culture:

1   Mutual learning about cultures requires an awareness of cultural differences in all questions, which supports a division into the own and the other – an important point in the multicultural education discourse;
2   The focus on culture makes it easier to include global aspects, e.g. cultures of different nations and people.

The focus on culture has been criticized by educationalists but the name 'intercultural'/'multicultural' is very strong.

It should be mentioned that, from the beginning of its development in Germany, there was a second main concept within multicultural education. This concept focused on racism, discrimination and inequality – barriers that have to be overcome before mutual exchange is possible.

Multicultural education with a focus on local diversity has helped to open schools, curricula and schoolbooks for diversity due to migration (cf. Hoff 1995). In 1996, the Standing Conference of the Ministers of Education and Cultural Affairs launched a recommendation on multicultural education, which can be taken as a sign of its formal acknowledgement (Standing Conference 1996).

Some universities and teacher training institutions offer courses for teachers or student teachers to qualify in multicultural education in extended graduate courses, e.g. additional courses of studies after the first teaching qualification, with a focus on German as a second language besides multicultural contents so that more teachers are qualified in this subject than ever before. These courses, often first conceptualized in the period of migrant education and according to its philosophy, have now changed not only their names, but also their content. In contrast to this positive development, most student teachers are not obliged to deal with multicultural education during their studies at all.

Intercultural communication

Intercultural communication has always had a strong relationship to international communication since it was originally examined mainly with regard to business communication. Misunderstandings in communications with migrant workers led to research in intercultural communication in Germany – between migrants and Germans (cf. Hinnenkamp 1989). In the following years, more research was done on intercultural communication in Germany, mainly in the workforce and in institutional settings.

There are two points to be underlined: first, nearly all of these examinations dealt with the situation where the German person is representing the institution or is a superior person in the workplace. Until now, it has hardly been taken into consideration that in a multicultural society migrants in the second or third generation can be at least equal colleagues, and even superiors, or those representing the institution. Secondly, there is only very little research on intercultural communication in schools, despite the fact that intercultural communication often takes place in this institution. Instead, there is a strong interest in intercultural communication in foreign languages and their didactics. So the global perspective wins an important field whereas, in Germany itself, the local diversity should be of at least equal importance.

A further point should be mentioned with regard to intercultural communication that is related to multicultural education: the focus on culture. The similarity lies in the fact that cultural differences are taken as given, which not only divides into the own and the other but also predicts behaviour and misunderstandings (cf. Hinnenkamp 2001). While the determining factors of intercultural communication are still under discussion, there are already many hints that it depends very much on the communication partners whether they regard themselves as belonging to different groups or not. These approaches in intercultural communication research are close to those in multicultural education where the complexity of belonging is increasingly taken into consideration.

Media education

Neither media education nor political education have played a dominant role in multicultural education in Germany so far.

Though migration and its consequences are an important part of the media discourse in multicultural societies, media are in general reluctant and do not always support diversity. While the media discourse on migration and multiculturalism is, in general, not on education but more on (dis)integration, there are some topics that are directly related to education. At present this is the question of the integration of migrant students depending on their knowledge of German.

Pivotal points in the media discourse are:

- bilingual education is not supported, sometimes even rejected;
- the political reduction of mother tongue teaching is only seldom questioned;
- a lack of German is regarded as a failure of the parents and the child him- or herself;
- the lack of German is regarded as a direct path into unemployment or even a criminal career;
- the lack of German is related to the ethnic communities. Sometimes

media refer to a 'ghetto' in order to describe ethnic communities. The functional infrastructure is seen as a hindrance to integration and a lack of willingness to learn German;

- the use of languages other than German in schools (even in breaks) is questioned;
- media in the mother tongues of the migrants – especially satellite TV – are described as a hindrance to learning German and adopting the German culture;
- the role of the Muslim religion is seen as rather ambivalent but in general as 'strange' and a contributing factor to the lack of successful integration;
- the multicultural society is often questioned or regarded as having failed.

The ambivalent and often negative role of media becomes obvious even in this brief portrayal. Media education needs to deal with this.

The role of Europe

The challenges of the European Union in 1993 and the implementation of the European dimension into the educational system in Germany, due to the European directive of 1988, gave main impulses to broaden the concept of multicultural education to European and global perspectives (The Council 1988). The European dimension has gained high relevance in all states though there is a strong dominance on languages and student exchange while the implementation of European aspects in all subjects is of lesser relevance. The European dimension has shown a way of overcoming national education and of opening up for international aspects, but it has played an ambivalent role in the development of multicultural education. European education and multicultural education were used nearly as synonyms in the late 1980s and early 1990s, and this had an interesting side effect: while multicultural education had only reluctantly been accepted into the educational administration, the word now became quickly accepted (cf. Luchtenberg 1996). Certainly, there is a necessity for global openness, even more so in the light of a coming united Europe for European education, but the danger is, that the more multicultural education is regarded as global or European education, the less interest there will be in local diversity and the challenges it provides.

Challenges

Migration into Germany in the past 50 years has led to many important changes in the school system and in educational research. The paradigmatic change from migrant education to multicultural education is the most important one, especially since multicultural education gains increasing acceptance. Yet, we are far from having solved the problems that result in migration. There are still many challenges to be met.

There is an approach which regards multicultural education as an umbrella term with the two components:

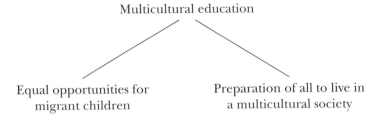

Multicultural education

Equal opportunities for migrant children

Preparation of all to live in a multicultural society

As well as the PISA study (OECD 2001) the annual school statistics also show that the requirements for the first component are far from being fulfilled in Germany. According to statistics published by the Standing Conference of the Ministers of Education and Cultural Affairs (Kultus-ministerkonferenz 2003), nearly 20 per cent of migrant students left school in the year 2000 without gaining a certificate – which is about double the amount of German students. Most juveniles with a migrant background attend a 'Hauptschule', which is the lowest secondary school within the German selective school system (cf. Jonen and Boele 2001). In 2000, nearly 40 per cent of migrant students left school with a secondary school leaving certificate of the 'Hauptschule' while only 28.5 per cent of the German students left school with only this qualification. The most important difference between both groups can be found in the results for a certificate that qualifies students to begin a study at a university, at a polytechnic or at a college. While 40 per cent of the German students reached this level, only 13 per cent of the non-German students did so.

Further facts undermine the poor situation of migrant children in the German school system:

*   they attend special schools – especially those for children with learning difficulties – far more than German students;
*   they have to repeat classes more often than German students;
*   they stay longer in a preschool class.

The PISA study has given some hints on how to answer the question why this is so, though it has, by far, not explained all the facts (OECD 2001).

*   The PISA study has shown that in Germany school fails to close the social gap between the students. Migrant students are particularly affected by this fact since many migrant families still belong to socially disadvantaged groups.

- A special part of the PISA study within the German evaluation has found that teachers were not able to find out which of their students had the lowest ability in reading. German teachers lack a competence in diagnosis as it is not taught at university during their teacher training.
- A main problem is the lack of support that students in general and migrant students in particular experience in the German school system. This is partly due to its selective structure, in which students are sent to different schools when they fail in one, or, at very least, they have to repeat one grade. It can be assumed that the half-day school also does not leave enough time to give weak students further help and assistance or to coordinate extra lessons like mother tongue teaching and German as a second language.

It must be noted that a lot of special programmes have been established in the last years but most of them are only locally applied in some schools. Examples of these are:

- Bilingual literacy classes in Berlin ('Zweisprachige Klassen'), Hesse ('Koala'), parts of North-Rhine/Westphalia ('Schubile'): Here mainly Turkish students who attend a regular class learn to read and write in both languages within a coordinated system of mother tongue teaching, team teaching and classroom teaching. The German students are not forced to learn Turkish but some learn at least a bit. In the following grades of the primary school texts are read in both languages and grammar knowledge is deepened. Secondary schools are not included so far.
- Turkish is taught as a regular language in secondary schools in some regions.
- New programmes have been developed in different states, e.g. in Bavaria and North-Rhine/Westphalia, partly in schools, partly in preschool institutions where not only the children are addressed, but also their mothers. The latter learn German (sometimes with the explicit aim that they are thus better prepared to help their children with their homework), but, in order to support bilingual competence, they are also encouraged to work with their children at home, in the same subjects that have been dealt with in school or kindergarten and using their mother tongue.

While such bilingual programmes are being developed in some institutions, the mainstream discourse in politics and media has turned in a different direction. The general discussion about a new immigration law ('Zuwanderungsgesetz') has deepened the call for integration, which is increasingly regarded as a debt that migrants have to pay.

Different measures are asked for in schools:

- Tests for school beginners in order to make sure they know enough German to follow a regular school class. Partly bilingual tests are being considered, but not everywhere.
- Besides the criticism of such tests and their construction as well as questioning the facts they really give, the crucial question is, what should be done with and for those children who fail the test?
- Different answers to this question occur, which include the proposals to send them to a preschool until they have learnt enough German or to give them a crash course until the school year starts.
- The idea of using the preschool institutions for language teaching is also being discussed. This would affect mainly kindergartens. Here, another problem occurs: kindergarten teachers are by no means qualified to teach languages and most institutions do not see their task as such a strict preparation for school.

In this new political and media debate on the integration of migrant students, integration has to be understood as the demand that migrant students have to learn enough German before school so that they do not trouble the school. Logically therefore, the focus is mostly on German, but certainly not on bilingualism or intercultural communication. Citizenship education is also not discussed; though it would help migrant students to cope with their special situation and probably also help them to understand the political situation in Europe. This would also form a connection to the European dimension. (Intercultural) educationalists do not deny that the problem of school failure is strongly connected with insufficient knowledge of German. But they see the proximity of the programmes and measures so far discussed to a deficit-oriented migrant education while the structure, programmes, curricula of the institution school are not, or only slightly, questioned, as might be necessary and appropriate in a multicultural society. Simple measures could, for example, be:

- to train all teacher students in German as a second language so that the math teacher or the teacher in chemistry knows about the difficulties of migrant students in coping with a subject in a target language;
- to refer to German as a second language in the curriculum for German;
- to integrate the mother tongue teachers and allow for more team teaching.

The improvement of migrant students' school careers is one of the big challenges for education in Germany in the coming years. To cope with the mixture of local and global aspects is another one. This can be examined with regard to languages:

- Due to the development in Europe the interest in languages has increased since the late 1980s as administration, schools and parents have realized the necessity of linguistic competence for the future of students.
- A new type of 'Bilingual Classes' were created. In general they address German students in regular classes, where they are taught more of their first foreign language (normally English) than is usual in classes five and six. In addition to this, they are taught one or two subjects like geography or social studies in the target language from class seven onwards.
- Furthermore, a foreign language is now taught in primary schools.
- 'Multicultural learning' has become a goal in all language classes (English, French etc.) and foreign language didactics deal with multicultural learning. This type of multicultural learning focuses on British or French studies, either on contacts or exchanges with students in the countries of the target language or the study of the foreign culture.

Thus, the international view increases the interest in European languages but denies at the same time the necessity of promoting mother tongue instruction (cf. Luchtenberg 2002). This situation in schools has an interesting parallel in the media, where broadcasting in the mother tongues of the immigrants has been dramatically reduced in recent months.

There is a necessity for a multicultural education that combines dealing with local, European and global diversity.

There are also challenges with regard to media, the influence of which as regards an acceptance of multiculturalism and migration is so high because most people have no chance of finding out different facts themselves. Their only chance of relativism is to compare several media. This already demands a certain media competence that is best gained at school. Media education plays an important role in the German curricula, though it is not part of a specific subject. So far, multicultural media competence is not yet in the curricula, though it seems very important to teach students how to deal with the many ways in which the media can influence our understanding of a diverse society. Multicultural media competence can be understood as part of multicultural education and multicultural communication and as a measure – among others – of meeting the educational challenges of migration.

To sum up, many challenges, which result from migration into Germany, are still to be met. Thus migration has turned out to be a fairly permanent one and has turned Germany irreversibly into a multicultural and multilingual society. While in the early days of migrant education most educational programmes for migrant students either aimed at a later return of those students into their countries of origin or were directed towards a full assimilation into the German society, concepts of multicultural education take it – if often only implicitly – for granted that the migration is a permanent one. In the light of this fact, it is astonishing that there is such little reflection on a citizenship education that addresses migrant students (cf. Luchtenberg 2003). This is all the more astonishing since such a necessity has been reflected worldwide, as well as in Europe, for many years (cf. Banks 1997; Bell 1995; Friebel 1996; Hahn 1998; Ichilov 1998; Lynch 1992). There is an astonishing disparity between a multicultural education that emanates from the assumption of a multicultural society with permanent migration and the lack of enabling students – migrants as well as Germans – to understand the political conditions of this multicultural society and – beyond that – its place in Europe and in the world.

There are also numerous challenges due to varying forms of migration to be found in the multiculturalism Germany still has to accept.

Recent forms of migration

Politics and education have to reconcile the fact that not all immigration is permanent, because there is an increasing trend towards transmigration processes (cf. Pries 2001). Permanent migration has been understood as a more or less unidirectional movement from one nation state to another, including the possibility of remigration as a second step that can be regarded as a unidirectional movement as well since it is also a permanent process. Now we face different forms of migration in the late twentieth and start of the twenty-first century where globalization plays a key role. Transmigration is understood as a specific type of migration in transnational social spaces (Glick Schiller *et al.* 1997; Pries 2001). It is shown that migrants develop multidirectional patterns of migration with different social and spatial relations. These patterns may differ between groups as well as between individuals. These shifts in social reality challenge the framework for analysis in social science as well as in educational theory and practice, though the group of asylum seekers and refugees has always been regarded as non-permanent migrants. The recent patterns of transmigration have been very much facilitated by the European Union where the workforce can work for an unlimited time in any of the member states, but also move to one or more other states during their working life. This has involved change for a migrant's migration possibilities, as well as for teaching.

Transmigration is furthermore characterized by another phenomenon: there are not only more highly educated migrants than in the usual work migration, but many of them do not migrate on their own because they belong to international operating companies that send them abroad (often with their families) for a certain amount of time.

There is a further aspect that has to be taken into consideration: even those migrants who have decided to live in Germany permanently, many of whom gain German citizenship, are still closely connected with their country of origin. This fact is supported by the government in their home countries who feel in a way responsible for their (former) nationals who live abroad. Thus there is also a situation of diaspora for some migrants. To some extent there were always transmigration processes but the present situation is challenging due to two phenomena: short term migration becomes more and more common, and it becomes more relevant in a situation where a country such as Germany has just begun to adapt to the idea of being a multicultural society.

Short term migration includes students and young people for courses, au pairs as well as employees in international companies who have been sent abroad for a short period. They normally know the length of their stay in advance. This can be different for other persons in the transmigration process who often decide during their migration to return to their country of origin and later on to migrate again, or they migrate into a third country after having finished their job in the second country.

What are the consequences of the above-mentioned phenomena when regarded in the light of multicultural education and the necessities resulting from permanent migration? For example, how is integration to be defined in this context and what is the effect on language education?

Integration

It has to be questioned whether the model of integration in the concept of multiculturalism is compatible with transmigration where migrants live in more than one social and spatial context, either at the same time, in consecutive periods or in a way where social and geographical spaces are split or overlap. How can integration be defined in such a context when even in the context of permanent migration aspects of social, economic and political participation are not at the centre of discussion?

Migrants who come on a short term contract to Germany are normally in a financially secure position since a company or an institution either sends them or they have got work permission in Germany as, e.g. IT workers. Students may be an exception but they are at least basically funded.

Integration has a different notion with regard to migrants in a transmigration concept: there are nearly no complaints about them living in rather closed communities as applies to the Japanese communities in Germany – a fact that is in sharp contrast to the discussion about Turkish ghettos. It could be supposed that the obvious non-integration within the group of short term migrants with regard to social life is seen as a guarantee of return whereas it is regarded as being a sign of self-exclusion within the group of long term or permanent migrants.

If integration of non-permanent migrants follows a different pattern, one has to ask what integration means in their case? Obviously everyone living abroad must obey the law of that country, but what else could integration then mean?

If integration is related to participation, most transnational migrants have the advantage of participating in a general way in the economic life. Yet, this is applicable to most migrants who live in ethnic quarters, but their integration is denied because of living in these quarters. Non-permanent migrants do not live per se in a diaspora since it is possible to live relatively independent from the country of origin as well as from the present country. There are, of course, diaspora-like communities of non-permanent settlers.

As discussed earlier, language is a crucial part of the discussion with regard to the integration of migrants. Again, the attitude changes with regard to short term migrants in the context of transmigration.

Language education

Language education for non-Germans focuses far more on fluency in German than on bilingualism, as was shown on p. 45. We have to ask whether children from families with a high mobility are sufficiently trained in the way multicultural education works, i.e. high concentration on German, consideration of the first language and integration into the regular class and what the alternatives could be. Furthermore, it can be stressed that at least for employees in a qualified job in international companies, English is more often the language spoken at the workplace than German. Yet, it has to be considered that they live their daily life in a German-speaking country where they face barriers when participating in shopping, sport clubs or chats with neighbours or colleagues after work if they do not speak German.

Models for transmigration and the tackling of (language) education in Europe do exist. This concerns the international employees in European institutions like the European Patent Office in Munich. Their children usually attend the European school in Munich where they are taught together with German students. The European Schools are official educational establishments controlled jointly by the governments of the member states of the European Union. In all these countries they are legally regarded as public institutions (Schola Europaea 2003). A student can finish a European School with a European Baccalaureate so that he/she will be able to study in other European countries than their home country or the country where he/she gained the certificate. Students work for competence in their home language, German and English. There are only three European schools in Germany (Frankfurt, Karlsruhe and Munich) so that this model is only accessible for a few transnational migrant families.

Could the German school offer a similar approach for students of these families? The strong focus on German as a second language can certainly only be part of offers to these students. On the other hand, regular schools will probably not be able to offer courses in English or in the first languages, especially if one regards the poor range of mother tongue tuition with regard to permanent migrants. There is no solution to this problem at the moment.

Political education

We have considered political education as highly important with regard to the formation of a multicultural society in which all members have the right of diversity but also the obligation to work on the cohesion within this society. There are still many hindrances to acceptance and inclusion for migrants – as individuals as well as ethnic groups.

What are special challenges with regard to transmigration and short term migration? First, variety and diversity within society is increasing, especially regarding social status. On the one hand, this offers a chance of dealing with the socio-economic status of migrants, demonstrating that migration is often, but not necessarily related to poverty and deprivation. There is, of course, a danger here of following the political idea of dividing into 'good' and 'poor' migrants. On the other hand, there is a general opportunity to deal with the economics of migration, its impact on the first and second generation, showing the increasing participation in small businesses and small to medium-sized companies. These topics also gain importance because political education will be closer related to economics in the future. The economic ties often lead to the countries of origin – of permanent migrants as well as of short term migrants: there is a close connection between this fact and the discussion of a political diaspora, self-exclusion or participation.

Political education that deals with transmigration will also deal with the phenomenon worldwide and contribute to the understanding of globalization as regards the future of the students.

Multicultural education for all

Multicultural education has only recently gained some reputation in Germany and is still far from fulfilling the requirement 'Preparation of all to live in a multicultural society' (cf. diagram p. 51), which is due to permanent migration into Germany. Therefore it is certainly an irritating situation that multicultural education currently has to work on the question of how to deal with short term migration. Yet, there is the necessity not only to find concepts for the children of short term migrants, but also to integrate this part of migration into the concept of multicultural education. Part of this is to cope with new status groups: multicultural education has a strong focus on social education – this can be explained by the fact that work and refugee migrants were so far mainly underprivileged and marginalized. Transnational migrants are often persons with high qualifications and a good social standing. It has to be asked whether the social education approaches have to be modified with regard to this latter group. Mutual learning as well as combating racism and racial discrimination are as important with regard to transmigration as they have always been with regard to work migration. Now the global aspects gain importance in a very special way since the presence of short term migrants – and their children in schools – belong at first glance to the high diversity in Germany due to migration, but at a further glance they also represent the worldwide relationships.

There is another, more practical point to be considered: so far, schools have nearly no concepts for students who enter school in the course of a school year, but this can easily happen in families with high mobility. In addition, these students will often only stay a year or even less. Nevertheless, and in particularly due to their mobility and school changes, they require much attention – it is necessary to ascertain their competencies and discover where they need more support.

The challenges of transnational migration have only recently been considered and, although it would certainly not be appropriate to put transnational migration into the middle of multicultural education, it has to be considered. This is especially the case because these migrant students will all be together in classes, so that a broad range of concepts has to be put together to find a suitable education for all students. To some extent, this development leads to a new mixture of local, European and global aspects of multicultural education. This is certainly a task that can only be solved in a European, if not global approach.

Intercultural communication

The new mixture is also applicable to intercultural communication: intercultural communication within a diverse society is concerned with the daily life of all, because it takes place in professional or private life 'at home' and is thus different from intercultural communication with foreigners – either in their home country or when they come to Germany for business or tourism. Migrants who settle in Germany for a short time do not become part of daily life as permanent migrants, but they are not only more involved in daily life than foreigners but communication takes place here. It also has to be considered that permanent migrants and short term migrants are involved in this new form of intercultural communication. Furthermore, this applies to schools, too.

Media education

Media in Germany prefer international topics in contrast to multicultural questions (cf. Luchtenberg and McLelland 1998). If they refer to Germany's multicultural society, they often do so in a negative tone. There are no analyses so far as to how media deal with transmigration or short term migration. Such analyses are certainly worthwhile – especially with regard to the question as to whether a difference can be found between highly qualified migrants and work migrants on a short term basis. Since integration is one of the main topics in the media at present, it has to be examined how far this topic is related to transmigration.

Media education that is understood as an multicultural media education will mainly train students to find out media manipulation about migration, migrants and multiculturalism, but it enables them to discover the differences between an inner and outer perspective, where the latter refers to global or European aspects. Now, in-between aspects become relevant as well.

The role of Europe

As has been stated in several sections, globalization and Europe gain new relevance when transmigration or short term migrations are considered. The European development is an important issue here because the European Union not only supports transmigration in the described sense by its legislation, but also adds further aspects by pushing the development of European identity, which means that a new social and geographical space emerges. Yet, transmigration is not limited to European migrants, as the search for IT workers has quite recently shown.

Multicultural education that is open for transmigration and short term migration – and it has to be open because of the fact that both are part of the diverse society in Germany – must of necessity focus on the situation in Germany (inner perspective), while still connecting this with European and global aspects (outer perspective). This is necessary because of the strong relations of transmigration to the outer perspective; this can be understood as a chance to reconcile both aspects of multicultural education.

Challenges

We now find a paradoxical situation in Germany: the country and its educational bureaucracy have begun to accept the situation of permanent migration and to look seriously for concepts to improve the learning conditions for students with a migration background as well as to implement concepts to prepare all for life in a multicultural society. It is paradoxical because the need to deal with non-permanent migration and its impact on education has arisen at this selfsame moment. This could be understood as a setback, an understanding that would cause damage to all kinds of multicultural education. It can also be understood as a challenge and chance to open up for new tasks and a broader understanding of multiculturalism and multicultural education. Here – as in multicultural education with a focus on a multicultural society due to permanent migration – a lot of research and educational development has to take place with regard to the achievement of migrant students. There are nearly no concepts of how to deal with students who will attend school in Germany only for a limited time. It might be worthwhile to consider a model that is tested with regard to children of circus artistes and workers: a school in their country of origin would be a base school for them and provide them with a portfolio about their achievements, their learning material etc. This portfolio would have to be continued in the school that they attend in Germany so that the next school – or their base school – can assess them according to their results in Germany.

The other challenge concerns the discussion within the German society about integration and the conditions of a multicultural society. The conditions within a multicultural society are indeed tackled by the fact of an increasing non-permanent migration since this poses new questions about cohesion and participation. The classical countries of immigration face a similar problem so that most probably common solutions will have to be found.

Summing up this chapter, we have to state that the migration pattern in Germany, as well as in other parts of the world, has become more complex. At the same time, PISA has shown that the present educational approach in Germany is not adequate for its migrant students so that it will be difficult both to improve the present situation as well as to consider further challenges. Yet, there is a chance that the different levels of multicultural education discussed will contribute to the further development of a multicultural education that is able to meet new tasks.

References

Bade, K. (ed.) (2002) 'Migration in der europäischen Geschichte seit dem späten Mittelalter', *IMIS-Beiträge* 20, Osnabrück: IMIS.

Banks, J. A. (1997) *Educating Citizens in a Multicultural Society*, New York: Teachers College.

—— (ed.) (2003) *Diversity and Citizenship Education: Global Perspectives*, San Francisco: Jossey-Bass/Wiley.

Die Beauftragte der Bundesregierung für Ausländerfragen (2001) *Migrationsbericht der Ausländerbeauftragten im Auftrag der Bundesregierung*, Berlin and Bonn.

Bell, G. H. (ed.) (1995) *Educating European Citizens. Citizenship Values and the European Dimension*, London: David Fulton.

Bundesgesetzblatt II Nr. 2 (1998) *Bekanntmachung über das Inkrafttreten des*

Rahmenübereinkommens des Europarats vom 1. Februar 1995 zum Schutz nationaler Minderheiten, Bonn: Auswärtiges Amt: 57.

Bundesministerium des Inneren (2003) http://www.bafl.de/template/aktuelles/pressemitteilung_bmi/pressemitteilung_bmi_2003_01_08.htm 9.8.03.

Council of Europe (2004) http://www.col.int/t/e/legal_affairs/local_and_regional_democracy/regional_or_minority_languages 10.5.04.

The Council and the Ministers of Education Meeting with the Council (1988) 'Resolution on the European dimension in education of 24 May 1988', *Official Journal of the European Communities* No. C 177: 5.

Friebel, W. (ed.) (1996) *Education for European Citizenship*, Freiburg: Fillibach.

Glick Schiller, N., Basch, L. and Szanton Blanc, C. (1997) 'From immigrant to transmigrant: theorizing transnational migration', in L. Pries (ed.) *Transnationale Migration*, Baden-Baden: Nomos: 121–140.

Hahn, C. L. (1998) *Becoming Political. Comparative Perspectives on Citizenship Education*, Albany: State University of New York Press.

Hinnenkamp, V. (1989) ' "Turkish man you?" – The conversational accomplishment of the social and ethnic category of "Turkish guestworker" ', *Human Studies* (Special Issue: Erving Goffman's Sociology, ed. by F. Ch. Waksler), 12 (1/2): 117–146.

—— (2001) 'Constructing misunderstanding as a cultural event', in A. di Luzio, S. Günthner and F. Orletti (eds) *Culture in Communication. Analyses of Intercultural Situations*, Amsterdam and Philadelphia: J. Benjamins: 211–243.

Hoff, G. (1995) 'Multicultural education in Germany: Historical development and current status', in J. A. Banks and C. A. M. Banks (eds) *Handbook of Research on Multicultural Education*, New York: Macmillan: 821–838.

Ichilov, O. (ed.) (1998) *Citizenship and Citizenship Education in a Changing World*, London: The Woburn Press.

Isoplan (2003) http://www.isoplan.de/aid/index.htm.

Jonen, G. and Boele, K. (eds) (2001) *The Education System in the Federal Republic of Germany 2000*, Bonn: Kultusministerkonferenz.

Kultusministerkonferenz (2003) http://www.kmk.org/statist/ausl_txt.pdf.

Luchtenberg, S. (1996) 'The European dimension and multicultural education: compatible or contradictory concepts', in Th. Winter-Jensen (ed.) *Challenges to European Education: Cultural Values, National Identities, and Global Responsibilities*, Frankfurt: Peter Lang: 281–293.

—— (1997) 'Stages in multicultural theory and practice in Germany', in R. J. Watts and J. J. Smolicz (eds) *Cultural Democracy and Ethnic Pluralism. Multicultural and Multilingual Policies in Education*, Bern: Peter Lang: 125–148.

—— (2002) 'Bilingualism and bilingual education and its relationship to citizenship from a comparative German–Australian viewpoint', *Intercultural Education* 13 (1): 49–61.

—— (2003) 'Ethnic diversity and citizenship education in Germany', in J. A. Banks (ed.) *Diversity and Citizenship Education: Global Perspectives*, San Francisco: Jossey-Bass/Wiley.

Luchtenberg, S. and McLelland, N. (1998) 'Multiculturalism, migration and racism: the role of the media. A comparative study of Australian and German print media', *Journal of Intercultural Studies* 19, 2: 187–206.

Lynch, J. (1992) *Education for Citizenship in a Multicultural Society*, London and New York: Cassell.

OECD (eds) (2001) *Knowledge and Skills for Life. First Results from PISA 2000*, Paris.

Pries, L. (ed.) (2001) *New Transnational Social Spaces*, London: Routledge.

Schmidt-Fink, E. (2003) 'Statistik', *Ausländer in Deutschland* 2: 18.

Schola Europaea (2003) *Report of the Secretary-General of the Board of Governors of the European Schools (2002) and Statistics*, http://www.eursc.org/SE/htmlEn/IndexEn_home.html.

Standing Conference (1996) *Empfehlung Interkulturelle Bildung und Erziehung in der Schule*, Bonn: Sekretariat der Ständigen Konferenz der Kultusminister der Länder in der Bundesrepublik Deutschland.

Statistisches Bundesamt (2003) http://www.destatis.de/basis/d/bevoe/bevoetab4.htm 9.8.03.

4 Collective solidarity and the construction of social identities in school

A case study on immigrant youths in post-unification West Berlin

Sabine Mannitz

The state school has been affected by fundamental changes in Germany[1] in the wake of labour immigration and of the national reunification. The post-war labour immigration and more particularly the consolidation of the former guest workers' stay since the 1970s implicated German schools in the challenge to cope with multinational, multilingual and multi-faith pupils. The German unification made it necessary to redefine collective solidarity. Both of these moments imply tasks of integration that compete with each other – posing societal membership against the national one – but that also interact with each other in practice. School is an excellent place to study such contestations, interactions and learning processes. It is a place of institutionalized communication between the generations, the public and the private, and, last but not least, the national majority and (immigrant as well as other) minorities. School teaches children civil values and propagates norms about the ways in which conflicts of interest between different groups should be solved, in which the public and the private should be balanced and one should participate in wider society. It is hence an important agent in promoting the existing consensus in respect of the social and political order and of the related imagination of a shared community of solidarity. Yet, since democracies are principally open for change, the crucial challenge is not to be seen in the guarantee of a reproductive cycle but in the task of qualifying all pupils for their participation in the democratic argument over defining the consensus and the collective good. What possibilities are foreseen to adapt the existing order and its sense of cohesion to a changing society? What place is suggested for immigrants, and what effects has the German unification had on the definition of crucial common goals?

This chapter aims to highlight the interrelation between the tasks of the German state schools to foster national solidarity as well as social integration in a wider sense, and the formation of collective identities. The focus is hereby set upon adolescents from immigrant families: how do they learn to conceive of themselves vis-à-vis others in Germany? How relevant is this allocation for the social construction of identity in their daily lives? The issue is approached by summarizing related findings from my research in a secondary school in Berlin,[2] with the topical case in point being boundary formations in the post-unification setting. I shall introduce and examine the classifications which informed the educational discourses and practices in the school, which is situated in the borough of Neukoelln, i.e. a district with an average rate of 22 per cent foreign residents and 30 to 40 per cent in the school's immediate neighbourhood. I aim to investigate what normative expectations regarding social cohesion were spelled out in the educational interaction during my fieldwork there, and follow this up by observing how they were responded to by youths from immigrant families in their identity narrations.

The chosen research site is, of course, as individual a school as any. At the same time, it is one of the general relay stations between the state and the population that are to organize social order and cohesion by means of communication. As such, they have to fulfil a distinct task in collective socialization, which makes any school a social field of significant meaningfulness – not irrespective of, but rather inclusive of its possible particularities. In this premise, I follow Bourdieu's notion, saying that social contestation for the power of classification in the public as a whole plays a key role in organizing social relations and identities (Bourdieu 1987). Whether the involved actors accept, fight against or simply ignore the categories that are presupposed in hegemonic discourse, involves a process that relates to specific social acts of communication. This understanding involves the necessity of directing attention to the small-scale social field in order to trace the changes in or likewise the (re)production of meanings, classifications and hierarchies within the context of their generation.

To examine the relations between dominant discourse in school, the perception of relevant group boundaries and identity narrations of young foreigners[3] in post-unification Berlin, the argument proceeds in four steps. First, I shall summarize very briefly what general attitude marks the reception of pupils from immigrant families in German schools. The second section argues that the state school has meanwhile arrived at the crossroads of competing modes of civic and of societal integration. This is illustrated by the way in which pertinent topics are represented in textbooks which are powerful mass media and the most tangible expressions of the normative agenda in education. After this account, a third part introduces the concrete situation of the school in question and explains how different groups were construed and assessed there. The identity categories applied by adolescents from immigrant backgrounds are finally analysed against the background of the competing discourses within the described field.

Regarding the conceptualization of groups and their collective solidarities, I will argue that the young 'foreigners' – as they called themselves –

were ahead of the national bias inherent to traditional models of incorporation. Their statements reveal complex processes of integration or rather discursive assimilation that concerns modes and methods in deliberation which transcend national bounds.

Immigrant pupils in German schools

The ways in which children from immigrant families are catered for in German schools is an issue that has received increased attention since the publication of the OECD PISA study 2000 (Baumert *et al.* 2001). The international comparison of pupils' achievements pointed to a number of grave disproportions. Children from immigrant families proved to be significantly less skilled than their German peers in reading and comprehending the German language. And they came off much worse than pupils from comparative immigrant groups in other countries of the OECD survey. This indicates a serious disadvantage. For the pupils concerned, opportunities are limited if they lack the basic prerequisite of mastering the residential country's lingua franca. Conversely, Germany misses chances of making good use of its human resource potential. The causes of this lose–lose situation are numerous.

In the first place, the circumstance that Germany, for decades, normatively ignored the fact that it had indeed become an immigration country since the end of the Second World War is responsible for a lack of conceptual tools for handling the immigrants' reception. The policy of hiring labourers from abroad on a temporary basis gradually developed into a de facto immigration from the 1960s to the 1980s. But irrespective of the consolidation of the former guest workers' stay, the official political creed remained that the FRG should not be regarded as an immigration country. The fact was 'coped with' that a considerable number of foreigners were part of the population, but the German state, particularly under the conservative government that held office throughout the 1980s until 1998, showed no willingness to aim at the long term incorporation of the labour immigrants; it merely reacted on an *ad hoc* basis. A remarkable gap developed over time between the societal reality of immigration and the official political (non-) recognition of the demographic change (see Bade 2000 and Bade and Weiner 2001). The outcome is an ambivalent mixture of partial inclusion – in institutions of civil society, the job market and most welfare provisions – and simultaneous exclusion (in the form of fairly restrictive conditions) regarding formal political citizenship. It has, however, become part of the common certainties that the former guest worker population (and their offspring) will stay in the country as de facto immigrants.

A corresponding mixture of contradictory trends marks the situation in schools: from the 1970s onwards the 'guest workers' started to bring their families over. Their children enrolled in German schools. This development meant new challenges for schools and teachers. But the sudden diversity in the school's clientele became neither the subject of any nation-wide policy, nor did it warrant exceptional public attention. It was left up to local societal routines and to the political principle of subsidiarity. Amplified by the West German structure of federalism, the different states have come to apply their own strategies in coping with pupils from (the various types of) immigrant families. In the realm of language education, for instance, the whole range exists in Germany from remigration ori-ented instructions in foreigners' mother tongues in one state, bilingual primary education and multilingual schools that draw on cognitive argu-ments in another state, or grammar schools that include minority lan-guages as further modern languages in the programme whenever a certain number of pupils ask for it. Comprehensive reports and evalua-tions about all the different approaches and about their usefulness do not exist (Reich *et al.* 2002).

The unsystematic way of integrating foreign pupils in the system of German schools was treated for most of the time as a side issue and, apart from the clientele concerned, only bothered a small group of experts and practitioners. Among the insiders, it was, however, no secret that the pre-dominant indifference towards the situation of children from immigrant families led to their disproportionate school failure (Kornmann and Klin-gele 1996). The negative PISA outcome has carried this observation into the wider German public. But who or what is to blame for these pupils' bad school performance? Who or what needs to change? The (ideologi-cally informed) judgements diverge on the point of whether the major problem which these pupils face is lacking parental support or rather a lack of adequate support and target-group concepts on the part of the state school. An agreement over the controversy and necessary con-sequences is far from being reached; nevertheless, the debate follows one interesting common axiom: the diagnosis of bad school results, insuffi-cient linguistic competence and the lack of parental support is inter-twined with an assessment of the immigrants' degree in cultural and social integration. (The lack of) lingual skills have received most of the attention in this context, and this is no coincidence.

Language is an instrument to enable communication and participation, but it is also a medium that contains social and cultural memories.[4] This is, on the one hand, why native languages, their handing down as well as the experience of their loss, are loaded with emotions of belonging and identity; it is, on the other hand, also the reason why language acquisition is commonly understood as an immediate expression of migrant parents' efforts to encourage their children in getting settled and projecting their future in the country of immigration. The extent to which the national language is mastered by immigrants and their children is hence regularly taken as a standard to measure not only their integration in a wider sense but, more specifically, their demonstrable willingness to participate in collective identification, in brief, to allow assimilation to happen in the next generation. This very argument seems plausible at first sight, but it follows a national bias that deserves critical attention: international and transnational relations mark the world to an unprecedented degree – can the relations between language, culture and social identity still be conceptualized as being nationally bounded under these circumstances? What do the changes imply for the state school's role as an agent of social integration in the general meaning of civic education?

School at the crossroads of integration modes

In present day school education, different integration requirements interact with each other in a number of ways. Diverging from original trajectories, the state school of the present has to integrate pupils from different nationalities who might or might not be future citizens in the formal judicial sense.[5] Historically, state education followed a nationalist programme which both reflected and also produced collective identities based on nation and language. Social cohesion was created within the national societies by means of stressing traits of the own in contrast to those of other nations, and this method of projecting and creating collective identities as national ones has been highly effective. Certainly, a number of factors worked together in the construing, shaping and reproducing of nations and 'their' states as reified collective actors of first modernity. But state schools played a major role in the making and the consolidation of this process (Gellner 1983; Anderson 1991).

Several developments have questioned this arrangement which has combined social and civic rights with the territorial expansion and the political sovereignty of an 'imagined community' (Anderson 1991) since the end of the Second World War. National sovereignty has come under pressure from the increased international interdependence of political decisions and economic flows. The European nation states have become engaged in processes of globalization, and they have themselves experienced various moments that undermine the national self-image: mass immigration has made populations multinational; social diversification and the European unification enterprise have qualified the national colouring of collective identities; many forms of public representation as well as political participation are no longer tied to the formal condition of citizenship today but can be exercised by foreign nationals in civil society.[6] These transformations of and within the nation states give reason to assume that schools no longer follow a particularly national agenda of civic enculturation. Be their pupils nationals or not, long or short term residents, part of the indigenous population or recent arrivals like refugees, with or without return orientation – schools have to prepare them all for their adult participation in society, as foreign residents or as citizens with the full range of political rights. Furthermore, new skills will have to be acquired in order to cope with increased diversity, also meaning that schools have to stimulate a different cognitive process than in the past (Luchtenberg and Nieke 1994). What sorts of collective bonds, norms and images are promoted these days?

Studying the guidelines for school education, normative shifts can be found in the programmes all over Europe to relativize national perspectives. Comparative analyses show that representations of the nations have undergone remarkable changes in school textbooks in the second half of the twentieth century. All over west Europe one has clearly sought to revise notions of national identities as revolving around sets of attributes, traditions and cultural heritages; national symbols and heroes are presented much more cautiously than 50 years ago when several countries still celebrated them as representatives of a glorious national past. Negative stereotypes of European neighbours have systematically been abolished from teaching materials since then (Pingel 1995: XI); and although following a specific sense of it in each case, one finds a general trend to the Europeanization of issues that were formerly presented to stress national uniqueness. To put it differently, the agenda of state education has become more and more universalistic in Europe, in the selection of relevant topics as well as in the ways of their presentation (Bertilotti *et al.* forthcoming 2004).

In Germany in particular, national themes do not figure prominently in school education. Owing to the experience of German Imperialism and National Socialism, the Federal Republic developed a positive self-image and became an accepted member in the western world by positioning itself as a liberal democracy rather than as a nation state. The constitutional order was established as the central point of self-reference. Consequently, German teaching materials in history or social studies have come to take a very pan-European, if not globalized, perspective and display recognizable reservedness in questions of national identity. This reflects clearly upon the lessons which were drawn from the past, and it applies to topical presentations of pre-1945 history as well as to the treatment of the 1990 unification: the fact that the GDR broke down and became part of the Federal Republic is represented in history textbooks without much excitement. In most cases, the demise of the GDR is explicitly located in the international context of revolutionary change in the socialist hemisphere with new attitudes of the Soviet leadership to their satellite states. The unification itself is widely presented in an objective fashion by giving brief accounts of the course of events (Bertilotti *et al.* forthcoming 2004). Nevertheless, the unification has in fact put national concepts back onto the educational agenda. In the attempt to reconstruct the nation after its formal reunion, the competitive balance of societal vis-à-vis formal political membership and nationality has become an issue of collective concern (Raethzel 1997: 183ff.). Syllabi and textbooks accordingly underwent revision. The nation is now no longer absent as before but a common denominator that is taken for granted – yet one that is associated with uneasiness and that needs taming: the fact that the event of the formal state unification in 1990 took place in a much more 'reserved' way than the opening of the Berlin Wall in 1989 is, for instance, assessed as 'certainly quite good this way' in the textbook that was mostly used in the school of my research (Ebeling and Birkenfeld 1995: 112).

The same book devotes a hundred pages to the 'History of the German Separation'. Strong emphasis within this unit is laid on post-war efforts of international reconciliation, so that divided Germany is placed into a setting of historical responsibility and of mutual recognition among international partners. And although the existence of two German states was once called an 'unnatural separation', it is made very clear that the two parts of the nation adapted quickly to living in the two different states and political power blocs after 1949: the phenomenon of mutual indifference, disapproval and 'alienation' between East and West Germans occupies several pages. The conclusion that is finally drawn is, however, no acknowledgement of the apparent weakening of national sentiments. It is the indication of a 'historical challenge' to overcome internal splitting. Willy Brandt is quoted with his comment on the Berlin Wall opening, to wit that 'what belongs together, grows together now' (Ebeling and Birkenfeld 1995: 152–157). The very reference to an organic community that 'belongs together' is most prone to be understood as prioritizing ethnonational over other forms of membership that consist of (so-to-speak nationally blind) procedures, pragmatic methods or instrumental competencies of participation in the public order.

In sum however, the message about the role of the nation has become more ambiguous since 1990. Not only have national tunes been taken up side by side with the general trend towards universalistic aspirations, but the two layers of discourse have also come to interact in a new way: the nation seems rehabilitated as one principle of collective organization but it is de-emotionalized at the same time by the prevalent style of objective historiography and the qualifying frame of international dependencies. While the breakdown of the GDR 'created a political momentum for change in the direction of political union that was without precedence' (Wiener 1998: 222), the nation is evidently too ambivalent and precarious a concept to allow for unbroken reactivation. On the other hand, invoking national solidarity is the most obvious option that suggests itself to establish common ground after a political unification that followed the conventional nation state rationale: Willy Brandt's certainty regarding the 'growing together' is taken up in most of the textbooks for contemporary history today.

Especially in view of multinational classes, school has to fulfil a difficult task at the crossroads of these integration modes, i.e. the universalistic ambition to foster general civic competences versus the particular goals on behalf of national solidarity. Inasmuch as national belonging is favoured to mobilize social cohesion, universalistic values may be spurned; foreigners face the risk of exclusion. Theoretically this is not a new insight but practically it did not really matter before 1989/1990. Constraints of nationally codified integration hardly played a significant role in the FRG before unification because immigrant diversity was never accepted anyhow as posing a special challenge, and the common platform of democracy and participation in civil society was dominating collective self-definition. By the late 1990s however, the immigrants and their children were to position themselves in a setting where not only national sovereignty had been reinstated but questions of collective identity had also been rediscovered to be 'centrally important' (Katzenstein 1997: 22). What place can foreign pupils possibly occupy in this setting? They belong to the (mostly permanent) population, but it is uncertain whether they are (or can ever expect to be) accepted as equal members in the community that 'belongs together'. Depending on how the latter is understood, access may not even be feasible (Raethzel 1997: 180f.). In respect of the influence which school may exert on the presentation of possible options, the central question is what concepts of difference, transmitted in practice, are significant.

Dominant images of difference: Germans and others

The school of my research had large numbers of pupils with different foreign nationalities. Pupils from Turkish, Lebanese and (formerly) Yugoslavian families were most numerous, but there were also children from Polish families or pupils whose families had immigrated from more far away countries like Sri Lanka. The rate of (ethnically) German children was approximately 40 per cent. How was this heterogeneity approached and assessed in school? The briefest answer is that the distinction of foreigners vis-à-vis Germans was a matter of routine in most teachers' daily practice and discourse, and it was connected to culturalist interpretations. The profound otherness of the foreign pupils was not only regarded as self-evident, but was furthermore assessed to be a negative circumstance and a major source of problems in school. An overwhelming majority of teachers expressed this with the opinion that the 'oriental families'[7] raised their children according to a completely different culture, which was held to be backward and a hindrance. In the same vein, the foreigners' mother tongue knowledge and use was neither accepted as normal circumstance nor appreciated as being an asset or useful skill but as a handicap that hindered participation, limited opportunities and prevented integration into German society.

In other words, the opinion was commonly held that the integration of the immigrants would essentially have to mean their assimilation – which was, however, estimated to be a fairly unrealistic vision. The fact that naturalization was not accepted as altering anything about the root of the problem is revealing in this context: the headmaster of the school saw a persistent problem due to cultural difference, and he regretted that one could no longer tell how many 'foreigners' were actually enrolled in the school. With more and more naturalizations, it became hard to classify the school's 'problematic clientele' as he put it. Many teachers felt overburdened by the circumstances, and they were more than willing to accept the convenient explanation that problems had to do with cultural differences. When it came to foreign pupils, the concept of cultural difference quickly ruled out all other possible explanations, such as social class or individual problems, be it in the context of a pupil's behaviour, his or her failure to reach a certain achievement level, or the refusal to join a class trip. As one teacher said:

> Especially regarding foreign pupils, role behaviour is . . . a bit backward. . . . There are hardly any possibilities to solve conflicts verbally, no willingness to compromise. And regarding the tensions between male and female teenagers, with our big proportion of oriental pupils, there are many failings.

A colleague of his judged that:

> Turkish pupils are victims of circumstance: Turkish parents fail insofar as little esteem is placed on the acquisition of the German language. The Turkish parents throw their children into the German school without any assistance. Turkish boys especially are often confronted with such unreal expectations by their parents that many are in danger of breaking. This pressure naturally produces ways of behaviour that we feel to be very unpleasant . . . The Turkish Parents' Association fails completely.

A third teacher, reacting to two Turkish pupils whom she heard talking in their mother tongue was most explicit as to what was going wrong: 'You talk Turkish, you stay in your own circles, you go shopping only in Turkish shops: integration cannot work like that!'

As these examples show, the foreigners, and among them most of all the 'orientals' were perceived as being in opposition to what school aims at. Assumed to reproduce outdated gender roles, to apply oppressive methods and insist on the significance of peculiar cultural traditions – all of which are irreconcilable with universalistic ideals – the foreign families represented the very antipode to modernity.[8] The understanding prevailed of a self-evident cultural hierarchy: the 'orientals' were marked negatively as a special group of foreigners, whose different cultures meant a danger of backlashes and splitting in society. Not only was their background seen as a negative liability, but it was also many teachers' understanding that 'orientals', more so than other immigrant groups, are reluctant to adopt anything of the modern German lifestyle. This may not be incorrect as an observation of individual pupils or families but such judgements were transferred most readily to larger groups, e.g. 'foreigners' or 'the orientals'. This perspective has far-reaching implications since it makes meetings at eye-level equally as unthinkable as the inclusion of the so-construed others into 'our' collective by means of naturalization.

In daily school life, therefore, the routine categorization of foreigners versus Germans entailed implications of differentiated modernity, social hierarchy, political legitimacy and cultural competence. It was far more than an objective distinction according to different nationalities, and it revealed that sentimental valuations of cultural belonging governed the imagery of 'us' and 'them' much more than one could expect when reading the ambitious education programmes. Ironically enough, the Germans have, however, no advantage over the foreigners when it comes to the cultural substance that is implicitly alluded to: the counterpart to the 'backward' cultures of the others is no appealing option as long as it operates in association with discredited Germanness. The following case from a lesson of history in grade nine casts a spotlight on the complexity of the inherent contradictions in this field.

> The lesson deals with the end of the German Empire on 9 November 1918. The teacher starts by asking if the class knows of further important events from German history that also happened on 9 November. Some of the pupils know that the Berlin Wall was opened on the 9 November; but a few Turkish girls declare right away that it does not count as an important event. . . . The lesson goes on with another pupil mentioning 9 November 1938, the night of pogroms against the German Jews, called the 'Night of Broken Glass' by the Nazis (*Reichskristallnacht*). The teacher explains this term and its cynicism and is then asked by a Turkish boy, 'Why didn't the Jews flee from Germany then?'

> *Teacher:* Well yes, why don't the Turks flee?
> *Turkish boy:* Why should the Turks flee?
> *Teacher:* Today there are murders, arson attacks and assaults on Turks – why don't the Turks flee?
> *Turkish girl:* The attacks are not carried out by the state!
> *German boy:* Things won't get *that* bad.
> *Teacher:* Exactly! That is what many Jews believed as well. And then you also have to consider what it means to go away: the Turks have after all property here, maybe a flat, a shop, money in the bank. If people were told, 'You are only allowed to take with you what you can carry in two suitcases, and the rest belongs to Germany', who would want to leave then?! It was just like that with the Jews at that time.

This act of translating history was pedagogically well-intended to stimulate the pupils' empathy. But it works with a twofold exclusivism and reproduces polarized concepts which are coloured by ethno-national

ideology in favour of cultural homogeneity: following the bias of otherness, it treats Jewish Germans of 1938 as if they had been foreigners and to
some degree even reconfirms the idea of their not belonging to the
German people. In the classroom it draws the line between Germans and
foreigners and moreover implies a possible opposition between culprit
and victim. Identification with either role would be absurd.

The lesson dialogue shows what impact National Socialism has left on
the post-war understanding of the Germans as a community with collective
responsibility. German nationality appears to entail a bundle of imagined
continuities that render it unsuitable for being translated into mere membership in a polity and also contribute to complicating identification.[9]
And even though one might object more principally that national membership is not suitable for defining an identity, the specific notional landscape in the German case makes expressions of identification with
Germanness much more problematic than elsewhere. This perspective was
explicitly shared by the pupils from migrant families. A 17-year-old girl
from a Lebanese family said, 'One can't feel one is a German ... and I
don't *want* to think of myself as German either, because being "typically
German" is somehow a deterrent in itself!' The conviction that belonging
to the German people implies a Jekyll and Hyde nature is also shared by
many born Germans. There is in fact no attractive political project or even
cliché connected with being a German national that could be stressed so
as to invite others to join in – apart maybe from the sophisticated appeal
of sober post-nationalism. The positive cliché of the Germans which one
finds in school textbooks and collective imagination draws upon the
proverbial industriousness of the Germans (which is ambivalent in itself
since the Nazis have perverted its potential, but which is still cited in
explaining the economic success of the FRG and of the GDR); yet the
economy can be joined anyway, irrespective of nationality, as consumer, as
employer, employee or businessman. Taking all this into consideration,
there is hardly any incentive for immigrants to blur the boundaries and
imagine themselves as being on a path towards Germanness. Apart from
pragmatic reasons, it is not attractive to enter a community that is defined
as sharing the historical burden of responsibility for the breakdown of
civility. The category of the Germans is neither open to comprise immigrant heterogeneity nor inviting in itself.

For the second and third generation of migrants this allocation table
poses special difficulties. Owing to the rather restrictive German nationality legislation as regards in-between options, such as dual citizenship, most
of the so-called 'foreign pupils' were in fact foreign nationals. At home, as
much as in school, this belonging was connected to sentiments of identity
and to expectations of continuity: the adolescents were expected by their
elders to see themselves as Turks, Croatians or Palestinians with their own
distinct culture. Yet even though nationality was in this way associated with
culture, emotional ties and collective identity on all sides of the hege-

monic categorization, all this did not quite match the mixed experience of distance and simultaneous belonging which many adolescents made in both of the 'two worlds'! Quite parallel to the dominant stereotype that prevailed of 'the foreigners' in their school, many pupils from migrant families experienced their parents insisting upon the maintenance of peculiar group boundaries and traditions that had lost meaning among the adolescents' peer groups in Berlin. Their own classifications were much more fluid, depending on the situation and the momentary social context. In some situations they deployed the prevalent categorization that distinguishes Germans from foreigners; in other situations they felt themselves to be both, or subverted the existing narratives and resorted to other lines of differences and of commonalities.

Reproduction and deconstruction of group boundaries: identity narrations of 'foreign' youths

Since the hegemonic discourse concerning the difference between Germans and foreigners offers hardly any reasoned arguments to sustain a self-confident positioning like seeing oneself as a legitimate 'other German' (Mecheril and Teo 1994), the concerned youths had to manoeuvre most carefully in a field of competing forces if they wanted to argue their genuine position *within* German society. Hardly any of them followed a trajectory of moving to the country which their parents or grandparents had once left behind. They felt much more at home in Berlin and held the emigration countries for less modern, nice as holiday destinations, but determined by traditionalism and narrow-mindedness. In this respect, a certain 'Germanization' became noticeable in their stereotypical perceptions of their own family backgrounds. They judged harshly the places of their families' origin according to criteria they had adopted in Germany. But when it came to their own position, none of my interlocutors wanted to be squeezed into such a stereotype. Instead, they all resorted to experiences that were apt to belie the dominant images and introduced further differences. Rather than adhering to absolute categories of belonging, they tended to express partial identifications that depended on situation and circumstance.

One frequently applied strategy was the general subscription to the grand categorization into Germans and foreigners, followed by an immediate sub-differentiation or further qualification of meanings. To quote one example: in a discussion with several pupils from Lebanese, Greek, Turkish, Kosovarian and Tamil families the participants all agreed that 'their mentality' (singular!) differed from 'the German mentality' (also singular!). But then all sorts of internal differences were pointed out that finally undermined collective attributions. A 17-year-old Palestinian girl explained that, 'We live in two different societies in a way, therefore none of us can be typical of either group'.

In spite of the strong contrast which she conceptualized as 'two differ-ent societies', her own uneasiness with being sorted into the resulting choice of groups led to a remarkable deconstruction:

Palestinian girl:	At our school it is like this, for example: the for-eigners are on one side, and the Germans are also more on their own ... because the Germans are completely different ...
Greek girl:	Every person is different. That has nothing to do with nationalities!
Palestinian girl:	But in our families, we stay with our parents until we get married. That is different among the Germans.
German girl:	For me it is like that. I'll move out of my parents' place soon.
Another German girl:	But there are also very strict German families.
Palestinian girl:	And among the foreigners, there are the Arabian-Turkish ones, the Muslims that means, and the others.
Croatian girl:	Yes, because principally the Polish are also for-eigners, but as they are Christians, they tend to be more like the Germans ... European somehow ... Sometimes one feels like, 'Where do I belong ultimately?' Should we found a new state for all who are half-and-half German?
Kosovo-Albanian boy:	That's only because you encounter barriers and then you realize that you are not accepted one hundred per cent as a foreigner here.

By the time of their adolescence, these young people had basically learnt to see themselves as the 'others' in Germany. They reproduced the domin-ant public representation of the immigrants, made it their common grounds for further argument – and final deconstruction. This is interest-ing in several respects. In identifying with the residual foreigner attribute, they distance themselves from Germanness whilst taking a position within the notional landscape of German society. This means they turn against the 'divisions rooted in their parents' pre-emigration cultural heritages' (Baumann 1996: 157). At the same time, however, the categorical contrast of Germans versus foreigners was evidently judged insufficient to encompass the complex social reality of multiple belonging and differenti-ated distinction. It was clearly recognized to be just a makeshift reaction to the collective exclusion of being 'not accepted one hundred per cent as a foreigner'.

Reflections regarding denied recognition became more pronounced in the young people's narrations about Berlin before and after the reunification. In this context, they also deconstructed the imagined community of the Germans by stressing gulfs as well as commonalities. Assessments of the social space and mental maps of Berlin were most instructive here: a widespread image in the German public depicts Kreuzberg and Neukoelln, (both boroughs belonged formerly to West Berlin) as desperate ghetto milieus of a poor immigrant population that encapsulates itself and spoils all possibilities of integration – quite parallel to the way teachers spoke of their foreign pupils in school. In contrast to this image, the foreign youths who lived there drew a very positive picture of their neighbourhoods and expressed strong attachment to these boroughs. In their explanations, the adolescents connected much of their homey sentiments to the disappearance of the Berlin Wall which had made them recognize differences between Germans and Germans, meaning in this case, East and West Germans:

> 'Be honest: it was a mistake to pull down the Wall, right?', I was asked by 17-year-old Kamil.[10] Together with his Kurdish friend Ferhat he went on explaining:
>
> *Ferhat:* The Nazis, the baldies ... they don't dare to come to our school or to Kreuzberg, because so many foreigners are around here. They only dare to go where foreigners are less numerous. ... It works out well here. At our school, there are no problems between foreigners and Germans.
>
> *Kamil:* On the whole, it's only like that since the Wall is no longer there. Every evening we go and try to rebuild the Wall but we can't manage, right Ferhat?! – He laughs, then continues: Formerly it was no problem. And we even went to throw bananas over the Wall so that they could have it better in the East! – You don't believe me, hm?! We threw kiwi fruit over the Wall for them! Probably they thought they were hand grenades; and now all the Nazis come here.

In the brief exchange, the East Germans are pictured as the ideal-type 'bad Germans', i.e. 'the Nazis'. For the two boys and their peers, otherness, stubbornness and the unwillingness to adapt to the terms of civility were clearly personified by certain Germans, namely those from the former GDR. Others expressed similar views: owing to the high number of immigrants, there were no problems with rightists at their school or in their residential quarters. They mobilized a protective collectivity along the lines of potential victimization: the danger seems averted wherever the structural minority holds a majority in terms of numbers. Since they saw right wing radicalism as a new phenomenon stemming from the former GDR, the opening of the Wall was interpreted to mark the beginning of siege and danger: 'It's only like that since the Wall is no longer there.'

The small example shows that, even though 'the Germans' were often cited as the contrast group for 'the foreigners', the boundaries were still permeable, and internal differences allowed an undermining of the bold taxonomy. Here, 'we' Westerners were put against 'them' from the East. Kamil's story about the exotic fruit he had thrown over the Wall illustrates that 'they' do not even share 'our' terms of trade and etiquette. Instead of appreciating the good deeds by being grateful and nice, the East Germans brought trouble and hostility. Kamil makes use of the prevalent image of otherness due to cultural difference, and he applies it to diversity within the Germans – arguing such a watershed is to be found along the lines of the former state border.

This way of constructing the otherness of the East Germans follows the fashion in which the Third World and some emigration countries are represented in geography lessons and textbooks: economically speaking, the underprivileged need our help, but in return they should try to meet our standards. Kamil's emphasis on 'our' economic superiority is hence not coincidental. It runs in fact in line with the messages that were taught in his school about the post-war modernization. After the catastrophes of two world wars, of Nazi totalitarianism, and the mass murder of the European Jews, the political ambitions of the Germans were profoundly discredited. The positive post-war project in the FRG – which the labour immigrants participated in – was the economic reconstruction together with international integration; and conversely, a functioning economy is taught in history classes to be the best foundation for a functioning liberal democracy and thus a remedy against Nazism. With the help of this argument, the myth of a better past before unification is put together: the former West is sketched as an idyll of economic wealth and social harmony. Wrapped up in this narration, pride and identification become visible with the economic success of the former West: 'we' *had* all sorts of fruit to throw them over the Wall. Kamil and Ferhat appealed to a level of solidarity and a shared view of the world with me as somebody from the West. This was held up against the bonds of the nation, and the two boys knew very well that the situation in post-unification Germany makes this alliance fairly plausible. The 'growing together' of Germans from East and West has proven to be anything but smooth or natural. On either side of the former border, mythical stories of the better past can still be found.

Having left school, all of the young people were forced more than before to leave their safe haven in Kreuzberg and Neukoelln. Hardly any of them could maintain their previous practice to simply avoid the Eastern parts of the city, since the vocational training institutions, the universities and colleges cover the whole city. The resulting encounters had a twofold effect: on the one hand they turned suspicion into certainties. Personal experiences of discrimination substantiated the idea that a deep abyss divided the East and the West in terms of civilization. When we met for interviews in the years 2000 and 2001, such confrontations played an enormous role; all of my interview partners came to speak of situations that had confirmed their assumptions of the xenophobic East. They felt restricted by a hostile surrounding of 'no-go-areas', and many of them expressed the wish 'to rebuild the Wall', the sooner the better. On the other hand, a notable identification push was caused by these experiences of discrimination: the young 'foreigners' became much more aware than ever before how much they felt at home in Germany and how much it hurt them to be treated as outsiders. The following statement is taken from an interview, conducted in February 2000 with a 20-year-old woman from a Croatian family. It is paradigmatic in a number of respects how she describes her classmates from East Berlin in the vocational training centre:

> They have a much more aggressive attitude towards foreigners than a normal German. I do not want to lump them all together, but the people from the West, who have already had a lot of contact with foreigners in school and who have many good friends among foreigners, behave completely differently and will do so for the rest of their lives. But those, they have always been isolated and have never been in contact with anybody else! When they meet somebody with a head-scarf now, that's just a big question mark for them.... The problem is that they have not grown up together with foreigners like the people in the West. Here it has *never* been a problem.... The Wall is no longer there, and everything has changed.

The 'Easterners' are again characterized as being in need of catching up, developing themselves and their civil competence. This perception resembles not only the dominant stereotype of the poor immigrant but is also a typical way in which people from the West tend to perceive those of the East. Instead of being modest and grateful as they should, according to this view, the former GDR Germans were described by my interviewees as being bossy and self-pitying and, at the same time, as narrow-minded, backward and aggressive. Considering this backlash, the pre-unification past was imagined as a time of harmony without *any* problems. Apart from the glorified projection which this idea implies, it also reflects upon a far-reaching identification with the foreigners' (supposed) role in West Berlin before the national relaunch. The picture that is drawn of the former GDR describes a state that has prevented people from learning tolerant and open behaviour in society, denoting a stage of pre-modern limitation which was overcome in the former FRG and West Berlin *with the help of the immigrants!* My interlocutors felt offended because the East Germans did not acknowledge how much the immigrants had contributed to the success story of post-war West Germany – economically anyway, but likewise in terms of having civilized the (West) Germans. This is recalled in the construction of the 'normal' Germans 'who have learnt to live with foreigners'. Given that the power to define normality is always a resource of the established (Elias and Scotson 1994), the very talk about the 'normal Germans' expresses ultimate feelings of belonging and is to be read as a strong claim for recognition.

When seen against this discursive background, the suggestion to re-erect the Berlin Wall is more than just an effectively relieving joke. It appeals to a different perspective on social cohesion than the national one. The logical consequence that alliances might even be established with some Germans from the former GDR was a further, puzzling experience: inasmuch as the 'Easterners' were seen as profiting from the national reunification, the 'foreigners' were surprised to find that, in their vocational schools, many classmates from East Berlin agreed that times had been better before 1989. Joking relationships were established upon this unexpected common view – an efficient means to cope with otherwise precarious and tense relations (Radcliffe-Brown 1952: 91f.). Based on these disturbing moments, some of the more thoughtful characters among my interviewees had indeed come to see the unification in relative terms and defined their own role, though as others, in very constructive ways. 21-year-old Meera, whose family had emigrated from Sri Lanka in the 1980s, was reflecting in this way upon the costs and benefits of being different when we met in June 2000:

> We had a kind of workshop in East Berlin once when I was a school-girl of grade eight or nine. All the children over there looked at us so strangely, and some dirty nicknames could be heard; but in a way they were also intimidated, for we were so many (with ironically lowered voice): Turks and Arabs, you know – I still remember that I found that quite funny! ... At the moment, unfortunately I do not have any contact with Germans from the East, except for one friend. ... I read an article some time ago with statistics saying that most East Germans do not like foreigners even though it is also a region where only a small number of foreigners live! That made me think. ... The preju-dices people from the East have against foreigners ... can be dispelled in personal contact! ... We had the advantage of enrichment by all the cultures. I have got to know so many cultures in school ... and therefore I will never be able to claim that I have something against somebody from this or that culture, after all I got to know these people: they had the same problems like me, and we could talk to each other about that!'

Meera shares the above cited opinions about the people from the East as representing backwardness; but she has, so to speak, adopted her own responsibility for making things better. She defines a positive role she may play herself in the process of growing together on the basis of a collective stigmatization of the people from the East: lacking a socialization that familiarizes with cultural heterogeneity, they are regarded as being unable to cope with plural society. Her argument presupposes a model of multicultural diversity; yet the underlying notion of otherness is reassessed positively as meaning a collective resource in terms of enrichment that entails the opportunity of learning tolerance. From this point of view, the immigrants appear as indispensable agents of social change because they embody plurality in society. Meera saw this as a chance to contribute to social development personally.

Even though Meera was among the most self-reflective in articulating this optimistic perspective, she was not the only one who had discovered such a positive solution. In search of possible ways out of the nationally codified dilemma of conceptual exclusion, the foreign youths made a virtue out of the attribution to be the others with the different cultures. The fact that group boundaries were sometimes reproduced in the same fashion that marked the dominant stereotype of the immigrants reflects upon the processes of assimilation they had gone through as regards reasoned arguments. At the same time however, this way of arguing did not prevent the young foreigners from assessing diversity in a principally positive manner. Their shared experience with being perceived as others produced a collective identity as foreigners in Germany, and this community of solidarity could only work on the basis that internal heterogeneity was accepted as being so normal that individual peculiarities of culture or of national belonging were in effect relativized as posing no threat to the group. It was thus the very diversity in a multinational, or as Meera described it, a multicultural school setting – which the German teachers regarded as a major source of problems – that had made these pupils accept the relative meaning of difference to such an extent that they could competently reassess the collective value of otherness.

Conclusion

The German unification has affected the school's integrative tasks in a number of ways. Not only were syllabi rephrased in order to adapt factual teaching contents, but issues of national identity were also brought back onto the educational agenda. This touches upon the preferred modes of fostering inner cohesion, upon criteria of legitimate membership, belonging and entitlements in the polity. Yet it competes with trends of denationalization, connected, for instance, with the German past, with the societal impact of immigration and the place of unified Germany in the transnational project of the European Union. The expectations regarding integration that are communicated through school are thus no straight continuum but weave a complex, at times contradictory fabric: traditional concepts of national enculturation were clearly rendered obsolete after 1945. However, the path that was followed instead in West Germany of binding collective commitment towards democratic consensus rather than towards the nation state, was not conceptualized in all its consequences – especially regarding the logical necessity of seeking to include the de facto immigrants in the citizenry. The societal reality of the Federal Republic and most of the educational agenda in the state schools complied with a post-national ethos that relates to democratic civil society rather than to the nation as the conceptual frame for integration. This setting allowed a far-reaching participation of the guest worker population, but more in the shape of a side effect than as a result of a decided political programme of inclusion.

The German unification disturbed this routine and confronted the enlarged collectivity with the need to develop a common self-image that ensures solidarity and social peace within the new state borders. The logical expectation that one should seek to advance the so-called inner unity in Germany after formal unification includes a variety of conceptual options. In the most popular version, the task to overcome the separation between former East and West has since been interpreted within the imagery of the nation as being a quasi-natural organic unity that starts to 'grow together' as soon as artificial barriers are dismantled. This way of envisaging collectivity competes with the understanding of civic integration as being a more comprehensive societal process detached from national membership. In fact, the unification has revitalized the possibility of polarization along the lines of nationality, and the increase in racist violence against 'recognizable' foreigners in Germany since the 1990s has clearly shown the risks involved in this approach. Fortunately, social reality comprises opportunities to discover alternative visions, as has been shown in this essay by using the empirical example of a group of young 'foreigners' from West Berlin.

It may seem evident that the place which foreigners can occupy will depend on the rules defined by the national majority in conceptualizing legitimate in- and outsiders. The foreign youths, however, managed to construct their own readings of the hegemonic discourse about Germans and others. Their versions of the social allocation table in unified Germany reflect upon processes of identification that question the conventional concepts of quasi-organic national solidarity. They rejected identification with their parents' national backgrounds as much as with Germanness, but they were willing to express identification with living in Germany and belonging there. While objecting against the assimilatory demands of 'Germanization', their discourses were specifically coloured by the German setting and its difficulties with conceptualizing the nation as a community that one could and would like to join. Being socialized into the ambivalence of German identity and its negative connotations, the quoted adolescents resorted to the common identity as foreigners in Germany, thus moving away from their parents' expectations and citing a social place *within* German society.

These young people had internalized the prevalent civil conventions, discourses and images surrounding Germanness and the related construction of otherness. They made use of these for strategic identity management and applied the means of othering to the East Germans that usually marks the representation of the immigrants, in Germany and in their school. This transfer reveals their familiarity with the rules of the game; yet it also reveals the highly contradictory experience of being accepted members in everyday social life while remaining widely excluded from the dominant collective self-image. They bridged the gap with partial and selective identifications, stressed positive moments like the good 'normal' Germans who represent tolerance, or economic rationality of post-war West Germany. Both are pragmatic in principle and were understood as being achieved together with the immigrants. The favourite mythical tale of perfect social harmony before 1989 combines these aspects in one condensed picture: it draws the image of a civilized society made up of 'normal' FRG Germans together with the immigrants and places them in a western world of pluralist modernity and wealth.

The creativity involved in these narrations deserves acknowledgement, but the driving forces are questionable: even the most positive perspectives that were developed by some of my interviewees regarding their possible role 'as others' have their roots in stigma management. In view of the influence of school, the creed is a standard phrase already in the normative rhetoric of educational guidelines that teaching should seek to dissolve polarization which creates stereotypical others in the search for self-definition. In practice, this challenge to deconstruct and question presumably self-evident boundaries between 'us' and others remains to be tackled, especially in settings where the difficulties of underprivileged living conditions tend to work in favour of hardening such concepts. In this respect, the young foreigners were in fact ahead of the nationally informed concepts of integration that were still and once again going round their school.

Notes

1 Since labour immigration marked a much shorter period in the GDR, and has not resulted in any longer term consolidation of the presence of the 'contract workers' there, the Federal Republic is my case of reference for the time before the 1990 unification.
2 The material results from my ten months of ethnological fieldwork in a secondary school in Berlin in the 1996/1997 school term and from interviews I conducted in between 1998 and 2001 with (then former) pupils from immigrant families I had come to know there. Regarding the age cohort, data collection spanned over their age from 15–17 to 20–22 years. The findings can only be summarized here. For further evidence see Schiffauer *et al.* 2004.
3 For two pragmatic reasons, I will use national labels and call pupils with a Turkish family background 'Turkish pupils' or speak of 'foreigners'; the first is readability, the second is the fact that it coincides with the emic vocabulary of my interlocutors. In the course of my argument it should anyway become clear that this labelling does neither denote essentialization nor legitimize exclusion.
4 The relations between mother tongues and national languages cannot be taken up in depth here. Language refers to cognitive skills. It patterns communication

and memories. Beyond that, language also reaches into different political fields, such as cultural, minority and identity policies: making use of a particular language in a particular setting can serve the purpose of staging one's origin. A common axiom in the literature is, however, that language acquisition goes along with a certain process of identification and can therefore be regarded as one marker of integration (see e.g. Byram and Leman 1990; Rampton 1995).

5 When understood as competence and practice of participation, citizenship applies to the immigrants who take part in crucial institutions of civil society. The gap between formal and informal citizenship is especially relevant for West Germany where the official creed to be no country of immigration prevented policies of enforced formal integration (Bade 2000: 338). The German nationality legislation has remained comparatively restrictive, and most former guest workers still hold the legal status of foreigners. In many respects of participation however, the migrant population in Germany achieves better than their counterparts in countries with more inclusive policies of formal integration, like the Netherlands (Thraenhardt 2000).

6 It has become impossible to cite all the works on this subject. To quote at least a few: Sassen 1996; Joppke 1998; Koopmans and Statham 1999; Kastoryano 2002.

7 All quotations are taken from the author's fieldnotes, single phrases in quotation marks as well as passages from lessons and interviews.

8 The representation of migration in the relevant teaching units points to the same direction: in German geography textbooks, the countries of emigration tend to be marked as backward and disunited by inner conflicts which are often related to parochial cultural traditions. Migration is mainly associated with intrinsic problems and poverty as push-factors, so that the immigrants appear as recipients (see Mannitz and Schiffauer 2004; Stoeber 2001).

9 The 'strong push in the negative direction' is a general characteristic of national identification patterns in West Germany (Rossteutscher 1997: 624).

10 Kamil's mother was German, his father Lebanese. In most situations he identified himself as being an Arab.

References

Anderson, B. (1991) *Imagined Communities: Reflections on the Origin and Spread of Nationalism*, London: Verso.

Bade, K. (2000) *Europa in Bewegung: Migration vom spaeten 18. Jahrhundert bis zur Gegenwart*, Munich: Beck.

Bade, K. and Weiner, M. (eds) (2001) *Migration Past, Migration Future: Germany and the United States*, Oxford and New York: Berghahn.

Baumann, G. (1996) *Contesting Culture: Discourses of Identity in Multi-ethnic London*, Cambridge: Cambridge University Press.

Baumert, J., Klieme, E., Neubrand, M., Porenzel, M., Schiefele, U., Schneider, W., Stanat, P., Tillmann, K.-J. (2001) *PISA 2000*, Opladen: Leske+Budrich.

Bertilotti, T., Mannitz, S. and Soysal, Y. (forthcoming 2004) 'Rethinking the nation-state: projections of identity in French and German history and civics Textbooks', in H. Schissler and Y. Soysal (eds) *The Nation, Europe, and the World: Textbooks and Curricula in Transition*, Oxford and New York: Berghahn.

Bourdieu, P. (1987) *Die feinen Unterschiede: Kritik der gesellschaftlichen Urteilskraft*, Frankfurt/Main: Suhrkamp.

Byram, M. and Leman, J. (1990) *Bicultural and Trilingual Education*, Clevedon: Multilingual Matters.

Ebeling, H. and Birkenfeld, W. (1995) *Die Reise in die Vergangenheit. Ein geschichtliches Arbeitsbuch*, Volumes 1–6, Braunschweig: Westermann.

Elias, N. and Scotson, J. L. (1994) *The Established and the Outsiders: A Sociological Enquiry into Community Problems*, London: Sage (1st edn 1965, London: Cass).

Gellner, E. (1993) *Nations and Nationalism*, Oxford: Blackwell.

Joppke, C. (1998) *Challenge to the Nation-State: Immigration and Citizenship in Western Europe and the United States*, Oxford: Oxford University Press.

Kastoryano, R. (2002) *Negotiating Identities*, Princeton: Princeton University Press.

Katzenstein, P. J. (1997) *The Culture of National Security. Norms and Identity in World Politics*, New York: Columbia University Press.

Koopmans, R. and Statham, P. (1999) 'Challenging the liberal nation-state?', *American Journal of Sociology* 105 (3): 652–697.

Kornmann, R. and Klingele, C. (1996) 'Auslaendische Kinder und Jugendliche an Schulen fuer Lernbehinderte in den alten Bundeslaendern', *Zeitschrift fuer Heilpaedagogik* (47) 1: 2–9.

Luchtenberg, S. and Nieke, W. (eds) (1994) *Interkulturelle Paedagogik und Europaeische Dimension. Herausforderungen fuer Bildungssystem und Erziehungswissenschaft*, Muenster and New York: Waxmann.

Mannitz, S. and Schiffauer, W. (2004) 'Taxonomies of cultural difference: Constructions of otherness', in W. Schiffauer *et al.* (eds) *Civil Enculturation: Nation-State, School, and Ethnic Difference in Four European Countries*, Oxford and New York: Berghahn.

Mecheril, P. and Teo, T. (eds) (1994) *Andere Deutsche: Zur Lebenssituation von Menschen multiethnischer und multikultureller Herkunft*, Berlin: Dietz.

Pingel, F. (1995) *Macht Europa Schule? Die Darstellung Europas in Schulbuechern der Europaeischen Gemeinschaft*, Frankfurt am Main: Diesterweg.

Radcliffe-Brown, A. R. (1952) 'On joking relationships', in A. R. Radcliffe-Brown (ed.) *Structure and Function in Primitive Society*, London: Cohen and West.

Raethzel, N. (1997) *Gegenbilder. Nationale Identitaet durch Konstruktion des Anderen*, Opladen: Leske+Budrich.

Rampton, B. (1995) *Crossing: Language and Ethnicity among Adolescents*, London: Longman.

Reich, H. and Roth, H.-J. (2002) *Spracherwerb zweisprachig aufwachsender Kinder und Jugendlicher*, Hamburg: Behoerde fuer Bildung und Sport.

Rossteutscher, S. (1997) 'Between normality and particularity – National identity in West-Germany', *Nations and Nationalism*, 3 (4): 607–630.

Sassen, S. (1996*) Losing Control: The Decline of Sovereignty in an Age of Globalization*, New York: Columbia University Press.

Schiffauer, W., Baumann, G., Kastoryano, R. and Vertovec, S. (eds) (2004) *Civil Enculturation: Nation-State, School, and Ethnic Difference in Four European Countries*, Oxford and New York: Berghahn.

Stoeber, G. (eds) (2001): *'Fremde Kulturen' im Geographieunterricht*, Hannover: Hahn.

Thraenhardt, D. (2000) 'Conflict, consensus, and policy outcomes: immigration and integration in Germany and the Netherlands', in R. Koopmans and P. Statham (eds) *Challenging Immigration and Ethnic Relation Politics*, Oxford: Oxford University Press.

Wiener, A. (1998) *'European' Citizenship Practice. Building Institutions of a Non-State*, Oxford and Boulder: Westview.

5   The education of migrants and minorities in Britain[1]

Sally Tomlinson

Introduction

Over the past 50 years Britain has become a multiracial and multicultural country. The 2001 census recorded that 7.9 per cent of the population of the UK as a whole, 4.6 million people, described themselves as from an ethnic minority. The majority were British citizens – settled minorities originally from the Caribbean, Africa, south Asian countries – notably India, Pakistan and Bangladesh, and from Hong Kong, and Cyprus. From the 1990s new patterns of migration were evident, with an increase in numbers of refugees and asylum seekers, an increase in temporary skilled migrant labour, and more movement of European Union nationals. Most social institutions, including education, gradually and with varying degrees of success, changed slowly to accommodate minority and migrant groups, although by 2001 there was an emerging backlash against multiculturalism, antagonism towards refugees and more hostility towards Muslims.

This chapter overviews patterns of migration and minority experiences in Britain, and goes on to examine the place of minorities in an education system which, by the 1990s, had become a competitive market place. Competition between schools was encouraged by parental 'choice' of school and media publication of examination results by school. Funding was devolved to schools and budgets were determined by pupil numbers, forcing schools to compete for the most desirable pupils. Re-elected in 2001, the New Labour government continued to support policies of diversity between schools, by specialist curricula and by religion. As in other countries, choice policies increased segregation in schools by social class, race and ethnicity, disability and special needs. While the educational achievements of all groups improved from the 1990s, there was considerable divergence between minority group performance; Caribbean, Pakistani and Bangladeshi pupils continuing to perform least well. Educational policies appeared to be creating new disadvantages for minorities. In particular, the national curriculum and citizenship education continued to reflect an Anglocentric viewpoint, funding for teaching

English as an additional language was minimal, there was limited teacher preparation for teaching training for a multicultural society, and anxiety over the extension of state-funded religious schooling.

Migration patterns

Major migrations to Britain after 1945 included both European 'displaced people' and new Commonwealth immigration. The labour of migrants from former colonial countries was actively sought and there was relatively large-scale immigration from the Caribbean, Africa, south Asian countries, Hong Kong and in the 1960s a large migration of Greek and Turkish Cypriot people. The forced expulsion of Asians from east Africa, and Vietnamese boat people in the 1970s and 1980s brought further migrant inflows and by the 1990s new patterns of migration were becoming established in Britain as in other countries. An increase in temporary skilled migrant labour has been encouraged by formalizing work permits. The Single European Act allowed more movement of EU nationals across borders, and there was an increase in transnational movement between countries. Civil wars in the 1990s brought in refugees and asylum seekers from Somalia, Ethiopia, Sri Lanka, Turkey, Iraq, Bosnia, Kosovo, west African countries, Afghanistan and other places, and more movement of the Roma from eastern European countries. Britain had undoubtedly become a multicultural country.

The majority of pre-1990 migrants were British citizens, and the latest census figures show that just under 8 per cent of the population are 'visible minorities', including people who claim 'mixed race' (Office for National Statistics 2003). Patterns of settlement and original job opportunities meant that minorities were mainly living in London and other large cities, and also in smaller northern towns where there was, up to the 1970s, employment in textile industries. By 2001 two London boroughs had more ethnic minorities than whites and census analysts have suggested that two cities; Leicester and Birmingham, will have non-white majorities by 2011. Minority ethnic groups have a younger age structure, some 43 per cent of Bangladeshi and 35 per cent of Pakistani groups being under 16 compared to 20 per cent of white groups, and it is becoming clear that a future workforce will draw heavily on minority young people. Numbers of more recent arrivals are difficult to ascertain, but there was an increase in refugees and asylum seekers to some 110,000 in 2001. Figures were exaggerated in the tabloid media and much hostile publicity given to both accepted and illegal migrants.

Migrant and minority experiences

Castles (2003) developed his notion of four 'ideal types' of incorporation of migrants and minorities in developed countries to explain the varied patterns of settlement, attachment and experiences. Assimilation policies – based on the US melting pot notion that immigrants would be 'Americanized' – were initially adopted in Britain, the assumption being that immigration should not create any social or cultural change in the majority society and that migrants' descendants would merge into the majority population. Castles' second model – that of differential exclusion – was never adopted in Britain, although it became the model for the guest worker system, in Germany and Switzerland, where migrants were accepted as workers but not as settlers. Despite much racism and postcolonial hostility to settlers, by the 1970s multiculturalism – described by Castles as the public acceptance of migrant and minority groups as communities which are distinguishable from the majority population in terms of language, culture and social behaviour – had become the most acceptable model for a future British society. A recognition of both cultural diversity and social, political and economic equality for minorities became an ideal goal, despite the persistence of racism and xenophobia. There was also some evidence that Castles' fourth type of migration, the growth of transnational communities whose members move between countries, ranging from multinational corporation employees to more modest economic migrants and their kin, was becoming important (Sklair 2001).

However, the slow and controversial move from the myth of a homogenous – white – British 'national identity' to the acceptance of a diverse multicultural society continued to create problems for policy-makers and minority groups.

Negative and xenophobic attitudes to settled minorities and discrimination suffered by the various minority groups in employment, housing, education and welfare services, have been well-documented over the past four decades (see Rex and Tomlinson 1979; Brown 1984; Skellington and Morris 1996; Modood *et al.* 1997) and four Race Relations Acts, the most recent in 2000, have attempted to deal with disadvantages and racial harassment. An important event was the publication of the MacPherson enquiry into the murder of the Asian teenager Stephen Lawrence in 1993, an enquiry eventually set up by the Home Secretary, which criticized the police and other bodies for institutional racism (MacPherson 1999). There has always been a dual attitude towards immigrant minorities in Britain. Their labour has been welcomed – apart from times of economic recession – when claims that 'they take our jobs' surface, and there have been persistent calls for immigration controls from the 1950s to the present-day. Despite most settlers having acquired nationality and citizenship rights the majority population does not generally accept that Britain is a multicultural and multi-faith country. Fascist groups continue to incite hatred of both settled minorities and recent migrants and asylum seekers. From 1997 the British National Party (BNP) began a campaign to incite people in northern towns to protest against Pakistani settlement and in elections in 2003 won a number of seats on local councils in the north.

In 1998 a Commission of Enquiry into the Future of Multi-ethnic Britain was set up with government endorsement. After taking evidence from groups around the country the Commission reported in 2000 (Parekh 2000). The report noted that among all groups there were conflicting loyalties, and that since there had been a devolution of power to Scotland and Wales, closer European ties, increasing globalization and an end to the 'British Empire' the notion of a British national identity needed rethinking. It also noted the 'aggressive hostility towards Islam' (2000: 10), hostility which increased considerably after the bombing in the USA on 11 September 2001, and the Iraq war in 2003. The Commission's report was itself greeted with extraordinary hostility by the media and the government, particularly its suggestion that the 'British Identity' needed rethinking. A year after the report's publication Hugo Young, a journalist writing in the liberal *Guardian* newspaper, suggested that 'all citizens of migrant stock, particularly Muslims', must ask themselves whether they 'actually want to be full members of the society in which they live' (Young 2001) and suggested that the (multicultural) ideology within the Commission's report 'can now be seen as a useful bible (sic) for any Muslim who insists that his religio-cultural priorities, including the defense of jihad against America, overrides his civic duties of tolerance, justice and respect for democracy' – an extraordinary claim to make about a report that was intended to defend multicultural democracy.

Although by the 1990s all settled minority groups had begun to improve their educational and skill levels and more were gaining non-manual jobs, differences had begun to emerge in socio-economic status, income, lifestyle, culture and identity between different ethnic minorities (Modood *et al.* 1997). There was an emerging Black and Asian middle class and considerable minority business success. Thus, Leicester, a city in which east African Asians settled in the 1970s had, by 2000, a thriving middle class whose children did well at school. Oldham, a northern town where rural Pakistani migrants settled to work in textile factories, had high unemployment, poorly qualified young people and high levels of racial segregation and tension (Harris and Bright 2001). In the summer of 2001 there were 'race riots' in several northern towns, which were variously attributed by the media to poverty and unemployment, fascist incitement of the White population, and drug taking. A report on the city of Bradford, produced in 2001 by a former head of the Commission for Racial Equality, concluded that the city had lost much of its industry and manufacturing and has 'struggled to redefine itself as a modern multicultural area and has lost its spirit of togetherness. As a result Bradford district has witnessed growing divisions among its population along race, ethnic and social class lines and now finds itself in the grip of fear' (Ouseley 2001). A Home Office-sponsored report on the riots regretted the loss of 'community cohesion' and suggested redefining the equality agenda so that the 'White community' did not feel left out, and managed to confuse the problems of settled migrants with new migrations by proposing a 'statement of allegiance' from migrants (Cantle 2001).

The education market post-1988

By the turn of the century it was obvious that the education system, never having adequately developed policies and practices to educate all young people for a multicultural society, faced new challenges. However, it is questionable whether changed educational policies and practices are of benefit to minorities or are designed to educate all young people within principles of equity and tolerance.

From the 1960s to the 1980s children of migrant and minority parents entered a school system in which overt selection for different kinds of schooling was gradually disappearing and comprehensive schooling was becoming the norm. School admission policies were coordinated by local education authorities and in those authorities where selection for grammar schools was phased out most pupils attended a neighbourhood school. Some 36 LEAs retained whole or partly selective systems, in which children of minority parentage did not do well (Rex and Tomlinson 1979). Central and local government were at least notionally committed to widening access to a broad secondary education for all social groups and education policy and practice changed slowly to accommodate minorities. Disadvantages experienced by minority pupils were associated with lack of English language teaching, low educational attainments, an Anglocentric curriculum, lack of funding, and teachers who while not overtly racist, held low expectations of the children from former colonial countries and had little or no training or awareness of minority educational issues. The report by the committee chaired by Lord Swann (Department for Education and Science 1985) noted the failure to produce national policies which would assist in the incorporation and successful education of minority children and the report itself provided an excellent blueprint for changes that would provide an 'Education for All' in a multicultural society.

However, from 1988, in England and Wales, a new framework for funding, administering and monitoring all aspects of education was created, and a national curriculum which retained an Anglocentric bias made mandatory in all schools. New policies and a retreat from 1980s teacher-led strategies to develop a multicultural curriculum (Aurora and Duncan 1996; Tomlinson 1990) were not intended to develop education suitable for a multicultural society. The then Prime Minister Margaret Thatcher made clear her hostility to any educational policies supporting multiculturalism or anti-racism (see Thatcher 1993).[2]

Funding was devolved to school level, school budgets were determined by pupil numbers and schools competed to attract 'desirable customers'. A diversity of schools was to be encouraged on the basis that schools should 'specialize' in some aspect of the curriculum, and selection of pupils by the schools became an important aspect of the system once again. Parents were told they had a 'choice' of school but in practice they could only express a preference with no guarantee of a place. Competition between schools was and continues to be fuelled by the annual publication of league tables of school performance in public examinations and schools are rewarded for the number of pupils they attract who can perform well for the school. In this educational climate, values of competition, individualism and separation are important, social and racial justice and equity less so.

Choice policies around the world have tended to increase segregation in schools by social class, race and ethnicity, disability and special needs (OECD 1994; Gerwirzt *et al.* 1995; Ball *et al.* 1996; Gillborn and Youdell 1999). Although in England since 1997, the New Labour government attempted palliative policies to improve schools and the education of poor children in inner city areas[3] other more punitive policies and the competitive situation between schools encouraged most schools to reject socially and educationally vulnerable students and orient themselves towards the perceived needs of the middle classes. Often these 'needs' were openly to move their children away from schools attended by minorities. Some of the emerging Black and Asian middle classes adopted similar strategies, with expressed preferences for selective or private schools, or schools with low proportions of minority pupils (Noden *et al.* 1998; Abbas 2002). However, 'choice' continued to be more problematic for middle class minorities. Research by Noden *et al.* (1998) showed that, despite expressed preferences and high aspirations for their children, minority families were less likely than Whites to get their children into high-performing schools. White parents, who before the market reforms had offered covert reasons for school preferences, were now openly able to express preferences for schools with few or no ethnic minorities.

Excluded pupils and failing schools

The education market also worked to encourage schools to get rid of students who disrupt the smooth running of the school or interfere with the credentialing of other pupils. In England, referral for special education has always provided one way in which minority – especially African-Caribbean – pupils have been removed from mainstream education. Black pupils were four times over represented in the old category of 'educationally subnormal' (Tomlinson 1982), and as 'emotionally and behaviorally disturbed'. In the 1990s, as the marketization of education became more established, the quickest way of removing undesirable pupils became through placements in 'Pupil Referral Units'[4] or through straight exclusion from schools, either temporarily or permanently. Gillborn noted in 1995 the 'Exclusions from school operate in a racist manner, they deny a disproportionate number of Black students access to main-stream education' (Gillborn 1995). Blair, studying differential school exclusions (Blair 2001), placed the issue in a broad social and historical perspective to show that Black working class pupils are criticized and excluded from school more than White students who commit similar 'offences'. Social class, race and ethnicity, special educational needs and behaviour problems have become filters through which the desirability or undesirability of particular pupils is understood. On most counts minority pupils, especially African-Caribbean pupils are less likely to be regarded as desirable by many schools.

A further policy which continues to disadvantage minorities has been the official targeting of schools – from 1993 – as 'failing' or 'in need of special measures' on criteria applied by the Office for Standards in Education (OFSTED), the new schools inspectorate created in 1992 (Tomlinson 1997). Schools move in and out of special measures, depending on whether their examination performance is thought to be improving, and some schools have been given 'Fresh Starts' with new headteachers and school names. Over the past ten years over 1,000 schools have been regarded as in need of special measures. The schools identified have largely been concentrated in deprived areas, especially in London, and attended by high proportions of minority pupils, second language speakers and from working class families. A school closed in 1995 after a court case, Hackney Downs School in London, had 80 per cent of pupils from minority or refugee backgrounds, 70 per cent second language speakers, a high proportion of children with special needs and a high degree of poverty (Tomlinson 1998). The press coverage of failing schools has always been negative and derisory and blame attached to pupils, parents and teachers. The 'naming and shaming of schools' as it came to be called, has provided a new way of scapegoating and disadvantaging minority pupils in urban schools. Nevertheless the government persists with this policy. At a launch of a declared new strategy to improve London schools in May 2003, Prime Minister Blair asserted that weak schools that fail to meet examination targets will close. On current performance information these are likely to be schools attended by large numbers of minority and refugee children.

School diversity

The first education white paper produced by the new Labour government (Department for Education and Employment 1997) demanded that comprehensive schools should develop their own distinctive identities and expertise, despite the fact that there was now a national curriculum for all schools, and comprehensives had in any case varied their ethos and priorities. After 1998 some 164 selective grammar schools remained in 15 LEAs, which affected the intakes of some 500 'comprehensive' schools. Other secondary schools could chose to have 'foundation' status, with their own admissions policies and special funding. Religious schools, formerly with voluntary aided or controlled status could remain as voluntary aided schools, again with their own admissions policies. These comprised some 700 schools; mainly Anglican and Roman Catholic, with 22 Jewish schools. Muslims, who had long campaigned for state-funded Islamic schools, were granted this right and four schools have so far acquired voluntary aided status. Other secondary schools were to be designated as community schools. Schools were to bid for extra money to specialize in an area of the curriculum – technology, languages, arts, sports and so on, and a level of selection by 'aptitude' for schools with specialist status was permitted. Some schools were to be designated as beacon schools, exemplifying good practice and were to get extra funding. Estate agents reported that house prices near beacon schools increased.

School diversity did not appear to favour minority pupils. Very few minority pupils had ever attended grammar schools, and foundation schools with specialist status became sought after by White middle class parents, as did church schools, whose criteria for admission usually required Christian baptism. A diversity of schools by religion has been heavily criticized for creating ethnic and racially separate schools. The government was, however, concerned to try to keep middle class children in inner city schools and to reassure minority parents that the schools were improving. A white paper in 2001 promised to identify 'gifted and talented children', especially in areas of disadvantage, and make special provision for them. An Academy for Gifted and Talented Youth was funded, based at Warwick University (Department for Education and Skills 2001). It is as yet unknown as to how many minority pupils are identified as gifted and talented.

In a further attempt to create city schools that would be attractive to middle class and aspirant parents, including minority parents, the government, via the 2002 Education Act, encouraged employers and business, local communities and charities to cooperate in the building of 'Academies', which were to include existing business-sponsored City Technology Colleges. By 2008, 30 of these Academies are expected to be in operation. Minority parents do see the creation of new schools partly under their control as a positive move. In Brixton, London, an area of high Caribbean settlement, Nelson Mandela is currently supporting a bid for a Brixton Academy for which campaigners will need to raise £2 million. The question remains as to whether a few excellent schools will help raise the educational performance of all minority pupils, and also raises questions concerning the abdication of the state from providing and paying for efficient schools for all pupils within a national education system.

Minority achievements

For minority students and their parents, the most important purpose of education is to provide opportunities to acquire educational credentials that will enable the young people to obtain good employment or move into higher education. Over the past 40 years there has been a slow but steady rise in the educational achievements of all school students, as measured by literacy levels and pupils entering for and passing public examinations. In the early 1960s fewer than 16 per cent of pupils 'passed' five subjects in the then General Certificate of Education. The development of comprehensive schooling, changed school policies and higher teacher expectations which encouraged more pupils to be taught and entered for public examinations – especially girls and minority pupils – were undoubtedly important factors in raising achievements. By 2001 over 50 per cent (more girls than boys) of pupils were passing the five General Certificate of Secondary Education subjects at the required level.[5]

The relative underachievement of ethnic minority pupils became a major issue from the 1960s onwards, with a series of research reports documenting the lower attainments of African-Caribbean, Pakistani and Bangladeshi pupils in particular. Research in the 1980s and 1990s continued to find these pupils making less progress than other pupils (Smith and Tomlinson 1989; Gillborn and Gipps 1996; Demack *et al.* 2000). Government policies to address the educational performance of minority students have included providing money for local authorities with significant numbers of minority students with an 'Ethnic Minority Achievement Grant' (EMAG)[6] and setting up a unit in the Education Department to monitor minority achievements. Gillborn and Mirza (2000) using information provided by 118 Local Education Authorities for EMAG purposes, summarized their findings as follows:

- National figures hide wide variations between local education authorities.
- African-Caribbean, Pakistani and Bangladeshi groups were still achieving less well in GCSE examinations than others at 16 and 'A' level examinations at 18.
- The gap between the achievements of African-Caribbean and Pakistani pupils has widened since 1988, although in a small number of LEAs Black students do as well as Whites.
- Pupils of Indian origin are the highest achieving group and in some cases out-performed Whites.
- Ethnic inequalities persist even when social class and gender differences are controlled for. Black middle class pupils do not achieve as highly as White middle class pupils.

Further confirming evidence comes from a longitudinal Youth Cohort study funded by the Department for Education. The YCS data shows that while attainments in all groups have risen since 1989, African-Caribbean and Bangladeshi pupils are least likely to have benefited, in that the gap between them and their White peers is as wide as a decade ago (Demack *et al.* 2000). Indian and Chinese pupils are the highest achievers and have improved their performance year on year. However, these groups are more likely to be in families with higher incomes. Chinese pupils are more likely to attend fee-paying schools, and Indian parents are most likely to pay for private tuition and want fee-paying or selective schools (Abbas 2002). The factors which are now regarded as important in the underachievement of Caribbean students in particular continue to be teachers low expectations, lack of awareness of equity issues,[7] stereotyping, school exclusions, institutional racism, an Anglocentric national curriculum, and the unequal social and economic position of Black parents. The government has, in 2003, instigated an ethnic minority achievement strategy, labelled 'Aiming High', and has suggested that schools could in future set separate exam targets for different ethnic groups (Shaw 2003), a suggestion not popular with headteachers or minority parents.

Minority students have always entered Colleges of Further Education at 16 in larger proportions than White students, to obtain educational and vocational qualifications, and in the 1990s, with an expansion in university places, more minority students began to attend universities. Students from Indian and Chinese groups are more likely to enter higher education than any other group; Caribbean, Pakistani and Bangladeshi students, especially women, being less likely to apply, although the situation began to change in 2000 with more Bangladeshi women applying. Minority students are more likely to be studying part time, and attend 'new' universities – formerly urban polytechnics – rather than old traditional universities. There is some evidence that policies of charging fees for tuition, and expecting students to take loans for their maintenance, has led to fewer working class and minority students applying for higher education.

There is as yet, little information on the educational achievements of refugee and asylum seekers, or Roma children. Rutter has pointed out that cuts in public expenditure and the required delegation of LEA budgets to schools have reduced the power of local authorities to plan for the arrival and education of refugee children (Rutter 2001). What evidence is available suggests that the education system has not yet found ways of helping these children to achieve, and little funding has been forthcoming for English language teaching.

Curriculum issues

In 1988 a national curriculum was introduced into schools in England and Wales, comprising three core and seven foundation subjects, all with heavily prescribed content developed by working groups chosen by central government. There was considerable government interference with the working groups recommendations, particularly the English and history groups (Cox 1995; Phillips 1998). Cox, Chair of the English working group, has described the way the then Conservative government and its advisors considered that the curriculum had been taken over by left wing progressives and multiculturalists, criticisms even being made of suggestions for bilingual education. Prime Minister Thatcher attempted to impose her view of British history on the history working group, and a working group set up officially in 1989 to produce guidelines on multicultural education in all subjects, had the publication of its report blocked by ministers (Tomlinson 1993). Although in 1985 Lord Swann's report on the education of all children, had recommended a rethink of the curriculum to reflect the pluralist nature of society, there was much hostility to the idea that an Anglocentric curriculum needed to change. Mrs Thatcher's memoirs document her antagonism to any suggestion of multiculturalism or anti-racism, and a multicultural curriculum was presented by critics as a threat to traditional British values and heritage and even as political subversion. A former Bradford headteacher, whose views had led to his resignation in 1984, wrote that continued references in the national curriculum to cultural diversity, equality for women and the handicapped and to personal and social education, were all evidence that the curriculum was dominated by left wing zealots (Honeyford 1990). Duncan Graham, first Chair of the National Curriculum Council, wrote after his resignation that 'it was made starkly clear to NCC by Ministers that whatever influence it might have would be rapidly dissipated by entering what was widely seen as a no-go area (multicultural education)' (Graham 1993: 132). The national curriculum in its original form was generally agreed to be unworkable and in 1993 Sir Ron Dearing was appointed to 'slim down' the content (Dearing 1993). After a further review a new version, *Curriculum 2000*, prescribed the subjects to be taught from 2000, including a new subject, citizenship education, to be taught from 2002.

The MacPherson report on the murder of Stephen Lawrence contained over 70 suggestions for combating racism, four of these referring to education (MacPherson 1999). One of these was that 'consideration be given to the amendment of the national curriculum aimed at valuing cultural diversity and preventing racism, in order to better reflect the needs of a diverse society'. There was subsequently a rhetorical commitment from central government to prepare all young people for a multicultural society. *Curriculum 2000* was to be the means to 'help young people develop spiritually, morally and physically ... becoming healthy, lively, enquiring individuals capable of rational thought and positive participation in our ethnically diverse society' (Qualifications and Curriculum Authority 1999). However, there was little guidance for teachers as to how to achieve this aim and some policy confusion. For example, while pupils at 11 could make a short historical study of 'an African, American, Asian or Australasian society' they could choose to study 'Romans, Anglo-Saxons, and Vikings in Britain' instead.

The notion of citizenship education within the curriculum has also become problematic, as the whole notion of citizenship is a contested concept. There is social, historical and regional and cultural diversity within the 'majority' population, and ethnic minorities, although officially citizens, are largely unequal on a range of social and economic indicators (Modood *et al.* 1997), although sharing experiences of racism. In addition, government policies have been contradictory. Following the Home Secretary's review team who reported on the 'race riots' in Bradford in 2001 (Cantle 2001) which recommended a 'greater sense of citizenship based on common principles' the government introduced a Nationality, Immigration and Asylum Act (2002) which required a citizenship oath for new citizens, and allowed for regulations on the testing of citizens on life in Britain and knowledge of English.

In addition, the notion of teaching citizenship has never been popular in England. Various attempts to teach 'civics', and political education never became statutory, and although the National Curriculum Council did publish non-statutory guidelines on citizenship education in 1990 (National Curriculum Council 1990) there was no evidence that teachers used them. A report by an advisory group on citizenship education, produced in 1998 (Crick 1998) recommended that the teaching of citizenship and democracy in schools should be mandatory and prescribed programmes of study were prepared. However, as Figueroa (2003) has noted, there is no focus on citizenship in a diverse society, power and empowerment are not included, and there is no focus on institutional discrimination, gender and ethnic equality or anti-racism. There are attainment targets for citizenship education, but these do not include diversity, resolving conflicts, international or global issues. Despite this, the government insists that citizenship education will help create a more tolerant, equal society.

Teacher preparation

Intercultural awareness and preparation for teaching in multicultural societies has been slow to develop in all European countries (Craft 1996), and despite repeated assertions that teachers needed training to teach in multi-ethnic Britain, there has been minimal development in courses, research or literature. After the government took prescriptive control of teacher training through a Teacher Training Agency (TTA) in 1994, many university and local authority run courses disappeared and student teachers are now less likely to have any preparation in the area than in the 1980s. Despite government rhetorical assertions that teachers should help all young people towards respect for diversity and for an understanding of

Britain's role in Europe and the modern world, little effort is devoted to such a proposition. The TTA produced guidelines in 2000 which noted that 'every trainee teacher needs to understand how to prepare all pupils to play a part in a culturally diverse, democratic society which values everybody and accords them equal rights', yet there is little advice on how to bring this about. The document (TTA 2000) consists mainly of a repetition of academic research findings. The new Inspectorate created in 1992, the Office for Standards in Education, produced more useful guidelines for what is expected from schools, and has both commissioned work and carried out its own studies on the achievement of minorities (Gillborn and Gipps 1996). Teacher preparation of teachers of bilingual children and those teaching English as an additional language is also minimal, although there is now an agreed curriculum for teaching English to adults. The Parekh Report (Parekh 2000) recommended an extended programme of certificated training for specialist language teachers, but no funding has been forthcoming.

Although frequent attempts have been made to increase the numbers of ethnic minority teachers in schools (around 2 per cent of all teachers) there is little to attract minorities into teaching, and no government policies beyond exhortation to university departments and colleges to attract students.

Religious schools

Religion has recently assumed much more political significance in a global context and in the debate on the future of 'faith schools' in Britain. The 1944 Education Act was regarded as a compromise which allowed Anglican, Roman Catholic and a few Jewish schools to operate as 'voluntary aided' state schools and by the 1990s some 23 per cent of pupils were attending such schools. Although some of the schools accepted all faiths, a majority of the Anglican and Catholic schools required pupils to be 'Christian'. Middle class parents began to seek out the schools as a way of avoiding ethnic minorities, the academic performance of the schools is usually good and more parents have sought to 'choose' the schools. Prime Minister Blair has been an enthusiastic supporter of faith schools, supporting a review carried out by the Archbishops' Council which recommended an increase in Church of England secondary schools. A 2001 white paper noted that the government had 'increased the range of faith schools in the maintained sector, including the first Muslim, Sikh and Greek Orthodox schools' and that 'We want faith schools that come into the maintained sector to add to the inclusiveness and diversity of the school system' (Department for Education and Skills 2001). Critics have argued that faith schools, rather than promoting inclusiveness, are divisive, and the government has also faced unforeseen problems in its promotion of religious diversity. A technology college in Gateshead, in the north-east of England, partly sponsored by a millionaire businessman, was found to be teaching creationism,[8] in accordance with his beliefs, rather than Darwinian evolutionary theory!

Conclusion

This chapter has briefly overviewed some of the educational challenges and changes which face Britain in the early twenty-first century as migration patterns have changed and settled minorities have adapted differentially to the society in educational and economic terms. Although government is committed to raising the educational achievements of all minorities, market reforms ensure that there are winners and losers in the education market. Markets may be able to enhance the life chances of middle class minorities and those with higher incomes, leading to a situation described by William Wilson in the USA whereby 'talented and educated blacks, like talented and educated whites enjoy the privileges and advantages of their class situation' while other groups remain in disadvantaged positions (Wilson 1979). In addition, success on the part of minority groups can actually increase racism and xenophobia, particularly from 'poor Whites' or downwardly mobile groups who regard minorities as illegitimate competition for the collective goods promised by the state (Wimmer 1997).

There are distinct problems posed for minorities by the education market which cannot be dealt with by short term palliative policies such as singling out the 'gifted and talented'. There is little attention paid to the issue of Black pupil exclusions from schools or improved teacher preparation, and the most pressing issue of all – that of curriculum change to really prepare all young people for a multicultural society – has provoked little debate. The Commission on the Future of Multi-ethnic Britain found itself under severe attack for suggesting that:

> The unstated assumption remains that Britishness and whiteness go together like roast beef and Yorkshire pudding. There has been no collective working through of the imperial experience. The absence from the national curriculum of a rewritten history of Britain as an imperial force, involving dominance in Ireland as well as in Africa, the Caribbean and Asia, is proving from this perspective to be an unmitigated disaster.
>
> (Parekh 2000: 25)

To this can be added the public and seeming governmental ignorance about debates on race in Britain from the 1950s which result in the similar policy recommendations that have emerged on each occasion of public crisis in the race area (Ben-Tovim 2002). Like many other countries, Britain in the early twenty-first century is an uneasy and anxious country as far as issues of race, migration, religion – particularly Islam – and multiculturalism are concerned. Education in this climate faces unprecedented challenges.

Notes

1 Britain, or the United Kingdom comprises England, Wales, Scotland and Northern Ireland. Much of the educational data in this chapter refers only to education in England and Wales.
2 In Chapter XX of her (1993) memoirs Mrs Thatcher records that she 'could barely believe' the contents of one teacher training course which required students to consider gender and race issues.
3 Some important policies included Sure Start, a programme to help disadvantaged families with children aged 0–3 years, Education Action Zones to improve teaching in inner city areas, a New Deal to help unemployed young people 18–24, a Social Exclusion Unit set up in the Cabinet Office to study disadvantaged groups, Early Years and Childcare Partnerships and others (see Tomlinson 2001).
4 The 1993 Education Act allowed for the setting up of Pupil Referral Units for disruptive pupils excluded from school and others not in school. These units rapidly became a means for ridding schools of undesirable pupils, with an over-representation of Black pupils.
5 These improvements still leave almost half the school population at 16 without the qualifications to enter higher education or professional training.
6 The Ethnic Minority Achievement Grant – EMAG or EMTAG as it became known when travellers' children were included – replaced the Section 11 Grant given under the 1966 local government Act to local authorities with high numbers of minority pupils.
7 A recent study which highlighted teachers low expectations of Caribbean children was carried out by Shotte (2002). This study of children relocated from the island of Montserrat after a volcanic eruption found that the children – doing well in education on the island – rapidly lost interest and motivation in their London schools. The teachers stereotyped them as 'Oh, Caribbean', criticized their English and had low expectations of their performance.
8 Eric Vardy, a businessman in the motor trade, influenced the school towards the teaching that the world was literally 'created' in seven days rather than the study of Darwinian evolutionary theory.

References

Abbas, T. (2002) 'The home and the school in the educational achievements of south Asians', *Race, Ethnicity and Education* 5, 3: 292–316.
Aurora, R. and Duncan, C. (1996) *Multicultural Education, Towards Good Practice*, London: Routledge.
Ball, S., Bowe, R. and Gerwirtz, S. (1996) 'School choice, social class and distinction; the realisation of social advantage in education', *Journal of Educational Policy* 11, 1: 89–112.
Ben-Tovim, G. (2002) 'Community cohesion and racial exclusion, a critical review of the Cantle report', *Renewal* 10, 2: 43–48.
Blair, M. (2001) *Why Pick on Me: School Exclusion and Black Youth*, Stoke-on-Trent: Trentham Books.

Brown, C. (1984) *Black and White Britain*, London: Policy Studies Institute.

Cantle, T. (2001) *Building Community Cohesion*, London: Home Office.

Castles, S. (2003) 'Migration, citizenship and education', in J. A. Banks (ed.) *Diversity and Citizenship Education*, New York: Jossey-Bass.

Cox, C. B. (1995) *The Battle for the English Curriculum*, London: Hodder and Stoughton.

Craft, M. (1996) *Teacher Education in Plural Societies*, London: Falmer Press.

Crick, B. (1998) *Education for Citizenship and the Teaching of Democracy in Schools: Report by the Advisory Group on Citizenship*, London: Qualifications and Curriculum Authority.

Dearing, R. (1993) *The National Curriculum and its Assessment*, London: Schools Curriculum and Assessment Authority.

Demack, S., Drew, D. and Grimsley, M. (2000) 'Minding the gap: Ethnic, gender and social class differences in attainment at 16 – 1988–95', *Race, Ethnicity and Education* 3, 2: 117–143.

Department for Education and Employment (DfEE) (1997) *Excellence in Schools*, London: The Stationery Office.

Department for Education and Science (DES) (1985) *Education for All*, The Swann Report, London: HMSO.

Department for Education and Skills (DfES) (2001) *Schools: Achieving Success*, London: The Stationery Office.

Figueroa, P. (2003) 'Diversity and citizenship education in England', in J. A. Banks (ed.) *Diversity and Citizenship Education: Global Perspectives*, New York: Jossey-Bass.

Gerwirtz, S., Ball, S. J. and Bowe, R. (1995) *Markets, Choice and Equity in Education*, Buckingham: Open University Press.

Gillborn, D. (1995) 'Racism and exclusion from school', *Paper to European Conference on Educational Research*, Bath: University of Bath.

Gillborn, D. and Gipps, C. (1996) *Recent Research on the Achievement of Ethnic Minority Pupils*, London: The Stationery Office.

Gillborn, D. and Mirza, H. (2000) *Educational Inequalities: Mapping Race, Class and Gender*, London: OFSTED.

Gillborn, D. and Youdell, D. (1999) *Rationing Education*, London: Routledge.

Graham, D. (1993) *A Lesson For Us All: The Making of the National Curriculum*, London: Routledge.

Harris, P. and Bright, M. (2001) 'Bitter harvest from decades of division', *Observer* 15/7/01.

Honeyford, R. (1990) 'The national curriculum and its official distortion', *The Salisbury Review* 18, 4: 6–9.

MacPherson, Sir W. (1999) *The Stephen Lawrence Enquiry*, Cmd 4262 London: The Stationery Office.

Modood, T., Berthoud, R., Lakey, J., Nazroo, J., Smith, P., Virdee, S. and Beishon, S. (1997) *Ethnic Minorities in Britain: Diversity and Disadvantage*, London: Policy Studies Institute.

National Curriculum Council (1990) *Curriculum Guidance Eight; Education for Citizenship*, York: NCC.

Noden, P., West, A., David, M. and Edge, A. (1998) 'Choices and destinations in transfer to secondary schools in London', *Journal of Education Policy* 13: 221–236.

OECD (1994) *Schools: A Matter of Choice*, Paris: Centre for Educational Research and Innovation OECD.

Office for National Statistics (2003) *The National Census 2001*, London: ONS.

Ouseley, H. (2001) *Community Pride Not Prejudice: Making Diversity Work in Bradford*, Bradford: Bradford City Council.

Parekh, B. (2000) *The Future of Multiethnic Britain*, London: Profile Books.

Phillips, R. (1998) *History Teaching, Nationhood and the State*, London: Cassell.

Qualifications and Curriculum Authority (1999) *Review of the National Curriculum in England*, London: QCA.

Rex, J. and Tomlinson, S. (1979) *Colonial Immigrants in a British City*, London: Routledge.

Rutter, J. (2001) *Supporting Refugee Children in 21st Century Britain*, Stoke-on-Trent: Trentham Books.

Shaw, M. (2003) 'Don't set divisive Black targets', *Times Educational Supplement* 16/5/03.

Shotte, G. (2002) 'Education, migration and identities: Relocated Montserratian students in London schools', Ph.D. Study Institute of Education, University of London, London

Skellington, R. and Morris, R. (1996) *Race in Britain Today*, London: Sage.

Sklair, L. (2001) *The Transnational Capitalist Class*, Oxford: Blackwell.

Smith, D. J. and Tomlinson, S. (1989) *The School Effect: A Study of Multiracial Comprehensives*, London: Policy Studies Institute.

Thatcher, M. (1993) *The Downing Street Years*, London: HarperCollins.

Tomlinson, S. (1982) *A Sociology of Special Education*, London: Routledge.

—— (1990) *Multicultural Education in White Schools*, London: Batsford.

—— (1993) 'The multicultural task group: the group that never was', in A. King and M. Reiss (eds) *The Multicultural Dimension of the National Curriculum*, London: Falmer.

—— (1997) 'Sociological perspectives on failing schools', *International Studies in Sociology of Education* 7, 1: 81–98.

—— (1998) 'A tale of one school in one city: The case of Hackney Downs', in R. Slee, G. Weiner and S. Tomlinson (eds) *School Effectiveness for Whom?*, London: Falmer.

—— (2001) *Education in a Post-Welfare Society*, Buckingham: Open University Press.

TTA (2000) *Raising the Attainment of Minority Ethnic Pupils*, Guidance and resource materials for initial teacher trainers, London: Teacher Training Agency.

Wimmer, A. (1997) 'Explaining racism and xenophobia: a critical review of current research approaches', *Racial and Ethnic Studies* 20, 1: 17–42.

Wilson, W. J. (1979) *The Declining Significence of Race*, Chicago: University of Chicago Press.

Young, H. (2001) 'A corrosive national danger in our multicultural model', *Guardian* 6/11/02.

6   Discovering the ethnicized school

The case of France

Françoise Lorcerie

In France, the schooling policy of the migrants' children was drawn up in the early 1970s, due to the major changes in the influx context; the labour force flows during the years of economic expansion had transformed into a flow of families mainly of Algerian, Moroccan and Turkish origins. This policy, then called 'The Schooling of Migrant Children', aimed at integrating these children into French schools while maintaining their 'cultures of origin'. However, since the early 1980s, it was deemed necessary that this policy have new targets. Jacques Berque, a professor in the prestigious Collège de France, was commissioned by the minister of National Education in 1985 to report on this matter. He argued the need of a new political project for school and society, one which would be able to 'solidarize the presences', according to his words, and which would recognize the new 'Islamic–Mediterranean dimension of France' (Berque 1985).[1]

This revision pushed the government to take on the major sociological fact of this period, which was that immigrants were fast turning into ethnic minorities, and were permanently settled but were also exposed to a number of disadvantages in daily life, a situation in which Berque saw the potential risks in the light of the colonial experience.[2] He pushed the government to conduct a 'global pedagogy' of national identity, and he insisted on constructing new links of solidarity without denying cultural diversity, which implied putting aside the usual ideology of assimilation (Lorcerie 1998).

These perspectives were delayed by years of media controversies and political tergiversation (Feldblum 1999; Laborde 2001; Favell 1998). It wasn't until the end of 1998 that two important governmental initiatives were taken. First, the recognition of ethnic discriminations in the autumn of 1998 (this recognition was stimulated by the European programme against ethnic discrimination[3]), and second the taking into account of Islam by the public administration, along with the other denominations, such as the process of the setting up of a French council for Muslim cult, initiated under the aegis of the Ministry of Internal Affairs, in the summer of 1999, and achieved in 2003. Nevertheless, the school was not included in any of these changes.

School central administration wait-and-see policy gave rise to large scale disorders, whose ethnic nature became evident to the researchers during the 1990s. As various theoretical papers testified, this led to a shifting of the paradigm of analysing school issues (Aubert *et al.* 1997; Barrère and Martuccelli 1997; Lorcerie 1999; Perroton 2000b; Lorcerie and Philipp 2003; Lorcerie 2003). Since then, ethnicity and ethnicization processes have been recognized by educational scientists as key concepts for the range of issues under consideration. Due to this change of paradigm, a sensitive gap has emerged between scientific findings and official speeches and decisions. This has contributed to making the question of schooling young people of non-European descent a combined educational and political challenge.

This chapter will focus on the discovery of the modes of ethnicization of national school settings by French educational scientists. This approach, which is still developing, benefits from a new feeling of permission among scientists due to the recognition of ethnic discriminations within French space (Simon 1999), it is thought that new empirical data will soon be available. Taking into account the actual data as well as what is missing, we shall review successively the following questions: how does the ethnic status affect student roles, and how does scholastic experience influence the ethnic status of students; how does ethnicity affect the roles of students' parents; and how does ethnicity influence the roles of school agents; finally, to what extent does ethnonationalism take place at school.

First, we will take an overall look at the framework.

The ethnicized school: a complex research programme

The social theories of ethnicity aim, on the one hand, at explaining ethnic individual investments in connection with the social processes, and on the other hand, at delineating the social effects of these investments. One tries to understand what is the impact of social and political activity on ethnic attributions and claims and on ethnic saliency, and what effect ethnic categorization has on social interaction and on social relations, inasmuch as one may distinguish causes from effects, with everything being interconnected. Besides, the ethnicizing process – that is to say ethnic categorizing in the social trade – is essentially asymmetrical. It is rooted in the processes of social domination and ranking. In a national society, the state appears to be a powerful agent of ethnic processes. The status of the outsider, which is assigned to those named *immigrés*,[4] whatever their nationalities and birth places (they may have been born in France), is mainly defined through state history and current political action (Weber 1968; Elias and Scotson 1964; Lorcerie 2003, spec. 1st part).

Applied to the educational system, this approach defines a systemic programme of investigation. In the educational field as well as outside, when ethnicization processes spread out, they affect by hypothesis not only the experience of the minority children (to various extents), but also that of their majority peers and educators, who are actors in the same social interactions. The major questions of such a programme may be classed under three headings, each covering a number of different questions (see also Thomas 1994). One can ask whether and how:

1   The ethnic status of the individuals (students, parents, school agents) affects their social behaviour at school and the way they are treated.

> Ethnic status > roles of student, parent, educator.

2   School settings and practices influence the claiming of ethnicity or the attribution of ethnic status, and the salience of ethnicity.

> School practices > individuals' ethnic status or salience of ethnicity.

3   Educational structures, forms and contents (curricula, lessons, didactic aids) reflect ethnic domination and ethnonationalism or resist them, providing a critical understanding.

> Ethnonationalism and ethnic domination > educational structures, curricula and activities.

Here again, the distinction of these headings is artificial, they have to be mentally reinserted into a global systemic causal system. The diagram following gives a broad outline of how these questions fall into the systemic functioning.

The educational system is considered as a social organization. It is part of the national institutional system and is placed within the global social environment (figured as 1a in Figure 6.1), as well as within a local environment (1b) – both levels being interrelated in the constitution of society. The study of ethnicity at school leads us to consider how ethnic statuses and relationships which prevail in the social and political environment are manifested in the educational space. Moreover, the school produces social effects. Therefore, school may also be considered as a channel through which ethnic categorization is being modulated, whether intensified or reduced, if not produced, via the activities which are achieved within (arrow back towards (1)).

In the interactions that take place within the framework of each school, whether during or outside teaching activities (3), knowledge is generated and identities are invested by the students and the professionals (4). This may provide opportunities for processes of ethnic ascription and self-identification for the various actors. This may also foster a reflexivity upon ethnic processes (5). However, the higher administrative level should not be neglected if one wants to take into account the effects of school on the production of ethnicity and the way it is managed. Educational structures

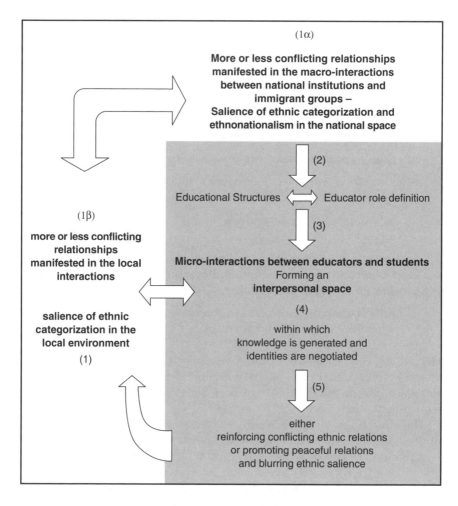

Figure 6.1 An analytical framework to study modes and stakes of ethnicity in educational systems.

Note
This diagram is inspired by and adapted from Cummins (1997: 424).

more or less prevent ethnic tensions within school space (2a). And professional norms, which are included in the training received by the agents and in the programmes taught, more or less help the professionals to be aware of the ethnic biases and problems, and to conduct learning activities in this domain (2b).

What information does French social science give us today?

Strange students[5]

What is the effect of the students' ethnic status upon their investment of student roles, and how do the scholastic settings and practices impinge on the ethnic self-identifications or on the ethnic salience among the students? New French studies on the ethnicized school have just begun to discover a major aspect of these questions, namely the ethnic salience in the social and scholastic experience of *majority* students. As for *minority* students, the findings of previous studies on the schooling of children of immigrants are being reconsidered in the light of the comprehensive theoretical framework of ethnicity, which leads to an overall reappraisal of the data.

'French' students and ethnicity

Almost nothing is known on how majority students, that is to say the 'French' pupils, react to the experience of ethnicity. In particular, what is the impact of scholastic experience on the ethnic attributions they make and on their own ethnic identification? The French studies dealing with the scholastic experience of students do not usually appeal to the paradigm of ethnicity; those which do are almost exclusively focused on the immigrants' children. A few observations nevertheless are available concerning 'French' pupils. Favre-Perroton brings to the fore the 'small White racism' of majority students assigned to a vocational school with many children of immigrants, which they perceive as degrading (Favre-Perroton 1999; Perroton 2000b). The large scale survey on violence and victimization in lower secondary schools (*collèges*) by Debarbieux and his team shows that certain school organizations incite a 'parting full of hatred' between pupils, fostering mutual ethnicization in addition to racist insults, while other modes of organization do not have this effect (Debarbieux *et al.* 1999: 71–93).

The effect of minority status on schooling is better documented.

Minority status students and ethnicity: the ethnic side of good behaviour

First of all it must be underlined that the ethnic side of scholastic behaviour or scholastic achievement cannot easily be shown empirically. If ethnicity may be an explanatory factor, it is always associated with other factors.

As regards students' behaviour, the theory of ethnicity does not allow for any simple prediction of what should prevail among minority students. In fact, conformity will probably prevail. In individual scholastic behaviour, minority ethnic status probably induces more often 'good behaviour' that insubordination or rebellion. But insubordination usually gets more public attention.

Goffman (1963) offered a useful framework when he distinguishes five strategies of 'stigma correction' in the interactions between a stigma bearer and the 'normal', suggesting that ethnic minority belonging is a tribal stigma. These strategies may be characterized with the help of two oppositions: on the one hand, the quest of similarity versus the quest of difference, and on the other hand, self-appreciation versus self-depreciation. These are:

1   assimilation, quest of conformity by stigma dissimulation or pretence (similarity + depreciation);
2   quest of excellence (similarity + appreciation);
3   buffooning, or submission to one's stereotyped role (differentiation + depreciation);
4   making use of one's handicap (differentiation + appreciation);
5   stigma reversal (differentiation + appreciation).

This systematic framework allows one to characterize the symbolic meaning of the main behavioural types displayed by minority students in their interactions with majority school agents in education. The most commented upon strategies are those which are forms of self-affirmation. A novel written for teenagers relates in a suggestive style how the writer, a young boy from a poor Algerian family, was going to become a social scientist. One morning he decided to sit in the front row of the classroom and to become the best pupil (type 2 strategy) (Begag 1986). The wearing of the veil by Muslim girls in school often shows the willingness to challenge the school staff by exhibiting one's religion in the name of human rights, which is supported by virtually all the other students (type 5 strategy) (Khosrokhavar 1997; Tietze 2002). It only signifies the submission to traditions and to the ethnic-religious group if the girls refer to their group of origin when defining their behaviour, which occurred in some cases for Moroccan or Turkish girls.[6]

But various studies on identity stating among young people of immigrant descent in scholastic settings show that non-differentiation is a prominent feature of these students' behaviour, which must be interpreted as a self-protection strategy (type 1 strategy). This is usual in situations where ethnic identity is a social stigma (Eidheim 1969), though concealed by media events, which favour critical episodes and ideological stakes around the 'right to be different'. Thus, in a simulation game, Cukrowicz asked his young interviewees to choose the place where they would like to live in a fictitious town whose map they had in front of them. Typically, the young Maghrebis choose to settle next to the 'French', while the reverse was not true (Cukrowicz and Duprez 1992). When young Algerian interviewees, previously students in a vocational school, relate their school memories, they talk about unfair treatments, and one would be tempted to interpret this as ethnic discrimination. However, they have explanations which don't refer to their ethnic status (Zirotti 1990), which comes under a type 1 logic. In a social psychology experiment, north African college students are asked to think about a project concerning the school curriculum which would take a better account of the variety of cultures. When the experimenter is a north African and the experimental place displays north African objects and signs, the individuals express a desire to include north African cultural items into the curricula much more frequently than when the experimenter and the experimental environment are 'French' (Vinsonneau 1996).

The ethnic side of school disorders

Earlier significant investigations led by Payet and Debarbieux in various lower secondary schools showed the virulence of ethnic-sounding conflicts in certain school communities (Payet 1992a, b, 1995; Debarbieux 1996; Debarbieux and Tichit 1997a, b). These conflicts, it is shown, turn into a mutual ascription of otherness between school agents and minority students, in a 'double process of ethnicization' that becomes a vicious circle (see p. 115, the section devoted to the relationship of teachers to ethnicity). As for the students, their bitterness is nurtured by a feeling of unfairness. Is this feeling a result of their scholastic experience, or has it been induced by their social experience outside the school? Couldn't it be fuelled by the ethnic humiliation they experience in their social environment?

Various studies establish that the children of North African immigrants tend to maintain a conflicting relation to school, notably at secondary school, without stating a clear causal connection. Thus, the National Education survey was carried out in 1995 by the National Institute for Economic Studies (INSEE) in order to know the opinions of secondary school students about their establishments. Globally, the students rejected the most negative images that were suggested, except for three groups who expressed harsh criticism: the students assigned to remedial sections, those who felt themselves to be on a lower level than their class, and those of North African origin (Héran 1996: 107–124). For all of these groups, an explanation in terms of 'relative deprivation' and resistance to scholastic categorization, such as 'bad' pupil, 'useless', naturally makes sense. For the North Africans, on the basis of an exacerbated sense of unfairness, the theory of intergroup conflict in an ethnic minority position leads one to expect this resistance (Guimond and Tougas 1994). But what impact does their scholastic experience itself have on their dispositions to criticism? In another survey carried out in some *collèges*, Payet and Sicot (1997) noticed that the foreign students expressed a sense of unfairness more often than the average student, that they had a worse global perception of their school, and that in their case there was a strong discrepancy between the punishments they said they received and the deviance they recognized.

Here again, the research didn't allow these peculiarities to be assigned to educational or extra-educational variables.

Zirotti (1997) tends to consider that the key factor is the collective dynamics induced by the social experience of stigmatization. North African pupils, he underlines, do not accept the scholastic ranking as evident, they suspect the teachers' judgements to be biased against them, they fight 'a sort of battle against educational categorization', which allows them to maintain a high level of expectation, whatever the school verdicts. They emphasize their protest claims at the decisive stages of their school careers. The resources for this battle no doubt arise from the family circles, but above all from the social group they make, on the basis of the 'collective experience of stigmatization and relegation in socially debased areas as well as in debased schools and classes'. Payet and Debarbieux, who have conducted various researches within the schools, tend rather to put forward the educational conditions in which minority pupils (and others around) achieve ethnicized modes of deviance, which they call 'an oppositional ethnicity'. They particularly bring into question the relationship between teachers and students, the scholastic climate and the pedagogical structure of the establishments (mainly the social inequality between the classes, due to a concentration of boys of north African origin in classes known as 'bad', see below p. 116). 'The position in the school structure contributes to making a claim of ethnic difference on the part of the actors' (Payet 1992b, 1997; also Debarbieux 1996; Debarbieux and Tichit 1997b).

The ethnic part of scholastic achievement

What is the effect of minority ethnic status upon scholastic achievement?

During the 1970s and early 1980s, this was the typical topic of the research conducted on the schooling of children of immigrants. It was largely assumed that the children of immigrants were underachieving. This question is not so popular now, others have superseded it in the media, such as scholastic violence supposedly due to children of immigrants or alleged Islamic threats in the educational space. However, the question of scholastic achievement has recently raised a new argument among the educational scientists in France, which has led to a step forward in the discovery of the ethnicized school.

Actually, the social theory of ethnicity is not able to answer this question simply. On the one hand, it states that the ethnic dichotomies are rooted in the global domination structure of society and connected with social ranking. On the other hand, it includes a probabilist theory of individuals' social action in connection with stigmatization: minority actors may adopt appreciation or depreciation behaviours, and they may also submit or resist dominant power relations; and the majority actors with whom they interact may also adopt different behaviours.

Concerning the scholastic achievement of minority students, the structural approach will provide an analysis in terms of cultural distance (Wac-quant 1987), it expects lesser achievement, at best similar results to those of children of similar socio-economic backgrounds. The interactionist approach of ethnicity, however, speculates on the social dynamics: it con-siders that scholastic achievement comes first from the individuals' com-bined actions and reactions, in the midst of the daily interactions through which school trajectories are built. It is in these interactions that ethnic status may play a part. An underachieving effect is not a priori excluded, nor is one of major success. Much depends on the actual and long term circumstances of the educational process.

Before the 1990s, rich data was unavailable in France for discussion. Up to that time, French statistics didn't provide any indicator of the immi-grant origin other than nationality, which excluded a significant part of the population under study, perhaps those who had best integrated.[7] In 1991, at the entreaties of the High Council for Integration, which had just been set up, ministerial statisticians accepted to exploit the data related to foreign birth in the studies pertaining to the integration of the children of immigrants. Thence, the Ministry of National Education used the data from a large sample, the panel of students who had begun secondary school in 1989 (Vallet and Caille 1996). Before that time, a single study conducted by Zirotti (1979) in one area had attempted to use statistics to highlight the ethnic building of scholastic careers.

Vallet and Caille's findings, far from closing the file, opened it larger than ever. They discovered a statistically strong advantage in favour of the immigrants' children on entering upper secondary schools (*lycées*), com-pared to other students of similar social status; an advantage which is not connected to the students' level of achievement nor to the teachers' benevolence towards them, but to the ambition of the wishes made by the families. Zirotti, on the contrary, had shown in 1979 a discriminatory bias against the Algerian students in the assessment of their capabilities at the end of the second year of *collège* – this being in accordance with what a number of school observers felt intuitively. The two researches arrived therefore at opposite conclusions. To explain this discrepancy, at least four hypotheses come to mind:

1   The findings are opposite because data collected from a school catch-ment's area cannot be compared with those taken from a national sample. There are important inter-school disparities in assessment practices, which national averages do not reflect.
2   The findings are opposite because the data gathered on a given origin (for instance the Algerians) cannot be generalized. There are import-ant achievement disparities according to the origins and migratory profiles. In the USA, these disparities nurture the argument on the ecological and cultural factors of scholastic achievement and minority assimilation processes.

3   The findings are opposite because both surveys are separated by some 20 years. In the meantime, the French school system has changed a lot, the second form assessment has been suppressed and a dialogue has been implemented between school staff and families at the end of the *collège*, concerning which paths to follow.

4   The findings are opposite because, in 20 years, the attitude of resistance to dominant social categorization and the refusal of ascription to an outsider status has increased among the students and families of immigrant origins. This last assumption arises from the actionist component of the ethnicity paradigm.

Hypothesis 1 points to the relative lack of data. In one case, the sample is too narrow to represent the range of possibilities, in the other it is broad but crushes the inter-school variation. Besides, the criterion taken by Vallet and Caille (1996) as an indicator of lower secondary scholastic achievements may be brought into question, i.e. gaining admission to upper secondary school (*lycée général*) at the end of *collège*'s fourth year. It doesn't measure directly the students' performance but the school's assessment policies, which tend to be 'lax in the establishments that are adrift' (Barthon 1998a). The ministry's survey also dodges the intra-establishment variation, whereas class building does not simply reflect differences of performance, but contributes to this variation (Payet 1997; Van Zanten 2001). Nevertheless, Vallet and Caille's (1996) overall finding is not surprising. Former French quantitative studies on immigrant children's scholastic achievements had already concluded for some time that scholastic performances were similar between students of foreign origin and nationals of similar social backgrounds (Boulot and Fradet 1988). Cases of better achievement are also known abroad.

Hypothesis 2, in addition to the preceding one, reflects the achievement variation according to the students' origins. Aren't the Algerians overselected? Isn't the stereotype of the immigrant who cannot be assimilated, nurtured by the colonial memories, reflected in the educational process? Indeed, Vallet and Caille (1996) find significant variations on the national scale depending on the origin. But the north Africans are among those who display a 'significant advantage', along with the students from south-east Asia and the Turks, while the Negro-African students and those from southern Europe do not differ significantly from the 'French', all other things being equal. Therefore, the discrepancies between the findings of the two surveys are not explained by collective or interactive characteristics which could be specifically detrimental to the Algerians in France: neither a communal culture typically distant from that of school, nor a 'quasi-caste' psycho-social schema would trap them into a self-defeating and oppositional vision of school, following the example of the young African-Americans Ogbu has observed in the USA (Ogbu 1978).

Hypotheses 3 and 4 respectively concern the evolution of the educational system and of the overall attitude of immigrant families in the face of the school. In 3, the educational system has turned out to be structurally less unequal and less unfair to the disadvantaged: such an assumption seems to have been confirmed over the past 20 years (Meuret 1999). This change is due partly to modifications in the structure of scholastic careers in *collèges* (suppression of the second form stage of orientation) and to the change in the orientation procedures at the end of the *collège* (dialogue with the families). Immigrant families have seized these new opportunities, in particular north African families who sometimes appear to force a decision from the school (Beaud and Pialoux 1999). Hypothesis 4 takes over from 3.

Hypothesis 4 states that immigrant students and families, bent towards social mobility, are effective actors within the educational system, able to mobilize more intensely than others in defence of what they perceive to be in their interest, despite being against the teachers' judgement. This behaviour doesn't fit the stereotype that these families are unable to bring up their children, but there is evidence shown by empirical data. Qualitative studies show that scholastic success may arise from logic such as that of individual or collective ambitions: for young north African boys and girls (Hassini 1997; Beaud 2002), for Algerian families launched on trajectories of upward mobility (Zeroulou 1988; Santelli 2001), not to mention other various success stories. Zirotti underlines the 'perseverance' of north African students in resisting the categorization made by school agents when they could 'compromise the social trajectory they have decided for themselves'. Education, he points out, is for these young a decisive stake, which is included in the family project of improvement (Akers-Porrini and Zirotti 1992). Besides, the families spend sizeable sums on this (Gissot *et al.* 1994).

Finally, 3 and 4 complement one another. They allow the relative advantage Vallet and Caille (1996) bring out in favour of the children of immigrants to be interpreted by implementing the paradigm of ethnicity. What explains this result is not a specific school-oriented ethos of the immigrant families (Zirotti 1997), but their propensity to mobilize for educational stakes, coupled with an ability to resist the verdicts of school agents. Immigrant families, in particular north Africans, use all eventual possibilities within their reach to improve their social status, and the new structure of orientation at the end of the lower secondary schools provides them with new opportunities. This type of family mobilization due to the educational stakes, however, goes back a long way (Léger and Tripier 1986: 122).

The effect of scholastic careers upon ethnic identities

Ethnic identities are entangled with other dimensions of the social identities of students (Lepoutre 1997; Alamartine 2003). Although there has been no systematic research on the question itself, the link has been suggested between the quality of scholastic experience, expressed by the level of achievement, and the identity options. For instance, minority boys who exhibit withdrawal practices into 'micro-societies of survival' are, or were, failed students (Bordet 1998).

Scholastic success fosters one's step to naturalization and identification as a French citizen, while failure is connected with opposite tendencies (Ribert 1998). Besides, it would seem that scholastic success or failure modulate the investment of Islam. The young practicing Muslims who succeed at school show concern for an identity separation from the 'French' and reject 'assimilation', whereas those who experience scholastic failure claim at first their dignity (Khosrokhavar 1997; Bouzar 2001).

The parents: choice of school and ethnicity

The discussion on the achievement levels at school (as above) leads one to consider that ethnic identity may be a resource for collective mobilization aiming at scholastic success in *minority* status groups. Certain researches have given sharp qualitative evidence of this kind of mobilization (Mazzella 1997; Lahire 1995).

As for *majority* status parents, what part does ethnic categorization play in their behaviour as parents of students? A matter which is being well-documented relates to the part ethnic categorization plays in the decision of not registering one's child in one's sector establishment. The studies on this question appeal to mixed methods combining statistical indicators of the choices of schooling and qualitative observations or interviews (Léger and Tripier 1986; Barthon 1998; Broccolichi and Van Zanten 1997). They find that those who free themselves from the sector constraints are more often upper or middle class families, notably teachers. Their choices are contextual preferences (a given establishment is chosen in an area of current daily mobility, which is connected to the family possibilities and to available information, whose range and quality are also socially different). Private schools accepted by the state are integrated into the range of choices. Choice criteria combine social, personal (relating to the child's advantage) and institutional domains (estimated quality of teaching, avoiding public sector dysfunctions). The ethnic criterion, rarely put forward as a motive of preference, is more often used as a motive of defiance towards a school. While the running of a school is relatively unclear, information on the ethnic composition of a school's body of students is relatively easy to attain due to people's visibility. With the help of social categorization, the ethnic criterion can finally summarize dangerous educational environments, as can be seen by families who avoid certain schools.[8] Thus the parents of majority students who use avoidance practices increase the tendency to social-ethnic polarization of the educational field.

School agents and ethnicity

Nothing has been written yet on the impact of *minority* status school agents on their roles in education. Indeed, there are still a very few of them.

The effect of the *majority* status on the professional behaviour of school agents in front of ethnically mixed students is better documented due to the recent contribution of French educational scientists in understanding the challenges of the ethnicized school. It is a morally delicate question: in the French social-institutional configuration, ethnicity is connected to professional difficulties and feelings of guilt much more than to wise management (but see Rinaudo 1998, 1999; Alamartine 2003, for outlines of intentional management of ethnicity). Some former precursory researches had documented the effect of teachers' ethnic categorizing on their judgements of the students. More recent studies show that ethnic categorization has an influence on teachers' relations to immigrant parents, accounting for a marked distance towards them. It also influences the decisions taken on the pedagogical structures of establishments. Finally it brings into play forms of ethic ambivalence and confusion in the face of such 'problems'. But much still remains to be investigated.

Teacher judgement and ethnic categorization

This line of research was taken up at the end of the 1970s by two daring studies: Zirotti's study, already mentioned, concerned the social-ethnic biases of different paths imposed on the students at the end of the second form of secondary schools (Zirotti 1979). The second was a study by Zimmermann on the variables of the teachers' feeling of attraction towards their pupils in nursery and primary schools (Zimmermann 1978). Zimmermann carried out his research in three nursery schools and two primary schools, all voluntary, with hierarchical support. He recorded the global opinions of the teachers on each pupil, as to whether they found them 'repugnant', 'rather unpleasant', 'indifferent', 'rather pleasant' or 'attractive, nice'. The schools were located in socially mixed areas. The findings confirmed the assumption that teachers spontaneously tend to integrate social categorization into their professional judgement. They exhibit strong prejudice against the children of immigrants, and a marked affective complicity with the children from upper social categories, with a tendency of reinforcing these tendencies from nursery school to primary school. More generally, it may be assumed that such cognitive biases operate in all their professional decisions, choices and actions.[9]

From class hierarchy to indirect discrimination: lower secondary school 'bad classes'

This context throws light on the professional choices which underlie the grading of classes in *collège* (Payet 1995; Debarbieux 1996; Debarbieux and Tichit 1997a, b; Barthon 1998; Debarbieux *et al.* 1999; Van Zanten 2001).[10]

Attention has been drawn to this question by Payet's detailed study (1995) on the pedagogical structure of two *collèges* in a suburb near the city of Lyon. This research showed that the school heads divide up the pupils into the various sections of the third form taking into account at the same time gender, scholastic levels and ethnic origins. Sometimes putting aside the wishes expressed by families, they favour a differentiating policy between two sub-groups: that of 'French' girls and north African boys. The former were assigned to the most valued section, the latter to less valued sections, whereas 'French' boys and north African girls were mixed in intermediary status classes. In that way, the school heads conformed to dominant gender and social-ethnic categorization, modulated by the scholastic profiles of students. They acted in order to minimize the risks of family and teacher discontent, wishing at the same time to contain scholastic disorders.

To what extent does the school staff appeal to ethnic criteria in dividing up the students into the classes and sections? This question was taken up by Barthon in her Ph.D. dissertation (1998), where she examined in detail the composition of first form classes in four different lower secondary schools located in a Parisian suburb. She built an index of dissimilarity between different sub-groups of students taking into consideration their level of achievement at the beginning of the year (good or bad), gender, socio-economic origins (low or high), and ethnic origins (children of immigrants or 'French').[11] She also examined the variation of this index between the four schools and every section of each school. She found that no 'Manichaean conclusion' could be stated about the way social and ethnic categorization was included in the pedagogical structure of the schools: it played a smaller part than that of scholastic achievement, and the combinations varied from one school to the other. It was suggested that the hypothesis of a regular separation of 'French' girls from north African boys should be rejected.

Nonetheless, every *collège* has 'good' and 'bad' classes at each level. Consequently, when the establishments receive socially and ethnically mixed student populations, those of immigrant origins tend to find themselves, along with 'backward' students, in 'bad' classes due to lower scholastic levels.[12] At the end of the lower secondary school, the students who are in 'bad' classes appear to be aware of the class hierarchy and of their inferior position. Research carried out in two *collèges* in a Parisian suburb found them prone to discouragement, pessimistic about their scholastic future, easily cynical and sometimes charging the teachers with racism (Van Zanten 2001).

Internal tension becomes extreme when the school transposes the social-ethnic divisions from an environment where the ethnic saliency is high and expresses conflicting social relationships into the educational space. An example was found in a small city *collège*, where 30 per cent were the children of executives and intermediary categories and 30 per cent north African children. The pedagogical structure put into effect scholastic and ethnic-social divisions in all the classes (Debarbieux *et al.* 1999: 90ff.). Contrary to what happened in popular primary schools in the surrounding areas, racism was virulent in the *collège* and the scholastic climate was highly debased. Certain classes were constantly punished and appeared to be entirely left out from an educational point of view.

Can we then speak of a tendency towards ethnic segregation throughout the pedagogical structure of schools? In this last case, we certainly can.

In the scholastic field, the concept of segregation points to a configuration which divides the body of students in such a way that certain categories of pupils are pushed aside and assigned to sections where they will receive an inferior scholastic education. The concept of 'discrimination' completes that of segregation. It emphasizes the fact that segregation processes arise from human action. As 'segregation', it is a normative concept. But it directly characterizes the kind of social action which generates unfair treatment towards certain individuals, compared to other individuals. Discrimination is said to be 'indirect' when an institutional provision, criterion or practice is *likely* to put certain individuals at a disadvantage when compared to others, irrespective of the intention of the social actors who maintain this provision, criterion or practice (see the European directive 2000/43, Chapter 1, art. 2). Thus, the concept of indirect ethnic discrimination qualifies the professional judgement implied in choosing and maintaining ethnically unfavourable pedagogical solutions: has the risk of minority students being penalized by this pedagogical solution been assessed at all, or not recognized or simply denied?

This concept seems to encompass the majority of questions asked about the hierarchy of classes in French lower secondary schools as regards the social paradigm of ethnicity: the hierarchical ranking of classes in *collèges* is more or less general, it seems to be globally instrumental in its aims at controlling the variation of scholastic achievement levels in order to manage it. It doesn't intend to prejudice any group of students. Nevertheless, such an educational device may be qualified as ethnically discriminatory from the moment when these sections receive mainly ethnicized minority children *and* confine them or risk confining them to scholastic failure. As such, the segregative configuration Debarbieux and Tichit (1997a, b) describe is clearly discriminatory, as are, to a lesser degree, a number of configurations with 'bad classes'.

Ethnicized school boundaries: dangerous places and noxious parents

If one finding should be retained from the recent sociological studies, the most constant and undoubted is the ascription of difficulty and danger to the places people live in and to the parents, on the basis of otherness which arises from both social-economic inferiority and ethnic difference. A variety of studies have brought to the fore, from individual or group interviews and *in situ* observations, the suspicion and contempt the school agents often nurture towards minority parents and their places of living, as well as their usual ignorance of these places and families (Léger and Tripier 1986; Payet 1992a, b, 1998; Debarbieux 1996; Poiret 1996, 2000; Perroton 2000a). Those holding both institutional power and social *normality* erect a boundary and maintain it by material barriers, removal practices, non-reciprocal interacting and discrediting words.

The discrediting activity through behind the scenes gossiping is one of the practical modalities of this power relationship. Here is an inaugural lecture in French sociology, many a time attested subsequently.

> The whole environment of The Gresillons is perceived on a disastrous mode and as generating scholastic failure: family life, that one thinks of as restless, noisy, perturbed by dogs barking with the TV on from morning till night, marked by money worries and parental quarrels; flats described as cramped and overcrowded, differing from middle class housing norms, not allowing anyone, in particular children, to 'isolate themselves' in order to work; family life – again – supposed at the same time to be totally deprived of communication and exchange; ... life in large housing projects, taken to be 'crazy' and characterised by tensions between neighbours; environment and buildings, depicted as sinister, lacking playgrounds and greenery, inciting the young to 'hang about the streets in gangs'; the students' parents, often said to be overburdened, too soft, taking no care of their children's sleep or health, seeking to get rid of them as much as possible, 'giving up' on bringing up their children, taking no interest (or too little) in their children's schooling and moreover being unable to follow it effectively due to lack of time and competence; families themselves whose perception is dominated by social problems: insistence on acts of violence towards children or between parents, on crime, alcoholism, finally all forms of destroying the family cell.
>
> (Léger and Tripier 1986: 173–174)

Today, one could add to this inventory Islam and the 'fundamentalist threat'.

Not everything in this speech is false but it is marked by stereotyping. This lecture and the language used construct and systematize moral inferiority, even danger, which legitimizes people's physical removal from schools. Those teachers who don't share this type of lecture and language are exposed to being treated as 'honorary stigma bearers', risking discredit while doing their best to protect the stigmatized (Goffman 1963).

The ethnicization of the school limits wrong-foots the official themes of the 'educational community' and 'parental partnerships', brought out by the 1989 Orientation Law on Education. It justifies the school agents' monopoly on schooling. As for the students, they take advantage of their parents' isolation to get extra freedom which may harm their education (Payet 1998).

Ethical ambivalence and the vicious circles of 'self-fulfilling prophecy'

If, for a majority of teachers in the disadvantaged areas, ethnicity (in the sense of ascription of difference) is used as an 'explanatory category' of social and scholastic settings, the norm of 'republican' equality and anti-racism is still present in their speech (Perroton 2000b). It is the only register to be displayed in formal communication. It is as if a game of what must be hidden and what may be said about ethnicity constituted a civility law amongst these teachers (Payet 1992b). As regards public action, ethnicity is signified by negative words that are kinds of metonymies, urging people to 'fight against': 'difficult' (school, area, students), 'violence'. . . . Such a game of what is hidden and what is overt puts ethnicity symbolizing on the register of bitterness and guilty conscience. It favours racist speech spreading behind the scenes (Debarbieux *et al.* 1999).[13]

This collective mood nurtures vicious circles and acts as a self-fulfilling prophecy (Merton 1957). It is well known that this schema turns people's fears into reality. It works only in the absence of a deliberate institutional control, Merton (1957) states. In the French educational field, this schema applies to the making of segregated classes. Social prejudice leads one to envisage immigrant teenagers as high-risk students. To protect certain classes, these students are put into separate classes. Hence, the risk is activated, the climate of the whole establishment is debased and its reputation of being a high-risk establishment increases. The same effect may be seen in the relation of schools to the local environment. By denigrating the local environment and families, teachers not only protect themselves from any parental intrusion in the school but also increase their status. 'But such representations also have negative effects: justifying the flight of families and teachers themselves, confirming and emphasizing the negative image of the school, they finally create obstacles for the implementation of a successful education, which should use opposite logistics', and in this way they induce as a counter-effect the depreciation of the teachers themselves (Léger and Tripier 1986: 179).

The extreme differentiation maintained between the environment and the school is to connect with a structural feature of the French school: its low strategic regulation. The school project (which is an administrative obligation) seldom works as a strategic piloting device, contrary to what the administrative doctrine asserts. In his survey on school violence, Debarbieux (1996) builds a school climate index, on the basis of how the students feel about their school, their area of habitation and their teachers, how aggressive they find the relationship between teachers and students and how they find the style of learning in that school. It appears that this index has approximately the same variations as that of social pre-cariousness and the proportion of children of immigrants. What does this result mean if not that, in the French social-institutional configuration, scholastic factors globally lack consistency compared to social factors?

Nevertheless, some cases are described where the vicious circle of a self-fulfilling prophecy is broken thanks to intentional scholastic action, as Merton (1957) suggests. Thus, in a small industrial town in the east of France, the children of north African workers who lived on a social housing project nearby were assigned to two different upper secondary schools. One of these received them as intruders and gave them very little help with their education, whereas in the other school, various devices had been set up to support them, which they were proud of, and their marks were clearly better (Beaud 2002). Such a mode of training requires an active reference to democratic values from the school agents, which is not ordinary in French educational space (Van Zanten 2001) and it implies the exercising of a professional leadership, usually around the school head, according to a compromise which the internal power relations may well hinder (Lorcerie and Darbon 2001).[14]

School and ethnonationalism: from prescribed curriculum to hidden curriculum?

Where do the ethnic biases exhibited by school agents come from? As stated above, they are presumably connected to the ethnic representations prevailing in French national space. More specifically, it may be assumed they are coupled with French ethnonationalism.

Let's call 'ethnonationalism' the ethnic orientation of nationalism or national feelings. Ethnonationalism is always concerned with both coexistence and tension with:

1 the civic contractualist orientation of democratic nationalism or national feeling. Besides, due to diverse ethnic belongings in the national space (this difference arises from social beliefs relative to the origins), ethnonationalism is also in a relation of coexistence and tension with;

2 minority ethnic identities implemented in social relations. From a sociological point of view, these relations are considered as dynamics

which mobilize actors – notably social and political establishments and state administration – and which shift into social struggles.

(Lorcerie 2003)

The French state school has traditionally been a vector of ethnonationalism. The 'patriot' type of ethnonationalism became prominent soon after the Third Republic was set up, following the 1870 defeat against Prussia. A number of historical studies show how historians and textbooks of the time devoted themselves to uniting the French and have them adhere to the new institutions, by erecting a national myth conveying a new pride in reference to the great Revolution and, in the long term, to the Gallic people.[15] Citron analyses the logic of this ethnicizing and, above all, statist historiography: 'The history invented for the school is the catechism of the religion of France,' she writes (Citron 1989: 25). It masks the state abuses of power, erases the social class and regional conflicts, personalizes 'the people'. Another historian praises the kind of political socialization produced by that presentation of the collective adventure, where France was regarded as universal and sacred:

> To be born French is to find in one's cradle a miraculously pedagogical history, advancing towards democracy through well-ordered sequences ... it is having for a homeland freedom, justice, tolerance ... There is no gap therefore between the empirical nation and the rational nation when identifying France to the universal principles of democracy.
>
> (cited in Nique and Lelièvre 1993: 116)

This form of national indoctrination at school was less marked during the interwar years, as a move of pacifism emerged among the school teachers (Loubes 2001). But the exaltation of the colonial deed, out of which the republicans had made a masterpiece of national (ethnicized) celebration at school (Maingueneau 1979; Nique and Lelièvre 1993), remained praised up until the 1980s. With regard to this, recent textbooks show terseness and distance, but the vision of the national past has not been reappraised (Citron 1989).

Hasn't ethnonationalism simply changed its form in the educational space? Erased from the prescribed curriculum, hasn't it passed into the hidden curriculum, following channels to be discovered, to finish by being taken over by ordinary professional gestures? This assumption, it may be noticed, conforms to the sociological theory of reproduction. If, on the one hand, school is the specific channel through which social status reproduction is achieved in our society, under the control of dominant groups (Bourdieu and Passeron 1970), and if, moreover, ethnonationalism is a mode of the social domination in national democracies (Weber 1968; Elias and Scotson 1964; Balibar 1988; Lorcerie 2003), one may expect that ethnonationalism will somehow become inculcated in a school which is a state apparatus.

At any rate, the French Ministry of National Education was slow in assuming the fight against discrimination, which the government had turned into a 'national cause' for the year 2002. Ethnic discrimination is not officially recognized as inducing particular scholastic needs for all the students, the fight against discrimination is not officially transposed into teaching contents. Consequently, available legal tools may not be ordinarily taught, and ethnicization processes may not be analysed as such with students (ethnonationalism being part of these), although there are certain exceptions.[16]

Notes

1 The Berque report was published at the 'Documentation française' (the official editor of the French government); it is the only report that has ever been written on this topic.

2 The young people of foreign origin, i.e. born in France from an immigrant parent or grandparent, account for 17 per cent of their age group. This national average covers strong local disparities (Tribalat 1997). As for foreign students, they account for 6.7 per cent of the total students in primary schools, and 6.1 per cent in secondary schools (source: Ministry of National Education, 1996 and 1997 respectively).

3 See Council Directive 2000/43 EC of 29 June 2000 *Implementing the principle of equal treatment between persons irrespective of racial or ethnic origin.*

4 There is no English translation for the word *immigré*, which is applied to immigrants as well as to children of immigrants or even grandchildren of immigrants, according implicitly to their ethnic origin

5 This title is borrowed from Jean-Paul Payet, who used it for his master thesis (1984) on relationships between students and school agents in a vocational school.

6 This behaviour doesn't fall into any of the types formulated by Goffman (1963): it is a conformity to the in-group, whereby the individual remains outside of the dominant symbolic world.

7 In particular, young French-Algerians are French born if they were born in France from parents born in Algeria during the colonial period.

8 Sylvain Broccolicchi, personal communication.

9 Such an assumption would be in accordance with the 'interpretive' theory of Hugh Mehan about teachers' constitutive action in their classes, and more generally with the theory of society constitution in sociology (Mehan 1992; Giddens 1984).

10 It is on the lower secondary school level that the question of class gradation upon combined scholastic and ethnic criteria has been best studied. The same question arises in vocational schools.

11 The index of dissimilarity measures here the frequency of assignment to different or identical sections of students with opposite characteristics.

12 Let's remember that the 'better results' gained by children of immigrants, as discussed above, appear at the end of *collège*, 'all things being equal', i.e. in particular at an identical social-economic level.

13 Parents are sometimes the only ones to be charged with radical otherness, their children being then seen as victims of their parents. Such a shifting was

observed, for example, in the school agents' positions during an operation managed to make them feel closer to the parents (Perroton 2000a).

14 British studies lead to the same conclusions (see Smith and Tomlinson 1989; Tomlinson 1991).

15 'Twenty centuries ago, France was called Gaul', wrote Camille Julian, then professor at the Collège de France (cited by Citron 1989).

16 This text is an adapted version of Chapter 1, Part III of Lorcerie 2003.

References

Akers-Porrini, R. and Zirotti, J.-P. (1992) 'Elèves "français" et "maghrébins". Un rapport différent à l'orientation scolaire', *Migrants-Formation*, 89: 45–57.

Alamartine, F. (2003) 'Des faits? Quels faits?', in F. Lorcerie (ed.) *Ecole, le défi ethnique*, Paris: ESF and INRP.

Aubert, F., Tripier, M. and Vourc'h, F. (eds) (1997) *Jeunes issus de l'immigration: De l'école à l'emploi*, Paris: CIEMI / L'Harmattan.

Balibar, E. (1988) 'La forme nation: Histoire et idéologie', in E. Balibar and I. Wallerstein (eds) *Race, nation, classe: Les identités ambiguës*, Paris: La Découverte.

Barrère, A. and Martuccelli, D. (1997) 'L'école à l'épreuve de l'ethnicité', *Annales de la Recherche urbaine* 75: 51–58.

Barthon, C. (1998a) 'Enfants d'immigrés dans la division sociale et scolaire: L'exemple D'Asnières sur Seine', *Annales de la Recherche urbaine* 75: 70–78.

—— (1998b) *Espaces et ségrégations scolaires: L'exemple des enfants d'immigrés dans les collèges de l'Académie de Versailles*, Ph.D., dir. M. Guillon, Univ. Poitiers.

Beaud, S. (2002) *80% au bac . . . et après? Les enfants de la démocratisation scolaire*, Paris: La Découverte.

Beaud, S. and Pialoux, M. (1999) *Retour sur la condition ouvrière: Enquête aux usines Peugeot de Sochaux-Montbéliard*, Paris: Fayard.

Begag, A. (1986) *Le Gone du Chaâba, roman*, Paris: Seuil.

Berque, J. (1985) *L'Immigration à l'école de la République*, Rapport au ministre de l'Éducation nationale, Paris: La Documentation française.

Bordet, J. (1998) *Les 'jeunes de la cité'*, Paris: PUF.

Boulot, S. and Fradet, D. (1988) *Les Immigrés et l'école: Une course d'obstacles*, Paris: L'Harmattan.

Bourdieu, P. and Passeron, J.-C. (1970) *La Reproduction: Eléments pour une théorie du système d'enseignement*, Paris: Editions de Minuit.

Bouzar, D. (2001) *L'Islam des banlieues: Les prédicateurs musulmans: nouveaux travailleurs sociaux?*, Paris: Syros.

Broccolichi, S. and Van Zanten, A. (1997) 'Espaces de concurrence et circuits de scolarisation', *Annales de la Recherche urbaine* 75: 5–19.

Citron, S. (1989) *Le Mythe national: L'histoire de France en question*, Paris: Les éditions ouvrières/Etudes et documentation internationales.

Cukrowicz, H. and Duprez, D. (1992) 'Les représentations des rapports sociaux entre communautés nationales: le cas des jeunes de Roubaix', *Revue française de sociologie* XXX–2: 257–279.

Cummins, J. (1997) 'Minority Status and Schooling in Canada', *Anthropology & Education Quarterly* 23, 8: 411–430.

Debarbieux, E. (1996) *La Violence en milieu scolaire, 1: Etat des lieux*, Paris: ESF.

Debarbieux, E. and Tichit, L. (1997a) 'Le construit "ethnique" de la violence', in C. Bernard and J.-C. Emin (eds) *Violences à l'école*, Paris: Armand Colin: 155–177.

—— (1997b) 'Ethnicité, punitions et effet-classe', *Migrants Formation* 109: 138–154.

Debarbieux, E., Garnier, A., Montoya, Y. and Tichit, L. (1999) *La violence en milieu scolaire, 2: Le désordre des choses*, Paris: ESF.

Eidheim, H. (1969) 'When ethnic identity is a social stigma', in F. Barth (ed.) *Ethnic Groups and Boundaries: The Social Organization of Culture Difference*, Bergen/Oslo: Universitetsforlaget; London: George Allen & Unwin: 39–57.

Elias, N. and Scotson, J. L. (1964) *The Established and the Outsiders: A Sociological Inquiry into Community Problems*, London: F. Cass.

Favell, A. (1998) *Philosophies of Integration. Immigration and the Idea of Citizenship in France and Britain*, London: Macmillan; New York: St Martin's Press.

Favre-Perroton, J. (1999) *Ecole et ethnicité: une relation à double face, thèse de doctorat*, Université de Bordeaux 2.

Feldblum, M. (1999) *Reconstructing Citizenship. The Politics of Nationality Reform and Immigration in Contemporary France*, Albany: State University of New York Press.

Giddens, A. (1984) *The Constitution of Society: Outline of the Theory of Structuration*, Cambridge: Polity Press.

Gissot, C., Héran, F. and Manon, N. (1994) *Les Efforts éducatifs des familles*, Paris: INSEE.

Goffman, E. (1963) *Stigma, Notes on the Management of Spoiled Identity*, Englewood Cliffs: Prentice-Hall.

Guimond, S. and Tougas, F. (1994) 'Sentiments d'injustice et actions collectives: la privation relative', in R. Bourhis and J.-P. Leyens (eds) *Stéréotypes, discrimination et relations intergroupes*, Liège: Mardaga: 201–232.

Hassini, M. (1997) *L'école: Une chance pour les filles de parents maghrébins*, Paris: CIEMI/L'Harmattan.

Héran, F., dir. (1996) 'L'école, les élèves, et les parents', *Economie et Statistique* 293.

Khosrokhavar, F. (1997) *L'Islam des jeunes*, Paris: Flammarion.

Laborde, C. (2001) 'The culture(s) of the republic in French republican thought', *Political Theory* 29, 5: 716–735.

Lahire, B. (1995) *Tableaux de familles*, Paris: Gallimard-Le Seuil.

Leger, A. and Tripier, M. (1986) *Fuir ou construire l'école populaire?* Paris: Méridiens Klincksieck.

Lepoutre, D. (1997) *Cœur de banlieue: Codes, rites et langages*, Paris: Odile Jacob.

Lorcerie, F. (1998) 'Berque, l'école, l'immigration: rencontre inopinée', in F. Pouillon (ed.) *Enquêtes dans la bibliographie de Jacques Berque. Parcours d'histoire sociale, REMMM*, 83–84: 171–194.

—— (1999) 'La "scolarisation des enfants de migrants", fausses questions et vrais problèmes', in P. Dewitte (ed.) *Immigration et intégration, l'état des savoirs*, Paris: La Découverte: 112–121.

—— (2003) *L'Ecole et le défi ethnique*, Paris: ESF and INRP.

Lorcerie, F. and Darbon, S. (2001) 'Encadrer les jeunes: Un lycée professionnel, un club de rugby', in D. Schnapper (ed.) *Exclusions au cœur de la cité*, Paris: Ed. Anthropos.

Lorcerie, F. and Philipp, M.-G. (eds) (2003) 'Enseigner en milieu ethnicisé?', livraison spéciale, janvier, *Revue VEI*.

Loubes, O. (2001) *L'Ecole et la patrie. Histoire d'un désenchantement, 1914–1940*, Paris: Belin.

Maingueneau, D. (1979) *Les Livres d'école de la République (1870–1914): Discours et idéologie*, Paris: Le Sycomore.

Mazzella, S. (1997) 'Belsunce: des élèves musulmans à l'abri de l'école catholique', *Annales de la Recherche urbaine* 75: 79–87.

Mehan, H. (1992) 'Understanding inequality in schools: the contribution of interpretive studies', *Sociology of Education* 65, 1: 1–20.

Merton, R. K. (1957) *Social Theory and Social Structure*, 2nd edn, Glencoe: The Free Press.

Meuret, D. (1999) 'Rawls, l'éducation et l'égalité des chances', in D. Meuret (ed.) *La Justice du système éducatif*, Bruxelles: De Boeck Université: 37–54.

Nique, C. and Lelièvre, C. (1993) *La République n'éduquera plus: La fin du mythe Ferry*, Paris: Plon.

Ogbu, J. U. (1978) *Minority, Education and Caste*, New York and London: Academic Press.

Payet, J.-P. (1992a) 'Ce que disent les mauvais élèves. Civilités, incivilités dans les collèges de banlieue', *Les Annales de la recherche urbaine* 54: 85–94.

—— (1992b) 'Civilités et ethnicité dans les collèges de banlieue: enjeux, résistances et dérives d'une action scolaire territorialisée', *Revue française de pédagogie* 101: 59–69.

—— (1995) *Collèges de banlieue, Ethnographie d'un monde scolaire*, Paris: Méridiens-Klincksieck.

—— (1997) 'La catégorie ethnique dans l'espace relationnel des collèges de banlieue: entre censure et soulignement', in F. Aubert, M. Tripier and F. Vourc'h (eds) *Jeunes issus de l'immigration. De l'école à l'emploi*, Paris: CIEMI/L'Harmattan: 207–218.

—— (1998) 'La ségrégation scolaire: une perspective sociologique sur la violence à l'école', *Revue française de pédagogie* 123: 21–34.

Payet, J.-P. and Sicot, F. (1997) 'Expérience collégienne et origine "ethnique": La civilité et la justice scolaire du point de vue des élèves étrangers ou issus de l'immigration', *Migrants-Formation* 109: 155–167.

Perroton, J. (2000a) 'Les ambiguïtés de l'ethnicisation des relations scolaires: l'exemple des relations école-familles à travers la mise en place d'un dispositif de médiation', *VEI Enjeux* 121: 130–147.

—— (2000b) 'Les dimensions ethniques de l'expérience scolaire', *L'Année sociologique* 50, 2: 437–468.

Poiret, C. (1996) *Familles africaines en France: ethnicisation, ségrégation, communalisation*, Paris: CIEMI/L'Harmattan.

—— (2000) 'La construction de l'altérité à l'école de la République', *VEI Enjeux* 121: 148–177.

Ribert, E. (1998) 'Les jeunes nés en France de parents étrangers face au choix de la nationalité', in I. Simon-Barouh (ed.) *Dynamiques migratoires et rencontres ethniques*, Paris: L'Harmattan: 219–232.

Rinaudo, C. (1998) 'L'imputation de caractéristiques ethniques dans l'encadrement de la vie scolaire', *Revue Européenne des Migrations Internationales* 14, 3: 27–43.

—— (1999) *L'Ethnicité dans la cité: Jeux et enjeux de la catégorisation ethnique*, Paris: L'Harmattan.

Santelli, E. (2001) *La Mobilité sociale dans l'immigration; Itinéraires de réussite des enfants d'origine algérienne*, Toulouse: Presses universitaires du Mirail.

Simon, P. (1999) 'L'immigration et l'intégration dans les sciences sociales en France depuis 1945', in P. Dewitte (ed.) *Immigration et intégration, l'état des savoirs*, Paris: La Découverte: 82–95.

Smith, D. and Tomlinson, S. (1989) *The School Effect – A Study of Multi-Racial Secondary Schools*, London: Policy Studies Institute.

Thomas, R. M. (1994) 'The meaning and significance of ethnicity in educational discourse', *International Review of Education* 40, 1: 74–80.

Tietze, N. (2002) *Jeunes musulmans de France et d'Allemagne: les constructions subjectives de l'identité*, Paris: L'Harmattan.

Tomlinson, S. (1991) 'Ethnicity and educational attainment in England: an overview', *Anthropology and Education Quarterly* 22, 1: 121–139.

Tribalat, M. (1997) 'Les populations d'origine étrangère en France métropolitaine', *Population* 1: 163–219.

Vallet, L.-A. and Caille, J.-P. (1996) 'Les elèves étrangers ou issus de l'immigration dans l'école et le collège français', *Les dossiers d'Education et Formations* 67.

Van Zanten, A. (2001) *L'Ecole de la périphérie. Scolarité et ségrégation en banlieue*, Paris: PUF.

Vinsonneau, G. (1996) *L'identité des jeunes en situation inégalitaire. Le cas des Maghrébins en France*, Paris: L'Harmattan.

Wacquant, L. (1987) 'Différence ethnique et différences sociales dans les écoles primaires de Nouvelle-Calédonie', *Actes de la recherche en sciences sociales* 70: 47–63.

Weber, M. (1968) 'Ethnic communal relationships', in *Economy and Society. An Outline of Interpretive Sociology*, New York: Bedminster Press.

Zeroulou, Z. (1988) 'La réussite scolaire des enfants d'immigrés. L'apport d'une approche en termes de mobilisation', *Revue française de sociologie* XXIX: 447–470.

Zimmermann, D. (1978) 'Un langage non-verbal de classe: Les processus d'attraction-répulsion des enseignants à l'égard des élèves en fonction de l'origine familiale de ces derniers', *Revue française de Pédagogie* 44: 46–70.

Zirotti, J.-P. (1979) *La Scolarisation des enfants de travailleurs immigrés*, tome 1. *Evaluation, sélection et orientation scolaires*, Nice: IDERIC.

—— (1990) 'Quand le racisme fait sens', *Peuples méditerranéens* 51: 69–82.

—— (1997) 'Pour une sociologie phénoménologique de l'altérité: la constitution des expériences scolaires des élèves issus de l'immigration', in F. Aubert, M. Tripier, and F. Vourc'h (eds) *Jeunes issus de l'immigration. De l'école à l'emploi*, Paris: CIEMI/L'Harmattan: 240–241.

7   New migration in Europe

Educational changes and
challenges – a perspective from
Greece

Soula Mitakidou and Georgios Tsiakalos

Immigrants in Greece

An impressive economic development in the last 25 years has transformed
Greece from a traditional country of origin to a host country of immigrants. In particular, as a result of radical political changes in eastern
Europe, Greece – a country of about 10 million citizens – has accepted
more than a million immigrants. Neither the Greek society, nor the Greek
state were prepared to deal with such a complex phenomenon, which put
to the test their value system and revealed invisible aspects of their character. The Greek society has a relatively 'open' character, in the sense that it
is inadequately organized and thus allows for many deviations in resolving
problems and situations and also that it offers possibilities for relatively
easy social advancement, being a non polarized society in terms of class
(Lambrianidis and Lymperaki 2001). Up to now, however, the 'open'
character of the Greek society has not contributed to a more tolerant attitude towards newcomers.

The global political and economic framework is formulating a type of
migration to the countries of south Europe that is quite different from
what migration used to be to the countries of north and central Europe in
the past. The main characteristics of this so-called 'new migration' are its
unofficial character, the large variety of nationalities and countries of
origin of immigrants, the central role played by the shadow economy, the
unofficial work markets for immigrants in each one of the host countries
and the – until recently – lack of basic immigration policy (Iosifidis 2001).

Few of the recent immigrants came to Greece through legal processes.
Most of them crossed the Greek borders illegally and even though some of
them legalized their status later, many of them have remained illegal. The
continuous flow of illegal immigrants is documented daily in a tragic way:
with deaths at the steep mountainous areas at the northern borders of the
country with Albania and Bulgaria, deaths at minefields that cover part of
the eastern borders with Turkey, and deaths by drowning at frequent
wrecks in the Aegean Sea (see Tsiakalos 2000, where many such incidents
are recorded). There are not detailed statistics but the number of people

that enter Greece illegally, compared to its population, is the biggest among the countries of the European Union. This is due to the fact that Greece has extended borders with three of the countries of the former Eastern bloc; it also has hundreds of islands, which neighbour the Asiatic coast, and thus lends itself to illegal landing.

The reference to the proximity of the Greek islands to Asia does not exclusively concern geography: it mainly concerns the political and economic situation that prevails in the countries of that area and forces millions of people to become refugees or immigrants. Thus thousands of Kurds from Turkey, Iraq and Iran; Afghans; Pakistanis; Bengalis; Indians; Palestinians; people from the Philippines, and from various African countries seek shelter in Greece. The largest number of immigrants and refugees in Greece, however, come from countries of east Europe, mainly from Albania and the Republics of the former USSR. All these newcomers to Greece may be grouped into three broad categories:

- Greek origin repatriates, members of native Greek minority groups, mainly from the former USSR and Albania;
- non-Greek legal immigrants or refugees;
- illegal immigrants.

There are distinct characteristics and particularities attached to each one of these groups. For instance, in terms of their legal status in Greece, newcomers are treated unequally by the Greek state. Indeed, individuals belonging to Greek minority groups from former USSR countries acquire Greek citizenship rather quickly. Contrary to the policy followed in the case of Greek origin repatriates from the former USSR, however, Greek origin repatriates from Albania face great difficulties in acquiring Greek citizenship, despite the fact that compared to repatriates from the former USSR they speak Greek. The ulterior motive of the Greek government to maintain a large number of Greek minority in Albania puts these immigrants in a peculiar situation: on the one hand, they legalize their stay in Greece easily and secure a status that gives them privileges in relation to other immigrants, on the other, however, it is harder for them to acquire the Greek citizenship than any other category of immigrants. Thus they remain 'foreigners' with significant negative consequences in their life. A serious consequence, for example, is that they are deprived of the prospect that Greek citizens are entitled to as citizens of the European Union, i.e. to immigrate to other more prosperous countries without any restrictions. After years of residence in Greece, they feel their status is precarious. 'Every three years we have to line up and take exams to prove that we are Greeks', said the president of the Federacy of Greek origin repatriates from Albania. 'The allegedly promising identity card allocated to Greek origin repatriates is annulled through special circulars that strip bearers of the few rights the card holds. We demand the obvious, we demand double citizenship, so that we may feel equal Greek citizens' (newspaper *Eleftherotypia*, 9 May 2003). The solution discussed at official level for Greek origin repatriates from Albania, i.e. double citizenship, constitutes a novelty for the Greek state, which, however, lacks legal basis and precedent. Therefore, problems related to integration in society and consequently integration in education are closely related with issues of external and internal affairs as well as public order (as the cases of the education of illegal immigrants described below will also indicate).

Concerning all other categories of immigrants and refugees, there are many limitations in the Greek law, the result being that several hundred thousand immigrants live in Greece in a state of illegitimacy. Ample reference to the ways and difficulties of legalization is made in a publication of the Jesuit Refugee Service of Europe (Barrett 2001):

> The regulation campaign in Greece started in 1998. The first phase was that of recording the foreigners and lasted for 5 months. Anyone missing the deadline was not allowed an extension. Those recorded were allowed to stay, work legally and proceed to the second phase that of acquiring the 'limited duration residence permit', or 'Green Card'. In order to acquire the Green Card, one of the conditions was to have collected a certain minimum number of social security stamps, very difficult for those working 'off the books'. The Green Card is issued usually for one year, but considerable delays in the process meant that not all applications were considered within a year of being made. In order to renew a much higher number of social security stamps were needed. Few migrants are able to provide that, and so very many were expected to fall back into irregularity once more.
>
> (Barrett 2001: 37)

The working conditions of immigrants in Greece, both legal but especially illegal, are characterized by instability, insecurity, irregularity, unacceptably low wages (usually much lower than the legal lowest wage) and low status. The particularities of the Greek economy, i.e. family businesses, long-established shadow economy, low living standards, inefficient state control and management seem to create the conditions that allow the development of a cheap work force (Psimmenos 2001). Despite the common racist argument that the percentage of unemployment among Greeks has increased due to the work of immigrants, there is scientific research that indicates that the work of immigrants creates more work opportunities than it fills (Ioakimoglou 2001). On the other hand, it is an unquestionable fact that the Greek economy has greatly benefited from the work of immigrants and in particular, illegal immigrants (Sarris and Zografakis 1999). Indeed, it is considered that Greece managed to reach the economic indicators that were required for its participation in the united European currency due to the work of immigrants. The low wages of immigrants, which by violation of the law are by far below the permitted lowest limit, allowed the Greek economy to develop at a rate much higher than its intrinsic possibility and mostly allowed its development in sectors such as rural economy, tourism, construction, which would have stagnated without the cheap immigrant workforce. This economic reality is obvious not only in the economic indicators but also in the everyday life of even the most remote village. With their work, immigrants revitalized economic sectors that had been threatened with extinction and contributed to the creation of new ones, thus producing surplus value and, consequently, prosperity. Moreover, the low wages of illegal immigrants gave many middle class Greek families the opportunity to improve their standard of living by taking advantage of the cheap services offered by immigrants (i.e. house cleaners, house maintenance and repair) that, under different circumstances, these families could not afford.

Questions related to education

According to official data, approximately 130,000 immigrant and repatriate children will attend Greek elementary and secondary classes in the academic year 2003–2004. The majority (51.6 per cent) are elementary school children, 8.5 per cent are kindergarten school children, 25.7 per cent junior high and 14.2 per cent senior high school children. In the district of Attica, metropolitan area of Athens, twelve out of a hundred students come from immigrant or repatriate families. The number slightly decreases in other districts (11.3 per cent in the district of Ionian islands, 9.8 per cent in central northern Greece, 8.6 per cent in southern Aegean and 8.3 per cent in Peloponnese) reflecting the settling patterns of immigrants in Greece (newspaper *To Vima* 24 August 2003).

The experiences of the Greek educational system with children that came from other countries was initially limited to children of Greek immigrants from abroad and later to children of Greek minorities from other countries. These were children of Greek repatriates who had not attended Greek schools in their host countries and had serious difficulties in attending mainstream schools. At that time, the attempt to cope with the educational problems of these children focused on three measures:

1   The announcement, in 1980, of reception or support classes with the professed purpose of facilitating these children's integration in the 'Greek society and the Greek way of thinking and behaving. In particular, the aim of these classes is to nurture the skills the students possess from their previous school experience as well as to develop the necessary skills for their future educational and professional evolution in the framework of the Greek education' (Ministerial decree 818.2/Z/4139/20-10-80).
2   The establishment, in 1985, of two schools in Athens and one in Thes-

saloniki for children of repatriates. In these schools, parallel to the Greek curriculum, the language of the country of origin was also taught. The same language was used when it was necessary for the comprehension of the Greek lesson. Despite the fact that these schools were established with the professed purpose of being equivalent to the German schools, the French schools and the American Colleges that have operated in Greece for years with great success, they have never achieved the same calibre.

3   A 'period of leniency' concerning assessment for the children's advancement to the next grade. So, two years after their arrival in Greece and their integration in Greek schools, repatriate students were allowed to proceed to higher grades with lower scores than their classmates whose mother tongue, i.e. Greek, was the language of instruction.

On the other hand, no specific measures were taken for the essential support of students in class, with the exception of support or reception classes when and if these were actually realized.[1] The negative aspects of support or reception classes are identified in:

- Their fragmentary character (even in schools that qualify, their creation depends to a large degree on the willingness of the principal and the teaching staff, who can either block or endorse their operation; reception classes are often formed one or two months after the beginning of the school year and after the children have begun in regular classes; their operation is easily discontinued if the teacher is considered necessary in another class or school).
- The lack of specific well-planned goals and a system of assessment of the results.
- The lack of appropriate and relevant teaching material.
- The lack of teaching staff training programmes (in-service training is often limited to one day seminars with presentations of general interest, such as the Greeks abroad or the significance of bilingualism).

Consequently, these experiences could hardly contribute to the acquisition of the know-how educators needed when, in the late 1980s and early 1990s, the large numbers of immigrants (refugees) began to arrive from the former Eastern bloc countries.

New migration – new challenges

In the case of refugees from the former USSR, school failure is considerable (see Tressou and Mitakidou 1997) and is only limited due to the fact that the group of Pontian[2] parents comprises of people of high

educational level and particularly positive attitudes to education. Therefore, they are involved in their children's education and compensate for
the gaps left by the official school.[3] Moreover, in the case of Pontian children, we are dealing with students with high subjective identification with
the indigenous population and consequently with everything the Greek
educational system entails in sectors that, in case of other immigrants, are
considered sensitive; for instance, the absolute dominance of the Greek
language; the ethnocentric elements of history teaching; the recognition
of Greece as the 'exceptional country'. As a result the allocation of the
student population at all levels of education is more balanced, that is,
there is a lesser dropout rate in the case of Pontian repatriate children. In
particular, the picture of Pontian students at all levels of education is as
follows: 39.5 per cent in primary school, 33.5 per cent in the first three
classes of secondary school, which is compulsory, and 22 per cent in the
higher three classes of secondary school, which is not compulsory (newspaper *Eleftherotypia*, 11 October 2003).

In the case of all other immigrant groups who have immigrated to
Greece since the late 1980s and early 1990s, however, statistics indicate
that the dropout rate, especially in the secondary part of compulsory education, is much higher than the corresponding percentage of the indigenous student population. In fact, the largest proportion of immigrant
children in Greek schools appears in primary schools (55.5 per cent)
while the corresponding percentage is 23.1 per cent in secondary compulsory school and it drops to 11.7 per cent in secondary non-compulsory
school (newspaper *Eleftherotypia*, 11 October 2003). These results are
coupled by data of unofficial longitudinal studies.[4]

The arrival of hundreds of thousands of immigrants who have different
home countries, different mother tongues, different relationships with the
indigenous population and are differently confronted by the indigenous
population has apparently posed new problems. Problems for which, as
the descriptions of the much 'easier' cases of Pontian children must have
indicated, the Greek educational system has not been prepared. Problems
that educators are likely to face when:

- they suddenly find themselves in classes in which 10 per cent and at
  times more than 50 per cent of the student population have no particular knowledge of the language of instruction, and at the same time;
- they do not possess the specific knowledge for teaching in mixed
  classes;
- they do not have the proper teaching material;
- they have little or no actual assistance from support and reception
  classes due to the problems identified above.

The philosophy of the educational programmes offered to children of
immigrants falls into the category of the 'sink or swim' type or else of the

'assimilate or fail' type. In this framework, it should come as no surprise that every now and then newspapers report cases of children, mainly from Albania, who, at the peak of their successful course at the Greek school are baptized Christian Orthodox. Another case in point indicating the significant shortages in the educational system with direct consequences in the daily reality of immigrant children and their families is the story of Odysseus Chenai, from Albania. Odysseus scored the highest in his class, which gave him the right to hold the Greek flag in the annual school parade for the national holiday of 28 October. The strong uproar Odysseus' distinction caused in the small rural community where he lived but also in the broader Greek society obliged the boy to withdraw from his right to hold the flag. His withdrawal, of course, did not guarantee a peaceful life for Odysseus and his family in their small community, since after the publicity faded and everyone returned to routine, the family had to live and interact with all those who opposed Odysseus' distinction and who were members of the dominant culture. These are incidents that are quite revealing for the Greek educational system and the Greek society in general.

Needless to say that in this framework, the children's mother tongue does not play any role, not even as a scaffold for the acquisition of skills and knowledge in the second language. Mother tongue maintenance classes are provided for by the law[5] but in real life they are not implemented, despite extended research data that indicates the significance of the mother tongue for the acquisition of the second language as well as for the balanced linguistic, cognitive and academic development of language minority children (Thomas and Collier 1997). The official outlook concerning the role of the first language is best captured in the statement of the person in charge of Special Programmes for the education of Roma children. To the question if Roma constitute a minority and consequently if they have the right to their mother tongue (Romanes), he answered:

> Greek Gypsies are a part of the Greek people and the Greek nation both through time and at present. They are not a minority. Therefore, we do not talk about a minority ... Some of the Greek Gypsies are Muslim in their religion. Muslim Gypsies are officially protected by the known treaty, which defines minority educational matters in Greece.[6]

With the last sentence reference is made to the Treaty of Lausanne between Greece and Turkey in effect since 1923, according to which it is determined among other things that 'Muslim minorities' in Greece and 'Christian minorities' in Turkey have the right to be taught through their mother tongue. The executive of the Ministry of Education considers that when Gypsies are Muslim they are a minority and therefore, have the right to their mother tongue. On the contrary, if they are Christian or atheist then they belong 'through time and at present to the Greek nation' and they are not 'protected' by international treaties, therefore it is not possible to teach them through their mother tongue.

There is also a parallel phenomenon, which requires description and interpretation. The official policy, as it is expressed in various relevant statements of the Ministry of Education, seems to take on a different orientation for the future: it aims towards an 'intercultural education' which could permeate the whole of the educational process and curriculum. The use of the expression 'different orientation for the future' is not random but refers to the known chasm between the rhetoric for a beautiful future, a rhetoric that draws on the most progressive ideas in the field of pedagogy, and an educational praxis which follows traditions like the ones described above. Thus for several years now, and with the support of the European Union, teaching materials have been in preparation for the advent of intercultural education. Regardless of the objections one may have for the quality of this teaching material, one could consider that serious changes are being prepared for the Greek education as a pedagogical answer to the challenges of new migration. However, the content of the curriculum revision, which has nothing to do with intercultural education, brings us down to the reality of the existing schools and reveals the fact that political leaders and policy makers often like to promote a beautiful virtual reality – 'potemkin villages' – and at the same time, they make sure they maintain the existent reality which condemns thousands of children to a subordinate existence.

The case of illegal immigrants

Despite the official concern for 'the control of dropout rates among foreign students and their integration in the educational system of our country,' (newspaper *To Vima*, 24 August 2003) there is no reference made for the children of illegal immigrants, who create a new phenomenon, at least in terms of its mass manifestation in education because they are the children who basically 'do not exist' for the authorities of the country. Even today and even when their presence has become visible to authorities or even when they have become legal, these children have a life history very different from other children: before reaching Greece, they have lived with their families for a period of time as illegal immigrants in another country – usually Turkey – and, consequently, have spent a long period of time outside school even though they were at school age.

The hundreds of thousands of immigrants who have crossed the Greek borders illegally include large numbers of children. Many Europeans cannot comprehend how it can be that in conditions of utter danger – for instance, in rotten ships that daily cross the Aegean – whole families travel. This is not random. Escape from wars, dictatorships, persecutions and poverty is mostly attempted for a better future for the children. Thus, contrary to common belief that illegal immigration concerns individuals, it is associated with whole families. That is, with children as well. Besides, even in the case of illegal migration of individuals, if it is successful, the whole family follows or a new family is created. Therefore, in order to pay for the fee of the illegal transportation – approximately 2,000–3,000 dollars to reach a European Union country by ship – all of the family's belongings are sold. Consequently, the decision to immigrate means a complete break from everything there was, everything they were.

Is education compulsory for the children of illegal immigrants?

All of the above examples relate to one basic question, which was rarely posed in the past and which is proving very significant in our effort to understand the particular problems ensuing from the new migration as well as the essence of some of the self-evident facts of our society: is education compulsory for the children of illegal immigrants?

If yes, then:

- How is their compulsory schooling secured?
- How are they enrolled at school?
- How is their irregular attendance checked?
- How are unwanted consequences, i.e. informing the police, evaded? (see Tsiakalos 2000 for many true stories of petty blackmail at school).

These are real questions, that is, they have appeared thousands of times and many activist members of academia have found themselves obliged to express their opinion and argue in order to enforce the right of certain children to participate in education. In doing that, they often realize that the application of the things they support necessarily leads to violation of the law and also of 'self-evident facts' that have become effective in many European educational bureaucracies – including the Greek bureaucracy, of course.

Considering the self-evident fact of compulsory education, it has been enacted exactly so that no adult and no adult institution may prevent a child from realizing his or her right to education, which is an individual human right. And precisely because it is the individual human right of a minor, in other words, a person who has no power and often no legal option to claim this right independently when it is at stake, that is why compulsory education has been legislated. Compulsory education means that when a child does not attend school then an adult or an institution is held responsible for that. From this perspective it becomes obvious that the education of children of illegal immigrants must be compulsory. Moreover, due to the particular precarious situation of parents, the responsibility for any violation of the children's right to education weighs on the state. Consequently, the particular questions posed above should concern local societies, educational authorities and educators. Nevertheless, in practice these questions are never posed because the official Greek policy on this matter by way of implementation is that we have no compulsory education for the children of illegal immigrants.

This position of the Greek state has been established as a negative tradition even vis-à-vis its citizens. No blame has ever been put – in the sense of legal responsibility – for the fact that the children of indigenous Roma in their overwhelming majority do not attend school. For the past year the Ministry claimed that 75 per cent of school age Roma children attended school, as opposed to 25 per cent that used to attend two years before. If one knows anything about the reality in the actual schools, one can see the discrepancy between the 'reality of the schools' and the 'virtual reality of the Ministry'. Even if it were true that only 25 per cent of the Roma children did not attend school, shouldn't, according to the law, responsibility be sought and laid? Instead of assuming responsibility, however, the mere 'identification' of the group's particular cultural traits usually suffices to justify the violation of the children's right to education. It becomes obvious that the violation of the right to compulsory education of children of illegal immigrants follows a negative tradition.

Is the right to education unquestionable and effective?

If the answer to the question 'is education compulsory for the children of illegal immigrants?' is negative – a surprising number of people feel that education should not be compulsory for the children of illegal immigrants, that is, they consider that compulsory education which is provided for in the Greek constitution does not apply in the case of people who are in the country illegally – then the new question is: at least, is the right to education effective?

Paragraph 1 of article 40 of the immigration law 2910/01 explicitly reports that 'all non-Greek children who live in Greece are subject to the minimum compulsory school attendance that Greek children are' and in paragraph 3 it continues that 'non-Greek children who live in Greece can be enrolled in public schools, even if their residence has not been officially settled and even with insufficient documents'.

Since the answer to the question 'are children of illegal immigrants entitled to education' is positive, the question that emerges automatically is: are schools obliged to accept them?

According to the law quoted above, principals of schools are obliged to enrol, in separate lists, students who have no permanent residence in Greece, even without the necessary documents. For the award of certificates of studies (e.g. certificate of studies of primary and secondary school), however, children have to submit all necessary documents that mostly confirm identification. Otherwise, certificates are not issued.

However, despite the fact that the regulation is clear, in practice this does not always apply. There are principals who claim that the regulation is not covered by the law – and the law allows for such 'convenient holes' – and therefore, they cannot implement it. The most common argument against enrolment that 'unwilling' principals invoke is the student's inability to prove that he or she belongs to the school district of the particular school. This can be proved with residence certificates but illegal immigrants cannot produce such certificates. The result is that there are schools in Greece which not even one immigrant student attends whereas the school next door may well accommodate a large number of immigrant students. Here is a characteristic example of this: two sisters from Albania, one of the first and the other of the fifth grade, were refused access to a particular school. The principal of the school refused to accept the children on the grounds that they did not have residence certificates. When the family's landlady went to certify their residence address, the principal threatened to report her to the revenue department for having rented her property without statement. The principal accepted the two girls only when the second author – Dean of the School of Education and prominent educator and citizen of the city of Thessaloniki – accompanied them – and reporters accompanied him – to school and stated that he would act as their guardian. The principal's excuse? She claimed that the children looked so smartly dressed as opposed to their parents that she had suspected that the parents had probably kidnapped them from Bulgaria.

It becomes obvious that despite the 'positive' official position, the ambivalent interpretations often offered by officials allow school principals to interpret and implement the law at will. To make things worse, quite recently, in August 2003, the Ministry of Internal Affairs and Public Order notified the Ministry of Education that schools have to check the residence and work permits of immigrant parents when they come to enrol their children and refuse enrolment if the parents' documents are not in order. The Ministry of Education passed the communication to every school but the reaction it triggered among organizations and activists in the country obliged the Ministry of Education to attribute the matter to 'bureaucratic entanglement' and withdraw the communiqué from the schools stating that enrolment will follow the procedures defined in the immigration law of 2001. The Ministry of Internal Affairs, however, has not responded so far.

Challenges

New migration can also be characterized as 'new' in terms of the way the European Union has decided to handle it. The European Union seems determined to turn Europe into a 'castle' that keeps out poor people who seek, in agony, a place in the land of affluence. In the field of education, the European Union policy has led to the re-emergence of phenomena that seemed to have been overcome decades ago. In particular, the new phenomena that appeared in the educational scene as a result of new migration are:

1   Failure to implement compulsory education for children of immigrants immediately, due to the fact that new migration is to a large extent illegal, anticipates a large number of illiterates and of children who will enter school at an older age. A problem that had almost been eliminated in Europe now reappears and authorities, educational systems and whole societies are not alert to its significance in the future.
2   Self-evident bureaucratic procedures associated with the children's enrolment in school either stretch the school's strict and absolute character or are unbending and thus function as mechanisms of exclusion from education.
3   Failure to secure compulsory education legally allows different handling by different principals. Consequently, there are schools with large numbers of children of illegal immigrants and schools with no such children at all.

It is easy to realize the serious implications that the educational system will face and also the huge cost society will have to pay when, in a few years, today's illegal immigrants will become legal – because they surely will. Then, we will have to deal with the existence of a large number of children and young adults without any education, with whatever social cost this involves. At the same time, the educational system will be asked to integrate children whose age will not correspond with their school experience. It will be an enormous challenge and policy-makers and educators do not possess the adequate knowledge and infrastructure to deal with it. This new problem is the result of the denial of European countries to recognize inevitable facts, such as the movement of millions of people from poor to rich countries. The reluctance to recognize facts leads to the reluctance to legalize the presence of hundreds of people which, in turn, leads to the exclusion of thousands of children from education. It is a challenge to which educators are obliged to respond.

Notes

1 A minimum of nine and a maximum of 17 children is the requirement for the creation of a reception class and a minimum of three and a maximum of eight students for a support class.
2 Pontian is the name that has prevailed for Greek minority people from the former USSR.
3 A good example of such compensatory programmes is the preparatory school organized by Pontian scientists of the Exact Sciences – often in Russian – for secondary school students.

4 Research data collected by Christos Tourtouras, Ph.D. candidate in the Department of Primary Education of Aristotle University in Thessaloniki, Greece.
5 Ministerial decision 2/354/Γ1/731/27-11-1995.
6 In *Proceedings of the Roundtable Religion and Cultural Identity: A Model for Intercultural Education for Greece of 2000*, December 1998, 67–68.

References

Barrett, L. (ed.) (2001) *Voices from the Shadows – Stories of Men and Women Living with Irregular Migration Status*, Brussels: Jesuit Refugee Service Europe.

Ioakimoglou, I. (2001) 'Immigrants and occupation', in A. Marvakis, D. Parsanoglou, and M. Pavlou (eds) *Immigrants in Greece*, Athens: Ellinika Grammata–Nikos Poulantzas Society.

Iosifidis, Th. (2001) 'Working conditions of three migrant groups in Greece', in A. Marvakis, D. Parsanoglou, and M. Pavlou (eds) *Immigrants in Greece*, Athens: Ellinika Grammata–Nikos Poulantzas Society.

Lambrianidis, L. and Lymperaki, A. (2001) *Albanian Immigrants in Thessaloniki*, Thessaloniki: Paratiritis.

Psimmenos, I. (2001) 'New work and unofficial workers in metropolitan Athens', in A. Marvakis, D. Parsanoglou, and M. Pavlou (eds) *Immigrants in Greece*, Athens: Ellinika Grammata–Nikos Poulantzas Society.

Sarris, A. and Zografakis, S. (1999) 'A computable general equilibrium assessment of the impact of illegal immigration on the Greek economy', *Journal of Population Economics* 12, 1: 155–182.

Thomas, W. and Collier, V. (1997) *School Effectiveness for Language Minority Students*, Washington DC: National Clearinghouse for Bilingual Education.

Tressou, E. and Mitakidou, C. (1997) 'Educating Pontian immigrants in Greece: successes and failures', *Early Education and Development* 8, 3: 323–338.

Tsiakalos, G. (2000) *Handbook of Anti-Racist Education*, Athens: Ellinika Grammata.

8 European perspectives on immigrant minority languages at home and at school

Guus Extra and Kutlay Yağmur

In this chapter we will focus on the status of immigrant minority (henceforward IM) languages at home and at school from three different European perspectives.

The first section goes into the utilization, value and effects of different *demographic* criteria for the definition and identification of (school) population groups in a multicultural society. Given the decreasing significance of nationality and birth country criteria in the European context, it is argued that the combined criteria of ethnicity and home language use are potentially promising long term alternatives for obtaining basic information on the increasingly multicultural composition of European nation states, cities and schools.

The second section offers *sociolinguistic* perspectives on the distribution and vitality of IM languages across Europe. In this context the rationale, methodology and first outcomes of the *Multilingual Cities Project*, realized in six major multicultural cities in different European Union (henceforward EU) member states, are presented. The project has been carried out under the auspices of the European Cultural Foundation, established in Amsterdam, and it has been coordinated by a research team at Tilburg University, the Netherlands.

The third section offers comparative perspectives on *educational* policies and practices in Europe in the domain of IM languages. Here we present major outcomes of a comparative study on the status quo of education in this domain in six EU countries. The report concludes with an outlook on how multilingualism can be promoted for all children in an increasingly multicultural Europe.

Demographic perspectives

As a consequence of socio-economically or politically determined processes of migration and marginalization of minorities, the traditional patterns of language variation across western Europe have changed considerably over the past decades (cf. Extra and Verhoeven 1998; Extra and Gorter 2001). The first flow of migration started in the 1960s and early

1970s, and it was mainly economically motivated. In the case of Mediterranean groups, migration initially involved contract workers who expected and were expected to stay for a limited period of time. As the period of their stay gradually became longer, this pattern of economic migration was followed by a second pattern of social migration as their families joined them. Subsequently, a second generation was born in the immigrant countries, while their parents often remained uncertain or ambivalent about whether to stay or to return to the country of origin. These demographic shifts over time have also been accompanied by shifts of designation for the groups under consideration in terms of 'migrant workers', 'immigrant families', and 'ethnic minorities', respectively.

As a result, most western European countries have a growing number of IM populations which differ widely, both from a cultural and from a sociolinguistic point of view, from the mainstream indigenous population. In spite of more stringent immigration policies in most EU countries, the prognosis is that IM populations will continue to grow as a consequence of the increasing number of political refugees, the opening of the internal European borders, and political and economic developments in Central and Eastern Europe and in other regions of the world. It has been estimated that in the year 2000 more than one-third of the population under the age of 35 in urbanized western Europe had an IM background.

Within the various EU countries, four major IM groups can be distinguished: people from Mediterranean EU countries, from Mediterranean non-EU countries, from former colonial countries, and political refugees (cf. Extra and Verhoeven 1993a, b). Comparative information on population figures in EU member states can be obtained from the Statistical Office of the EU in Luxembourg (EuroStat). An overall decrease of the indigenous population has been observed in all EU countries over the last decades; at the same time, there has been an increase in the IM figures. Although free movement of migrants between EU member states is legally permitted, most IM groups in EU countries originate from non-EU countries. According to EuroStat (2002), the EU population increased during 2000 by slightly more than one million. This growth was mainly due to the net inflow of 680,000 immigrants. In absolute numbers, net migration in 2000 was highest in Italy, followed by Great Britain and Germany. Together, these countries account for more than 60 per cent of the total net migration of the EU. None of the EU countries show a negative net migration. The lowest absolute levels can be found in Finland and Luxembourg. Without international migration, Germany, Greece, Italy and Sweden would have experienced a population loss. For most EU countries, non-EU nationals are the most numerous group in the immigration flows. In five countries more than 50 per cent of all immigrants are non-EU nationals, with Italy on top (71 per cent), followed by Austria (66 per cent), Germany (57 per cent), Sweden (56 per cent), and the Netherlands (52 per cent).

For various reasons, however, reliable demographic information on IM groups in EU countries is difficult to obtain. For some groups or countries, no updated information is available or no such data have ever been collected at all. Moreover, official statistics only reflect IM groups with legal resident status. Another source of disparity is the different data collection systems being used, ranging from nationwide census data to more or less representative surveys. Most importantly, however, the most widely used criteria for IM status, nationality and/or country of birth, have become less valid over time because of an increasing trend towards naturalization and births within the countries of residence. In addition, most residents from former colonies already have the nationality of their country of immigration.

There are large differences among EU countries as regards the size and composition of IM groups. Owing to labour market mechanisms, such groups are found mainly in the northern industrialized EU countries, whereas their presence in Mediterranean countries like Greece, Italy, Portugal and Spain is increasing. Mediterranean groups immigrate mainly to France or Germany. Portuguese, Spanish and Maghreb residents concentrate in France, whereas Italian, Greek, former Yugoslavian and Turkish residents concentrate in Germany. The largest IM groups in EU countries are Turkish and Maghreb residents; the latter originate from Morocco, Algeria or Tunisia. Table 8.1 gives official numbers of their size in 12 EU countries in January 1994.

According to EuroStat (1997) and based on the conservative nationality criterion, in 1993 the largest Turkish and Maghreb communities could be found in Germany (almost two million) and France (almost 1.4 million),

Table 8.1 Official numbers of inhabitants of Maghreb and Turkish origin in 12 EU countries, January 1994, based on the nationality criterion

EU countries	Maghreb countries			Total Maghreb	Turkey
	Morocco	Algeria	Tunisia		
Belgium	145,363	10,177	6,048	161,588	88,302
Denmark	3,180	368	404	3,952	34,658
Germany	82,803	23,082	28,060	133,945	1,918,395
Greece	333	180	314	827	3,066
Spain	61,303	3,259	378	64,940	301
France	572,652	614,207	206,336	1,393,195	197,712
Italy	77,180	3,177	35,318	115,675	3,656
The Netherlands	164,567	905	2,415	167,887	202,618
Portugal	221	53	28	302	65
Finland	560	208	142	910	995
Sweden	1,533	599	1,152	3,284	23,649
Great Britain	3,000	2,000	2,000	7,000	41,000
Total	1,112,695	658,215	282,595	2,053,505	2,514,417

Source: EuroStat 1997.

respectively. Within the EU, the Netherlands is in second place as the country of immigration for Turkish and Moroccan residents.

In most EU countries, only population data on nationality and/or birth country (of person and/or parents) are available. To illustrate this, Table 8.2 gives recent statistics of population groups in the Netherlands, based on the birth country criterion (of person and/or mother and/or father) versus the nationality criterion, as derived from the Dutch Central Bureau of Statistics. Moreover, Table 8.2 illustrates the recent growth of IM groups on the basis of the former, nowadays exclusively used, criterion.

First of all, Table 8.2 shows a longitudinal increase for all groups considered, except for Indonesians. More importantly, Table 8.2 shows strong criterion effects of birth country versus nationality. All IM groups are in fact strongly underrepresented in nationality-based statistics. However, the combined birth country criterion of person/mother/father does not solve the identification problem either. The use of this criterion leads to non-identification in at least the following cases:

- an increasing group of third and further generations (cf. the Indonesian/Moluccan and Chinese communities in the Netherlands);
- different ethnocultural groups from the same country of origin (cf. Turks versus Kurds from Turkey or Berbers versus Arabs from Morocco);
- the same ethnocultural group from different countries of origin (cf. Chinese from China versus Vietnam);
- ethnocultural groups without territorial status (cf. Roma).

Table 8.2 Population of the Netherlands based on the combined birth country criterion (BC-PMF) *versus* the nationality criterion on January

Groups	BC-PMF (2001)	BC-PMF (1999)	Nationality (1999)	Absolute difference (1999)
Dutch	N/A	13,061,000	15,097,000	2,036,000
Turks	331,000	300,000	102,000	198,000
Moroccans	284,000	252,000	128,600	123,400
Surinamese	315,000	297,000	10,500	286,500
Antilleans	125,000	99,000	–	99,000
Italians	35,000	33,000	17,600	15,400
(Former) Yugoslavs	75,000	63,000	22,300	40,700
Spaniards	31,000	30,000	16,800	13,200
Somalians	29,000	27,000	8,900	18,100
Chinese	36,000	28,000	7,500	20,500
Indonesians	403,000	407,000	8,400	398,600
Other groups	N/A	1,163,000	340,400	822,600
Total	N/A	15,760,000	15,760,000	4,072,000

Source: CBS 2000, 2002.

From the data presented in Table 8.2, it becomes clear that collecting reliable information about the actual number and spread of IM population groups in EU countries is no easy enterprise. Krüger-Potratz *et al.* (1998) discuss the problem of criteria from a historical perspective in the context of the German Weimarer Republik. In 1982, the Australian Institute of Multicultural Affairs recognized the above-mentioned identification problems for inhabitants of Australia and proposed including questions in their censuses on birth country (of person and parents), ethnic origin (based on self-categorization in terms of to which ethnic group a person considers him/herself to belong), and home language use. As yet, little experience has been gained in EU countries with periodical censuses, or, if such censuses have been held, with questions on ethnicity or (home) language use. Given the decreasing significance of nationality and birth country criteria, collecting reliable information about the composition of IM groups in EU countries is one of the most challenging tasks facing demographers. In Table 8.3, the four criteria mentioned are discussed in terms of their major (dis)advantages (see also Extra and Gorter 2001: 9).

As Table 8.3 makes clear, there is no single path to a solution of the identification problem. Different criteria may complement and strengthen each other. Verweij (1997) made a short tour d'horizon in four EU countries (Belgium, Germany, France, Great Britain) and in the USA in order to study criteria utilized in the national population statistics of these countries. In Belgium, Germany and France, such statistics have traditionally been based on the nationality criterion; only in Belgium has additional experience been gained with the combined birth country criterion of persons, parents and grandparents. For various reasons, identification on the basis of the grandparents' birth country is very problematic: four additional sources of evidence are needed (with multiple types of outcomes) and the chances of non-response are rather high. Verweij (1997) also discussed the experiences with the utilization of ethnic self-categorization in Great Britain and the USA, leaving the home language criterion out of consideration. Given the increasing identification problems with the combined birth-country criterion, Verweij, on the basis of Anglo-Saxon experiences, suggested including the self-categorization criterion in future population statistics as the second best middle and long term alternative in those cases where the combined birth country criterion would not suffice. Moreover, he proposed carrying out small-scale experimental studies on the validity and social acceptance of the self-categorization criterion, given its subjective and historically charged character (see also Table 8.3), before this criterion would be introduced on a nationwide scale.

Complementary or alternative criteria have been suggested and used in various countries with a longer immigration history, and, for this reason, with a longstanding history of collecting census data on multicultural population groups. This holds in particular for non-European English-

Table 8.3 Criteria for the definition and identification of population groups in a multicultural society

Criterion	Advantages	Disadvantages
Nationality (NAT) (P/F/M)	• objective • relatively easy to establish	• (intergenerational) erosion through naturalization or double NAT • NAT not always indicative of ethnicity/identity • some (e.g. ex-colonial) groups have NAT of immigration country
Birth country (BC) (P/F/M)	• objective • relatively easy to establish	• intergenerational erosion through births in immigration country • BC not always indicative of ethnicity/identity • invariable/deterministic: does not take account of dynamics in society (in contrast of all other criteria)
Self-categorization (SC)	• touches the heart of the matter • emancipatory: SC takes account of person's own conception of ethnicity/identity	• subjective by definition: also determined by the language/ethnicity of interviewer and by the spirit of times • multiple SC possible • historically charged, especially by Second World War experiences
Home language (HL)	• HL is most significant criterion of ethnicity in communication processes • HL data are prerequisite for government policy in areas such as public information or education	• complex criterion: who speaks what language to whom and when? • language is not always core value of ethnicity/identity • useless in one-person households

Notes
P = person
F = father
M = mother

dominant immigration countries like Australia, Canada, South Africa and the USA. To identify the multicultural composition of their populations, these four countries employ a variety of questions in their periodical censuses on nationality, birth country, ethnicity, ancestry, race, languages spoken at home and/or at work and religion. In Table 8.4, an overview of this array of questions is provided. For each country the last census is taken as the norm.

Both the type and number of questions are different per country. Canada has a prime position with the highest number of questions. Only three questions have been asked in all countries, whereas two questions have been asked in only one country. Four different questions have been asked about language. The operationalization of questions also shows interesting differences, both between and within countries across time (see Clyne 1991 for a discussion of methodological problems in comparing the answers to differently phrased questions in Australian censuses from a longitudinal perspective).

Questions about ethnicity, ancestry and/or race have proven to be problematic in all of the countries under consideration (see also Roosens 1989; Broeder and Extra 1998). In the USA, five racial categories have been distinguished (i.e. American Indian or Alaskan Native, Asian or Pacific Islander, Black, White, Other), and immediately afterwards two ethnic origin categories (i.e. +/− Hispanic origin). The racial classification has increasingly come under attack by the mixed race or multiracial movement and by those who argue that no racial classification exists or can be developed in such a way that biological variation is greater between than within racial categories (see Vermeulen 1999). In some countries, ancestry and ethnicity have been conceived of as equivalent, cf. the USA census question in 2000: *What is this person's ancestry or ethnic origin?* Or take

Table 8.4 Overview of census questions in four multicultural contexts

Questions in the census	Australia 2001	Canada 2001	South Africa 1996	USA 2000	Coverage
1 Nationality of respondent	+	+	+	+	4
2 Birth country of respondent	+	+	+	+	4
3 Birth country of parents	+	+	−	−	2
4 Ethnicity	−	+	−	+	2
5 Ancestry	+	+	−	+	3
6 Race	−	+	+	+	3
7 Mother tongue	−	+	−	−	1
8 Language used at home	+	+	+	+	4
9 Language used at work	−	+	−	−	1
10 Proficiency in English	+	+	−	+	3
11 Religion	+	+	+	−	3
Total of dimensions	7	11	5	7	30

the Canadian census question in 2001: *To which ethnic or cultural group(s) did this person's ancestors belong?* The Australian census question in 2001 only involves ancestry and not ethnicity, cf. *What is the person's ancestry?* with the following comments for respondents: *Consider and mark the ancestries with which you most closely identify. Count your ancestry as far as three generations, including grandparents and great-grandparents.* As far as ethnicity and ancestry have been distinguished in census questions, the former concept related most commonly to present self-categorization of the respondent and the latter to former generations. In what ways respondents themselves interpret both concepts, however, remains a problem that cannot be solved easily.

While 'ethnicity' according to Table 8.4 has been asked in the recent censuses of only two countries, four language-related questions have been asked in one to four countries. Only in Canada has the concept of 'mother tongue' been asked about. It has been defined for respondents as *language first learnt at home in childhood and still understood*, while questions 8 and 9 related to the language *most often* used at home/work. Table 8.4 shows the added value of language-related census questions on the definition and identification of multicultural populations, in particular the added value of the question on home language use compared to questions on the more opaque concepts of mother tongue and ethnicity. Although the language-related census questions in the four countries under consideration differ in their precise formulation and commentary, the outcomes of these questions are generally conceived of as cornerstones for educational policies with respect to the teaching of English as a first or second language and the teaching of languages other than English.

Derived from this overview it can be concluded that large-scale home language surveys are both feasible and meaningful and that the interpretation of the resulting database is made easier by transparent and multiple questions on home language use. These conclusions become even more pertinent in the context of gathering data on multicultural *school* populations. European experiences in this domain have been accumulated in particular in Great Britain and Sweden (cf. Broeder and Extra 1998 for an overview). In both countries extensive municipal home language statistics have been collected through local educational authorities by asking school children questions about oral and written skills in other languages than the national language and about the participation and need for education in these languages.

An important similarity in the phrased questions about home language use is that the outcomes are based on reported rather than observed facts. Answers to questions on home language use may be coloured by the language of the questions itself (which may or may not be the primary language of the respondent), by the ethnicity of the interviewer (which may or may not be the same as the ethnicity of the respondent), by the aimed at or perceived goals of the sampling (which may or may not be defined by national or local authorities) and by the spirit of times (which may or may not be in favour of multiculturalism). These problems become even more evident in a school-related context of pupils as respondents. Apart from the problems mentioned, the answers may be coloured by peer group pressure and the pupils' answers may lead to interpretation problems in attempts to identify and classify languages on the basis of the answers given. For a discussion of these and other possible effects we refer to Nicholas (1992) and Alladina (1993). The problems referred to are inherent characteristics of large-scale data gathering through questionnaires about language-related behaviour and can only be compensated by small-scale data gathering through observing actual language behaviour. Such small-scale ethnographic research is not an alternative solution to large-scale language surveys, but a potentially valuable complement. For a discussion of (cor)relations between reported and measured bilingualism of IM children in the Netherlands we refer to Broeder and Extra (1998).

Throughout the EU it is common practice to present data on regional minority (henceforward RM) groups on the basis of (home) language and/or ethnicity and to present data on IM groups on the basis of nationality and/or country of birth (see Extra and Gorter 2001). However, convergence between these criteria for the two groups appears over time, due to the increasing period of migration and minorization of IM groups in EU countries. Due to their prolonged/permanent stay, there is strong erosion in the utilization of nationality or birth country statistics. Given the decreasing significance of nationality and birth country criteria in the European context, the combined criteria of self-categorization and home language use are potentially promising alternatives for obtaining basic information on the increasingly multicultural composition of European nation states. The added value of home language statistics is that they offer valuable insights into the distribution and vitality of home languages across different population groups and thus raise the awareness of multilingualism.

Empirically collected data on home language use also play a crucial role in the context of education. Such data will not only raise the awareness of multilingualism in multicultural schools; they are in fact indispensable tools for educational policies on the teaching of both the national majority language as a first or second language and the teaching of minority languages. Obviously, a cross-national home language database would offer interesting comparative opportunities from each of these perspectives.

Sociolinguistic perspectives

In this section our focus is on the distribution and vitality of IM languages across different European nation states. Most sociolinguistic minority studies deal with RM languages rather than IM languages. In the former domain, however, we are faced with much diversity in the quality of the data. In some European countries, fairly accurate figures are available because a language question has been included in the census several times; in other cases, we only have rough estimates from insiders of the language group (usually language activists who want to boost the figures) or by outsiders (e.g. state officials who quite often want to downplay the number of speakers).

Given the overwhelming focus on processes of second language acquisition by IM groups, there is much less evidence on the status and use of IM languages across Europe as a result of processes of immigration and minorization. In contrast to RM languages, IM languages have no established status in terms of period and area of residence. Obviously, typological differences between IM languages across EU member states do exist, e.g. in terms of the status of IM languages as EU or non-EU languages (see Table 8.11), or as languages of formerly colonialized source countries. Taken from the latter perspective, e.g. Indian languages emerge in the United Kingdom, Arabic languages in France, Congolese languages in Belgium and Surinamese languages in the Netherlands. Most studies on IM languages in Europe focus on a spectrum of IM languages at the level of a particular nation state (e.g. LMP 1985; Alladina and Edwards 1991; Extra and De Ruiter 2001; Extra *et al.* 2002; Extra and Verhoeven 1993a; Caubet *et al.* 2002) or on one particular IM language at the national or European level (e.g. Obdeijn and De Ruiter 1998; Tilmatine 1997 on Arabic in Europe).

There are only few studies that take both a cross-national and cross-linguistic perspective on the status and use of IM languages in Europe (e.g. Jaspaert and Kroon 1991; Extra and Verhoeven 1993b, 1998; Fase *et al.* 1995; Ammerlaan *et al.* 2001). Extra and Gorter (2001) deal with both RM and IM languages from a European perspective. In this section we present the rationale, methodology, and first outcomes of the *Multilingual Cities Project* (MCP henceforth), realized in six major multicultural cities in different EU member states. The project has been carried out under the auspices of the European Cultural Foundation, established in Amsterdam, and it has been coordinated by a research team at Babylon, Centre for Studies of the Multicultural Society, established at Tilburg University, the Netherlands, in cooperation with local universities and educational authorities in all participating cities.

The aims of the MCP are to gather, analyse and compare multiple data on the status of IM languages at home and at school. In the participating cities, ranging from northern to southern Europe, Germanic and/or Romance languages have a dominant status at school and in public life. Figure 8.1 gives an outline of the project.

Due to processes of migration and minorization, all of these cities can be characterized as increasingly multicultural and multilingual. Apart from Scandinavian countries and to some extent Great Britain, there is no

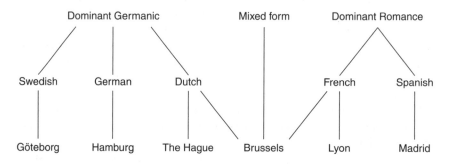

Figure 8.1 Outline of the Multilingual Cities Project (MCP).

European tradition of collecting home language statistics on multicultural (school) population groups. In fact, collecting home language data in some countries is even in conflict with present language legislation. This holds in particular for Belgium where traditional language borders have been legalized in terms of Dutch and/or French. Our method of carrying out home language surveys amongst primary school children in each of these cities partly derives from experiences abroad with nationwide or at least large-scale population surveys in which commonly single questions on home language use were asked. In contrast to such questionnaires, our survey is based on multiple rather than single home language questions and on cross-nationally equivalent questions. In doing so, we aim at describing and comparing multiple language profiles of major IM communities in each of the cities under consideration. For each language community, the language profile consists of five dimensions, based on the reported language repertoire (1), language proficiency (2), language choice (3), language dominance (4), and language preference (5). Derived from this database, we construe a (pseudo)longitudinal profile and a language vitality index for each language community. Our ultimate goal is to put these data in both cross-linguistic and cross-national perspectives. In sum, the rationale for collecting, analysing and comparing multiple home language data on multicultural school populations derives from three different perspectives:

- taken from a *demographic* perspective, home language data play a crucial role in the definition and identification of multicultural school populations;
- taken from a *sociolinguistic* perspective, home language data offer relevant insights into both the distribution and vitality of home languages across groups, and thus raise the public awareness of multilingualism;
- taken from an *educational* perspective, home language data are indispensable tools for educational planning and policies.

The questionnaire for data collection has been designed after an ample study and evaluation of language-related questions in nationwide or large-scale population research in a variety of countries with a history of migration and minorization processes (see Broeder and Extra 1998), and is also derived from extensive empirical experiences gained in carrying out municipal home language surveys amongst pupils both in primary and secondary schools in the Netherlands (see Extra *et al.* 2001, 2002). Table 8.5 gives an outline of the questionnaire.

In compliance with privacy legislation across different nation states, the database only contains home language data at the levels of municipalities, schools and grades; no data can be traced back to individuals. The answers to questions 9–12 make it possible to compare the status of birth country data and home language data as demographic criteria. The countries and languages explicitly mentioned in questions 9–12 are determined on the basis of the most recent municipal statistics about IM children at primary schools; thus, the list of languages for, e.g. Göteborg is quite different from the one used in Madrid. The language profile, specified by questions 13–17, consists of the following five dimensions:

- language repertoire: the number and type of (co-)occurring home languages;
- language proficiency: the extent to which the pupil can understand/speak/read/write the home language;
- language choice: the extent to which the home language is commonly spoken with the mother, father, younger and older brothers/sisters, and best friends;
- language dominance: the extent to which the home language is spoken best;
- language preference: the extent to which the home language is preferred to be spoken.

Table 8.5 Outline of the MCP questionnaire

Questions	Focus
1–3	personal information (name/code, age, gender)
4–8	school information (city, district, name, type, grade)
9–11	birth country of the pupil, father and mother
12	selective screening question ('Are any other languages than X ever used in your home? If yes, complete all the questions; if no, continue with questions 18–20')
13–17	language repertoire, language proficiency, language choice, language dominance and language preference
18–20	languages learnt at/outside school and languages demanded by pupils from school

The questionnaire has been tested on many occasions in the Dutch context. The Dutch questionnaire was translated into equivalent versions in French, German, Spanish and Swedish. It has also been tested in one primary school in each partner city. On the basis of the suggestions of local educational authorities and researchers, phrasing and wording of the questionnaires were further adapted. It was made sure that the basic questions on language were the same in all questionnaires. Basically, all six cities had the same questions, but one additional question on 'nationality' was added to the German questionnaire. This question was not included in any of the other cities.

Given the increasing role of municipalities as educational authorities in all partner cities, the project has been carried out in close cooperation between research groups at local universities and local educational authorities. In each partner city, this cooperation has proven to be of essential value. Table 8.6 gives an overview of the resulting database derived from the reports of primary school children in an age range of 4–12 years (only in The Hague were data also collected at secondary schools). The total cross-national sample consists of more than 160,000 pupils.

Local reports about the participating cities have been made available for Göteborg (Nygren-Junkin and Extra 2003), Hamburg (Fürstenau *et al.* 2003), The Hague (Extra *et al.* 2001), Brussels (Verlot *et al.* 2003), Lyon (Akinci *et al.* 2003) and Madrid (Broeder and Mijares 2003).

In this context, we focus on kernel outcomes of the project in The Hague as a case study. The Hague was chosen as the target city in the Netherlands because it belongs, together with Amsterdam, Rotterdam and

Table 8.6 Overview of the MCP database

City	Total of schools	Total of schools in the survey	Total of pupils in schools	Total of pupils in the survey	Age range of pupils
Brussels	117*	110*	11,500	10,300	6–12
Hamburg	231 public 17 catholic	218 public 14 catholic	54,900	46,000	6–10
Lyon	173**	42**	60,000	11,650	6–11
Madrid	708 public 411 catholic	133 public 21 catholic	202,000 99,000	30,000	5–12
The Hague	142 primary 30 secondary	109 primary 26 secondary	41,170 19,000	27,900 13,700	4–12 12–17
Göteborg	170	122	36,100	21,300	6–12

Notes
* Dutch-medium schools only.
** *Réseau d'Education Prioritaire* only.

Utrecht, to the four largest and most multicultural cities of this country. Table 8.7 gives a specification of the total database for both primary and secondary schools.

Both the coverage of participating schools/locations and pupils are substantial. All in all, 135 schools and 41,600 pupils in an age range of 4–17 years participated in the survey. Some of the key findings are:

- 49 per cent of all primary school pupils reported that apart from, or instead of, Dutch one or more other languages were used in their homes;
- the same holds for 42 per cent of all secondary school pupils;
- 88 other home languages than Dutch could be traced in the total population of 41,600 pupils;
- the 21 most frequently reported languages had a coverage of 96 per cent of the total amount of references to other languages than Dutch.

Table 8.8 gives the ranking of these 21 most frequently reported home languages. The distribution of languages is presented under three columns: primary and secondary schools are taken together and separately. In each column, the top five languages are the same but their order of occurrence is different in the primary and secondary school categories.

For each of these 21 languages, a (pseudo)longitudinal language profile has been specified in terms of the earlier mentioned dimensions, based on seven age groups. Moreover, for each language group tabulated information is presented on the total number of pupils per age group, the birth countries of the pupils and their parents, and the type and frequency of co-occurring home languages. In this way, the survey has created an unprecedented amount of information on multilingualism in The Hague.

Derived from the home language profiles of these 21 language groups, a cross-linguistic and pseudo-longitudinal comparison has been made of the four dimensions of language proficiency, language choice, language

Table 8.7 Overview of the database in The Hague

Educational context	Total	Sample	Proportion %
Primary education			
schools	142	109	77
locations	158	123	78
pupils	41,170	27,900	68
Secondary education			
schools	30	26	87
locations	51	43	84
pupils	±19,000	13,700	72

Table 8.8 Ranking of 21 most frequently reported home languages

Nr	Language	Total PS/SS	Total PS	Ranking PS	Total SS	Ranking SS
1	Turkish	4,789	3,666	1	1,123	2
2	Hind(ustan)i	3,620	2,339	2	1,281	1
3	Berber	2,769	1,830	4	939	4
4	Arabic	2,740	1,941	3	799	5
5	English	2,170	1,219	5	951	3
6	Sranan Tongo	1,085	514	7	571	6
7	Papiamentu	893	682	6	211	9
8	Kurdish	678	399	8	279	7.5
9	Spanish	588	381	10	207	11
10	Urdu/Pakistani	547	390	9	157	13
11	French	535	256	11	279	7.5
12	Chinese	419	245	12	174	12
13	German	402	194	14	208	10
14	Somalian	288	224	13	64	17
15	Javanese	262	111	18	151	14
16	Portuguese	199	127	16	72	15
17	Italian	166	120	17	46	20
18	Akan/Twi/Ghanese	152	134	15	18	21
19	Farsi	131	71	19	60	19
20	Moluccan/Malay	130	63	20	67	16
21	Serbian/Croatian/Bosnian	116	54	21	62	18

Notes
N > 100.
PS = primary schools.
SS = secondary schools.

dominance and language preference. For this analysis, these four dimensions have been operationalized as follows:

- language proficiency: the extent to which the home language is *understood*;
- language choice: the extent to which the language is spoken at home *with the mother*;
- language dominance: the extent to which the home language is spoken *best*;
- language preference: the extent to which the home language is *preferred* to be spoken.

The operationalization of the first and second dimension (language proficiency and language choice, respectively) is aimed at a maximal scope. Language understanding is generally the least demanding of the four language skills involved, and the mother acts generally as major gatekeeper for intergenerational language transmission. The final aim is the construction of a language vitality index (LVI). Since the concept of ethnolinguistic vitality was introduced by Giles *et al.* (1977), the focus has been on its determinants rather than on its operationalization. Determinants have been proposed in terms of non-exhaustive and non-mutually exclusive lists of factors, clustered in status factors, demographic factors, and institutional support factors, as in the case of Giles *et al.* (1977), or in additional factors such as cultural (dis)similarity, as in the case of Appel and Muysken (1987). Moreover, a distinction has been proposed between the objective status of these factors and their subjective perception by minority and/or majority groups (Bourhis *et al.* 1981; Van der Avoird 2001).

In our case, the operationalization of language vitality is derived from the construction of language profiles, based on the self-reports of school pupils, in function of our ambition to carry out both cross-linguistic and cross-national analyses of large databases. The four above-mentioned language dimensions are compared as proportional scores, i.e. the mean proportion of pupils per language group that indicate a positive response to the question under consideration. The ultimate LVI is, in its turn, the mean value of these four proportional scores. This LVI is by definition an arbitrary index, in the sense that the *chosen* dimensions with the *chosen* operationalizations are *equally* weighted. In this context, it should be mentioned that from a conceptual point of view the chosen dimensions are more closely related than in many other large-scale attempts to operationalize multiple human properties in terms of an index. An interesting case in point is the widely used *Human Development Index* (HDI), proposed by the United Nations in its annual UNDP reports. The HDI measures the overall achievements in a particular country in three basic dimensions of human development, i.e. life expectancy, educational achievement and income per capita. For each of these dimensions, an index of multiple values is created. The ultimate HDI is based on the average of the three dimension indices. Also in this case, the chosen dimensions with the chosen operationalizations are equally weighted (for details see Human Development Reports 2002).

In Table 8.9, we illustrate the four language dimensions and the resulting LVI per language group in decreasing order of vitality for the database of The Hague.

Turkish emerges as the most vital IM language. Its status is only shared by Somalian and Farsi, in spite of the fact that Turkish has a longer intergenerational status as a language of immigration and minorization in the Netherlands. A remarkable outcome is also the higher vitality of Berber compared to Arabic; both languages occur and/or co-occur as home languages of the Moroccan community in the Netherlands. A relatively low vitality emerges for those languages that have been in contact with Dutch abroad as a language of colonization, in particular Hindustani (in Surinam), Moluccan Malay (in Indonesia), Sranan Tongo (in Surinam) and Javanese (in Indonesia). Papiamentu (spoken on the Dutch Antillean Islands) withdraws, however, from this general colonial picture. Relatively low vitality indexes finally emerge for English, French, German and

Table 8.9 Language vitality index per language group, based on mean value of four language dimensions (in %)

Language group	N pupils	Language proficiency	Language choice	Language dominance	Language preference	Language vitality
Turkish	4,789	96	86	56	50	72
Somalian	288	92	88	57	53	72
Farsi	131	92	84	54	53	71
Chinese	419	94	82	52	48	68
Urdu/Pakistani	547	94	80	46	51	68
Berber	2,769	94	83	43	42	66
Serbian/Croatian/ Bosnian	116	84	62	43	52	62
Papiamentu	893	87	58	40	46	58
Akan/Twi/Ghanese	152	89	69	37	33	57
Arabic	2,740	89	60	38	42	57
Portuguese	199	82	58	28	41	53
Kurdish	678	85	58	31	31	51
Spanish	588	84	53	25	36	51
Hind(ustan)i	3,620	89	40	18	30	44
English	2,170	83	29	21	37	42
Moluccan/Malay	130	74	39	14	30	42
French	535	68	32	19	25	37
Italian	166	67	30	14	26	37
Sranan Tongo	1,085	82	28	15	34	37
German	402	77	24	14	20	34
Javanese	262	73	23	6	16	28

Italian; in particular the three former languages have a higher vitality at school than at home in the Netherlands, due to their status of obligatory or optional school subjects.

The aim of the Multilingual Cities Project is to make available kernel data on the status of IM languages at home and at school in the six multi-cultural cities mentioned in Figure 8.1. All municipal reports include kernel data on the distribution and vitality of IM languages at home and at school. Moreover, we aim at analysing all municipal data from both cross-national and cross-linguistic perspectives. The outcomes of the municipal studies are made available in six local reports. The outcomes of the cross-national study will be made available in a comprehensive report in English.

Educational perspectives

In this final section, we present the major outcomes of a comparative study on the status quo of teaching IM languages in six EU countries, based on document analysis and on oral or written information supplied by key informants, as carried out by Broeder and Extra (1998). Being aware of cross-national differences in denotation, we will use the notion *community language teaching* (henceforward CLT) when referring to this type of education in the countries under discussion. Our rationale for the CLT concept rather than the concepts *mother tongue teaching* or *home language instruction* is motivated by the inclusion of a broad spectrum of potential target groups. First of all, the status of an IM language as 'native' or home language can change through intergenerational processes of language shift. Moreover, in secondary education, both minority and majority pupils are often *de jure* (although seldom de facto) admitted to CLT (in the Netherlands, for example, Turkish is a secondary school subject referred to as 'Turkish' rather than 'home language instruction'; see also the concept of *Enseignement des Langues et Cultures d'Origine* versus *Enseignement des Langues Vivantes* in French primary versus secondary schools).

The focus of Broeder and Extra (1998) is on three countries with relatively large numbers of IM groups (Germany, France, Great Britain), on two countries which partially share their language of public use (the Netherlands and Flanders/Belgium) and on one of the Scandinavian countries (Sweden). In all the countries involved in this study, there has been an increase in the number of IM pupils who speak a language at home other than or in addition to the dominant school language in primary and secondary education. The schools have responded to this home-school language mismatch by paying more attention to the learning and teaching of the national standard language as a second language. A great deal of energy and money is being spent on developing curricula, teaching materials and teacher training for second language education. CLT stands out in stark contrast to this, as it is much more susceptible to an ideological debate about its legitimacy. While there is consensus about the necessity of investing in second language education for IM pupils, there is a lack of such support for CLT. IM languages are commonly considered sources of problems and deficiencies, and are rarely seen as sources of knowledge and enrichment. Policy-makers, headteachers, and teachers of 'regular' subjects often have reservations or negative attitudes towards CLT. On the other hand, parents of IM pupils, CLT teachers, and IM organizations often make a case for having IM languages in the school curriculum. These differences in top-down and bottom-up attitudes emerge in all the countries under consideration.

From a historical point of view, most of the countries in the Broeder and Extra study (1998) show a similar chronological development in their argumentation for CLT. CLT was generally introduced into primary education with a view to family remigration. In the 1970s, this argumentation was virtually abandoned. Demographic developments showed no substantial sign of families remigrating to their source countries; instead, a process of generation building and minorization came about in the target countries. This development resulted in a conceptual shift, and CLT became aimed at combating disadvantages. CLT had to bridge the gap between the home and school environment and to encourage school achievement in 'regular' subjects. Because such an approach tended to underappreciate ethnocultural dimensions, a number of countries began to emphasize the intrinsic importance of CLT from a cultural, legal and economic perspective:

- in cultural respects, CLT can contribute to maintaining and advancing a pluralist society;
- in legal respects, CLT can meet the internationally recognized right to language development and language maintenance, in correspondence with the fact that many IM groups consider their own language of key value to their cultural identity;
- in economic respects, CLT can lead to an important pool of profitable knowledge in societies which are increasingly internationally oriented.

The historical development of arguments for CLT in terms of remigration, combating deficiencies, and multicultural policy is particularly evident in some German states. In France and Great Britain, cultural policy is tied in with the respective national languages to such an extent that CLT is only tolerated in its margins. Taken from a historical perspective, cultural motives have played a more important role in Sweden. It should, however, be noted that multicultural arguments for CLT have not led to an educational policy in which the status of IM languages has been substantially advanced in any of the countries involved in this study.

The target groups of CLT in primary education are considered disadvantaged groups in virtually all countries focused upon in Broeder and Extra (1998); only Sweden has an explicit home language criterion rather than a socio-economic status or generation criterion for admission to CLT. Actual enrolment in CLT varies widely not only between countries (cf. enrolment figures in the Netherlands versus Flanders), but also between groups (cf. the enrolment percentages of Moroccan and Turkish pupils versus those of southern European pupils). Variation in enrolment is determined by a combination of factors, such as the attitudes of IM parents and pupils, and majority headteachers and teachers, and the geographical distribution of IM groups (which will decide whether or not numerical criteria can be met). As yet, comparative cross-national studies on the actual causes of this differentiated picture are not available.

There are remarkable differences in status between CLT in primary and secondary education in EU countries. A comparison of the parameters shown in Table 8.10 makes clear that CLT in secondary education has gained a higher status than CLT in primary education.

In primary education, CLT is generally not part of the 'regular' or 'national' curriculum, and, consequently, it tends to become a negotiable entity in a complex and often opaque interplay of forces by a variety of actors, in contrast with other curricular subjects. The higher status of CLT in secondary education is largely due to the fact that instruction in one or more

Table 8.10 Status of CLT in European primary and secondary education

CLT parameters	Primary education	Secondary education
Target groups	• *de jure*: mostly IM pupils from specified source countries • de facto: mostly subset of IM pupils	• *de jure*: mostly all pupils • de facto: mostly subset of IM pupils
Arguments	mostly in terms of a struggle against deficits: • bridging the home/school gap • promoting school success in other ('regular') subjects rarely multicultural policy: • promoting cultural pluralism • promoting knowledge of languages in a multicultural and globalizing society	mostly multicultural policy: • promoting cultural pluralism • promoting knowledge of languages
Objectives	rarely specified skills to be reached with CLT	commonly specification of oral and written skills to be reached with CLT
Evaluation	rarely judgement/report figure for CLT: 'language' in school report = national standard language	examination and report figure for CLT: national standard language is explicitly referred to and separately evaluated in school report
Minimal enrolment	relatively high number of pupils: specified per class, school or municipality	relatively low number of pupils: specified per class, school or municipality
Curricular status	not perceived as 'regular' education: instead of other subjects or at extra-curricular hours	regular optional subject in regular free timetabled space
Funding	• by national, regional or local authorities • by consulates/embassies of source countries	by national, regional or local authorities
Teaching materials	rarely originating from country of settlement, often from abroad/source country	commonly originating from country of settlement

Source: Broeder and Extra 1998: 107.

languages other than the national standard language is a traditional and regular component of the (optional) school curriculum, whereas primary education is highly determined by a monolingual habitus (see Gogolin 1994). *Within* secondary education, however, CLT must compete with languages that, in their turn, have a higher status or a longer tradition. The hierarchy of languages in secondary education is schematically represented in Table 8.11 in six categories with descending order of status. The overlap between categories three and five has remarkable consequences for the upgraded status of southern European languages as IM languages in northwestern Europe. With regard to category six, it should be noted that some countries provide instruction and/or exams in non-standard language varieties. In France, for instance, pupils can take part in examinations for several varieties of Arabic and Berber (see Tilmatine 1997); Dutch schools provide instruction in Moluccan Malay (as an alternative to Bahasa/Indonesian) and Sweden offers Kurdish (as an alternative to Turkish).

Table 8.11 Hierarchy of languages in secondary education, in descending order of status (categories 1–6)

	1	2	3	4	5	6
English	+		+			
French		+	+			
German		+	+			
Danish			+			
Dutch			+			
Swedish			+			
Finnish			+		+	
Portuguese			+		+	
Spanish			+		+	
Italian			+		+	
Greek			+		+	
Basque				+		
Frisian				+		
Gaelic				+		
Arabic					+	
Turkish					+	
Berber						+
Kurdish						+

Notes
1 Often compulsory subject.
2 Often optional subject as 'second foreign language'.
3 National languages of EU countries, often supported by positive action programmes at the EU level.
4 Regional minority languages, often supported by positive action programmes in the region and/or at the EU level.
5 Immigrant minority languages, often offered to immigrant minority pupils only.
6 Rarely offered non-standardized immigrant minority languages.

Another remarkable fact is that in some countries (particularly France, Belgium, and some German federal states), CLT in primary education is funded by the consulates or embassies of the countries of origin concerned. In these cases, the national government does not interfere in the organization of CLT, or in the requirements for, and the selection and employment of teachers. A paradoxical consequence of this phenomenon is that the earmarking of CLT budgets is often safeguarded by the above-mentioned consulates or embassies. National, regional or local governments often fail to earmark budgets, so that funds meant for CLT may be appropriated for other educational purposes.

CLT may be part of a largely centralized or decentralized educational policy. In the Netherlands, national responsibilities and educational funds are gradually being transferred to the municipal level. In France, government policy is strongly centrally controlled. Germany has devolved governmental responsibilities chiefly to the federal states with all their mutual differences. Sweden grants far-reaching autonomy to municipal councils in dealing with educational tasks and funding. In Great Britain, there is a mixed system of shared national and local responsibilities (cf. the ministerial guidelines for special target groups versus the guidelines of the local educational authorities).

In general, comparative cross-national references to experiences with CLT in the various EU member states are rare (e.g. Reich 1991, 1994; Reid and Reich 1992; Fase 1994; Tilmatine 1997; Broeder and Extra 1998), or they focus on particular language groups (e.g. Tilmatine 1997; Obdeijn and De Ruiter 1998). With a view to the demographic development of European nation states into multicultural societies and the similarities in CLT issues, more comparative research would be desirable.

As yet, language policy in Europe has largely been considered as a domain which should be developed within the national boundaries of the different EU member states. Proposals for an overarching EU language policy are laboriously achieved and non-committal in character (see Coulmas 1991). The most important declarations, recommendations or directives on language policy, each of which concepts carry a different charge in the EU jargon, concern the recognition of the status of (in the order mentioned):

- national EU languages as first, second or foreign languages;
- 'indigenous' or RM languages;
- 'non-territorial' or IM languages.

On numerous occasions, the EU ministers of education have declared that the EU citizens' knowledge of languages should be promoted (see Baetens Beardsmore 1993). Each EU member state should promote pupils' proficiency in at least two 'foreign' languages, and at least one of these languages should be the official language of one of the EU states.

The European Year of Languages, celebrated in 2001 in cooperation between the European Commission and the Council of Europe, gave new impetus and visibility to European activities in this domain by a whole variety of activities. Among the most important ones, in February 2002, were the Education Council's adoption of a detailed working programme on improving foreign language learning and the plea for the promotion of language diversity and language learning. At the Barcelona European Council of March 2002, the heads of state and government of all 15 EU member states called for further action to improve the mastery of basic skills, in particular by teaching at least two foreign languages from a very early age.

Promoting knowledge of RM and/or IM languages has not been included in these statements. The European Parliament, however, accepted various resolutions which recommended the protection and promotion of RM languages and which led to the foundation of the *European Bureau for Lesser Used Languages* in 1982. Meanwhile, the Bureau has member state committees in almost all EU countries and it has recently acquired the status of *non-governmental organization* (NGO) at the levels of the Council of Europe and the United Nations. Another result of the European Parliament resolutions is the foundation of the European MER-CATOR Network, aimed at promoting research on the status and use of RM languages. In March 1998, the *European Charter for Regional or Minority Languages* came into operation. This Charter was framed by the Council of Europe in 1992 and it has been ratified by an increasing number of member states. The Charter is aimed at the protection and promotion of RM languages, and it functions as an international instrument for the comparison of legal measures and other facilities of the EU member states in this policy domain.

As yet, no such initiatives have been taken in the policy domain of IM languages. It is a remarkable phenomenon that the teaching of RM languages is generally advocated for reasons of cultural diversity as a matter of course, whereas this is rarely a major argument in favour of teaching IM languages. In various EU countries, the 1977 guideline of the Council of European Communities on education for IM children (*Directive 77/486*, dated 25 July 1977) has promoted the legitimization of CLT and occasionally also its legislation (see Reid and Reich 1992; Fase 1987). Meanwhile, this guideline is totally outdated. It needs to be put in a new and increasingly multicultural context, it needs also to be extended to pupils originating from non-EU countries, and it needs to be given greater binding force in the EU member states. The increasing internationalization of pupil populations in European schools, finally, requires a language policy for *all* school children in which the traditional dichotomy between foreign language instruction for indigenous majority pupils and home language instruction for IM pupils is put aside.

There is a great need for educational policies in Europe that take new realities about transnational multiple identities and multilingualism into account. Processes of both convergence and divergence should be dealt with. The former relate in particular to the increasing status of English as lingua franca for international communication, the latter to the emergence of 'new' minority languages next to 'old' and established ones across Europe. At the request of the European Commission, the Language Policy Unit (2002) of the Directorate General for Education and Culture drafted a working document for consultation with at least three remarkable pleas. The first plea is to accept the idea of English as lingua franca ('shared medium') for cross-national communication in an enlarging Europe. Within Europe, English is rapidly gaining ground as the first foreign language in education, and is thus displacing other languages traditionally taught in European schools. The second plea is to enlarge the range of languages other than English to choose from, given the widely advocated idea that our learning institutions should be places that 'celebrate' linguistic and cultural diversity. And the third plea is the creation of an inclusive view of languages. The range of languages on offer should include both smaller and larger national European languages, RM and IM languages in Europe, and the languages of Europe's major trading partners throughout the world.

Derived from an overarching and inclusive conceptual framework, *priority languages* should be specified for the development of curricula, teaching methods and teaching training programmes. Such activities should be part of a common referential framework. Both in Europe and abroad much experience has been gained in specifying language proficiency targets (cf. the European Council *Framework of Reference* for determining different language proficiency levels). Underscoring the oft-announced plea for the learning of three languages by all EU citizens, we suggest the following principles for the implementation of this plea at the primary school level:

1   In the primary school curriculum three languages are introduced for all children:

   - the standard language of the particular nation state as a major school subject and language of communication across other school subjects;
   - English as lingua franca for international communication;
   - an additional third language opted from a variable and varied set of priority languages at the national, regional and local level of the multicultural society.

2   The teaching of all these languages is part of the regular school curriculum and subject to educational inspection.

3   Regular primary school reports contain information on the children's proficiency in each of these languages.

4   National working programmes are established for the priority languages referred to under (1) in order to develop curricula, teaching methods, and teacher training programmes.

5   Part of these priority languages may be taught at specialized language schools.

Given the experiences abroad (e.g. the Victorian School of Languages in Melbourne, Australia), language schools can become expertise centres where a variety of languages are taught, if the children's demand is low and/or spread over many schools. In line with the proposed principles for primary schooling, similar ideas could be worked out for secondary schooling where learning more than one language is an established practice. The above-mentioned principles would recognize multilingualism in an increasingly multicultural environment as an asset for all children and for the society at large. For further inspiration on the concepts proposed we refer to *Multilingualism for All* (Skutnabb-Kangas 1995) and *The Other Languages of Europe* (Extra and Gorter 2001). The European Union, the Council of Europe, and the UNESCO could function as leading transnational agencies in promoting such concepts. The UNESCO *Universal Declaration of Cultural Diversity* (last update 2002) is highly in line with the views expressed here, in particular in its plea to encourage linguistic diversity, to respect the mother tongue at all levels of education, and to foster the learning of several languages from the youngest age.

References

Akinci, M.-A., De Ruiter, J. J. and Sanagustin, F. (2003) *Le plurilinguisme à Lyon. Le statut des langues à la maison et à l'école*, Paris: L'Harmattan.

Alladina, S. (1993) 'South Asian languages in Britain', in G. Extra and L. Verhoeven (eds) *Immigrant Languages in Europe*, Clevedon: Multilingual Matters: 55–65.

Alladina, S. and Edwards, V. (eds) (1991) *Multilingualism in the British Isles* (Volume 1: *The Older Mother Tongues and Europe*; Volume 2: *Africa, the Middle East and Asia*), London and New York: Longman.

Ammerlaan, T., Hulsen, M., Strating, H. and Yağmur, K. (eds) (2001) *Sociolinguistic and Psycholinguistic Perspectives on Maintenance and Loss of Minority Languages*, Münster and New York: Waxmann.

Appel, R. and Muysken, P. (1987) *Language Contact and Bilingualism*, London: Edward Arnold.

Baetens Beardsmore, H. (1993) *European Models of Bilingual Education*, Clevedon: Multilingual Matters.

Bourhis, R., Giles, H. and Rosenthal, D. (1981) 'Notes on the construction of a "Subjective Vitality Questionnaire" for ethnolinguistic groups', *Journal of Multilingual and Multicultural Development*, Volume 2: 145–155.

Broeder, P. and Extra, G. (1998) *Language, Ethnicity and Education: Case Studies on Immigrant Minority Groups and Immigrant Minority Languages*, Clevedon: Multilingual Matters.

Broeder, P. and Mijares, L. (2003) *Plurilingüismo en Madrid*, Madrid: Centro de Investigación y Documentación Educativa.

Caubet, D., Chaker, S. and Sibille, J. (eds) (2002) *Codification des langues de France*, Paris: L'Harmattan.

CBS (2000/2002) *Allochtonen in Nederland*, Voorburg/Heerlen: CBS.

Clyne, M. (1991) *Community Languages: the Australian Experience*, Cambridge: Cambridge University Press.

Coulmas, F. (1991) *A Language Policy for the European Community. Prospects and Quandaries*, Berlin: Mouton De Gruyter.

Directive 77/486 (1977) *Directive 77/486 of the Council of the European Communities on the Schooling of Children of Migrant Workers*, Brussels: CEC.

EuroStat (1997) *Migration Statistics 1996. Statistical Document 3A*, Luxembourg: EuroStat.

—— (2002) *Statistics in Focus. Population and Living Conditions, Theme 3 – 7/2002*, Luxembourg: EuroStat.

Extra, G. and De Ruiter, J. J. (eds) (2001) *Babylon aan de Noordzee. Nieuwe talen in Nederland*, Amsterdam: Bulaaq.

Extra, G. and Gorter, D. (eds) (2001) *The Other Languages of Europe. Demographic, Sociolinguistic and Educational Perspectives*, Clevedon: Multilingual Matters.

Extra, G. and Verhoeven, L. (eds) (1993a) *Community Languages in the Netherlands*, Amsterdam: Swets & Zeitlinger.

—— (eds) (1993b) *Immigrant Languages in Europe*, Clevedon: Multilingual Matters.

—— (eds) (1998) *Bilingualism and Migration*, Berlin: Mouton De Gruyter.

Extra, G., Aarts, R., Van der Avoird, T., Broeder, P. and Yağmur, K. (2001) *Meertaligheid in Den Haag. De status van allochtone talen thuis en op school*, Amsterdam: European Cultural Foundation.

—— (2002) *De andere talen van Nederland: thuis en op school*, Bussum: Coutinho.

Fase, W. (1987) *Voorbij de grenzen van onderwijs in eigen taal en cultuur. Meertaligheid op school in zes landen verkend*, Rotterdam: Erasmus Universiteit.

—— (1994) *Ethnic Divisions in Western European Education*, Münster and New York: Waxmann.

Fase, W., Jaspaert, K. and Kroon, S. (eds) (1995) *The State of Minority Languages. International Perspectives on Survival and Decline*, Lisse/Exton: Swets & Zeitlinger.

Fürstenau, S., Gogolin, I. and Yağmur, K. (eds) (2003) *Mehrsprachigkeit in Hamburg. Ergebnisse einer Sprachenerhebung an den Grundschulen in Hamburg*, Münster: Waxmann.

Giles, H., Bourhis, R. and Taylor, D. (1977), 'Towards a theory of language in ethnic group relations', in H. Giles (ed.) *Language, Ethnicity and Intergroup Relations*, London: Academic Press: 307–348.

Gogolin, I. (1994) *Der monolinguale Habitus der multilingualen Schule*, Münster and New York: Waxmann.

Human Development Reports (2002) HTTP:/hdr.undp.org/reports/global/2002/en/pdf/backone.pdf and <-backtwo.pdf>

Jaspaert, K. and Kroon, S. (eds) (1991) *Ethnic Minority Languages and Education*, Amsterdam/Lisse: Swets & Zeitlinger.

Krüger-Potratz, Jasper, D. and Knabe, F. (1998) *'Fremdsprachige Volksteile' und deutsche Schule*, Münster and New York: Waxmann.

Language Policy Unit (2002) *Promoting Language Learning and Linguistic Diversity*.

Commission Working Document for Consultation, Brussels: Commission of the European Communities, Directorate General for Education and Culture.

LMP (Linguistic Minorities Project) (1985) *The Other Languages of England*, London: Routledge and Kegan.

Nicholas, J. (1992) *Language Diversity Surveys as Agents of Awareness Raising and Change in Education*, University of London (thesis).

Nygren-Junkin, L. and Extra, G. (2003) *Multilingualism in Göteborg. The Status of Immigrant Minority Languages at Home and at School*, Amsterdam: European Cultural Foundation.

Obdeijn, H. and De Ruiter, J. J. (eds) (1998) *Le Maroc au coeur de l'Europe. L'enseignement de la langue et culture d'origine (ELCO) aux élèves marocains dans cinq pays européens*, Tilburg: Tilburg University Press, Syntax Datura.

Reich, H. (1991) 'Developments in ethnic minority language teaching within the European Community', in K. Jaspaert and S. Kroon (eds) *Ethnic Minority Languages and Education*, Amsterdam/Lisse: Swets & Zeitlinger: 161–174.

—— (1994) 'Unterricht der Herkunftssprachen von Migranten in anderen europäischen Einwanderungsländern', in A. Dick (ed.) *Muttersprachlicher Unterricht. Ein Baustein für die Erziehung zur Mehrsprachigkeit*, Wiesbaden: Hessisches Kultusministerium: 31–46.

Reid, E. and Reich, H. (1992) *Breaking the Boundaries. Migrant Workers' Children in the EC*, Clevedon: Multilingual Matters.

Roosens, E. (1989) *Creating Ethnicity. The Process of Ethnogenesis*, Newbury Park: Sage.

Skutnabb-Kangas, T. (ed.) (1995) *Multilingualism for All*, Lisse: Swets & Zeitlinger.

Tilmatine, M. (ed.) (1997) *Enseignment des langues d'origine et immigration nord-africaine en Europe: langue maternelle ou langue d'état?*, Paris: INALCO/CEDREA-CRB.

Van der Avoird, T. (2001) *Determining Language Vitality. The Language Use of Hindu Communities in the Netherlands and the United Kingdom*, Tilburg University (thesis).

Verlot, M., Delrue, K., Extra, G. and Yağmur, K. (2003) *Meertaligheid in Brussel. De status van allochtone talen thuis en op school*, Amsterdam: European Cultural Foundation.

Vermeulen, H. (1999) 'Essentializing difference? The census, multiculturalism and the multiracials in the USA', in M. Foblets and C. Pang (eds) *Culture, Ethnicity and Migration*, Leuven/Leusen: Acco: 81–98.

Verweij, A. (1997) *Vaststelling van etnische herkomst in Nederland. De BiZa-methode nader bekeken*, Rotterdam: ISEO.

9 Sweden as a multilingual and multicultural nation

Effects on school and education

Tore Otterup

Introduction

There are very few countries where the whole population has a common ethnic origin and speaks only one language. It would mean that these societies have developed in isolation with few contacts with other peoples, cultures and languages. To find examples of such countries in Europe we would need to look to the outer fringes of the continent, e.g. Iceland (Hoffman 1994). The normal situation both in Europe and in the rest of the world is that a country is multi-ethnic as well as multilingual. Through the centuries both peaceful and hostile contacts have been maintained between nations. Borders have been moved back and forth depending on who were the stronger militarily and for this reason today there are many different groups of people, cultures and languages represented within most nations. Another reason is the migration between countries which has taken place over the centuries and which has become even more common during recent decades. However, the fact that a country is multilingual does not necessarily mean that its inhabitants are all multilingual. In Sweden, like in many other countries, it is mostly the linguistic minorities, which have had to develop multilingualism to be able to handle contacts with the majority population, while the rest of the country has remained monolingual. Changes concerning these matters have taken place in later years, at least on an official level.

Sweden has for a long time considered itself to be a largely monolingual country with Swedish as the national language, in spite of both Saami and Finnish having been spoken in the northern parts of the country long before the Swedish language was established.[1] Since Sweden was governed from the south and the political power had its seat in Stockholm it was obvious that Swedish became the common language in the whole of the country. For many centuries, however, the original population in the northern parts of the country was left to look after itself because of the limited interest in its culture and languages shown by central government. It was not until the latter part of the nineteenth century that a more active Swedification process towards the Saami- and Finnish-speaking inhabitants was introduced.

There have always been linguistic minorities in Sweden and two languages, Saami and Finnish, are also indigenous languages. Other linguistic and cultural minorities have come to the country through migration,
e.g. Roma and Jews. The more important migration, however, that has
had a more far-reaching impact on the Swedish society has taken place
since the Second World War and today shows no signs of abating.

Early linguistic minorities

The Saamis are generally considered to be the original population of the
Nordic countries. Today they live in northern Norway, Sweden and
Finland as well as on the Kola peninsula in Russia but it is not possible to
establish the exact date of their arrival in these areas. What can be ascer-
tained is that 2,000 years ago the Saamis lived all over present-day Finland
as well as northern Norway and Sweden (Helander 1984). The Saamis
have always been nomads because their livelihood was mainly hunting and
fishing and later reindeer breeding. When Scandinavians in the south
during the sixteenth century began to expand into the northern territories the areas occupied by the Saamis were reduced which in time made
them abandon their nomadic lifestyle. Some moved south to find work
and it is estimated that there are today 20,000 Saamis in Sweden (Korhonen 1997) most of whom live in the two main cities Stockholm and Göteborg. Today only 1,500 Saamis get their livelihood from reindeer
breeding.

The Saamis were subject to an extensive Swedification process from the
latter part of the nineteenth century lasting up until the 1950s. During
recent years, however, the position of the Saami has been strengthened
through new laws and this applies in particular to the northern Saami,
which includes about 75 per cent of all Saami speakers in Sweden. The
northern Saami dialect has rapidly developed and is today used in Saami
language newspapers, in fiction and on TV (Korhonen 1997). The language now also has scientific and other more sophisticated uses. Saami for
educational purposes is also being developed. There are Saami schools in
northern Sweden where Saami is taught and where Saami culture has
been integrated in the curriculum. At the University of Umeå there are
also university courses in Saami specializing in Saami history and culture.

For centuries Sweden and Finland were united and in that period a
variation of Finnish, or a Finnish dialect, was spoken in northern Scandinavia. When the border was drawn up along the Torne River after the war
between Sweden and Russia during 1808–1809, a unified area was split in
two (Wande 1997). This did not mean that contact across the border
ceased. To this day Finnish is the dominating language in the countryside
on the Swedish side of the border whereas Swedish dominates in towns
and larger communities. It is estimated by STR-T (the Swedish
Tornedalians National Organization) that today 50,000–60,000 people

speak Tornedalsfinnish. Unlike the Saamis, the lifestyle of the Tornedalians has not diverged from that of the majority of the population which is why there have been no or few conflicts between them. However, during the latter part of the nineteenth century the dominating nationalist-Romantic movement – *one people, one nation, one language* – saw Finnish speakers as a problem (Boyd 2002). The loyalty of the Finnish-speaking Tornedalians was in doubt since other parts of Sweden where Finnish was spoken had become Russian after the peace treaty at Fredrikshamn in 1809. These fears led to a certain persecution of Finnish speakers and the use of Finnish was prohibited in various fields, such as education. Most of the churches in the area which had been using Finnish for a long time switched to Swedish early in the 1900s (Arnstberg and Ehn 1976). This Swedification process lasted about 100 years and led to the functional dominance of Swedish in the Torne Valley.

What distinguishes the Tornedalians from the majority population in the same area is above all their bilingualism (Tornedalsfinnish and Swedish). The Tornedalians have used Swedish in official contexts and Finnish in private (Jaakkola 1974). Younger Tornedalians tend to switch languages and opt for Swedish which has led to many of them moving south in search of employment. In spite of the negative attitude towards Tornedalsfinnish during the past 100 years, even amongst its own users, there is now a noticeable change of attitude towards the language. This group has developed greater self-confidence and there is a movement to establish an independent norm for written Tornedalsfinnish or *Meänkieli* (literally 'our language') as the language is more often referred to nowadays. Work on standardizing *Meänkieli* is ongoing and in 1992 a 10,000 word dictionary was published, *Meänkielen sanakirjo, Tornedalsk ordbok* (Kenttä and Wande 1992) as well as, a few years later, a Tornedalsfinnish grammar, *Meänkielen kramatiikki* (Kenttä and Pohjanen 1996). Hyltenstam (1999: 133) maintains that today's Meänkieli can justifiably be referred to as a language in its own right as opposed to a dialect thanks to the current standardization process.

Gypsies, or *Roma* as the group is now called in Sweden, have certainly lived in Sweden since the sixteenth century (Fraurud and Hyltenstam 1999). According to earlier sources Roma lived in Stockholm as early as 1512. They may even have been in Sweden as early as the fourteenth century as claimed in other older sources (cf. Etzler 1944). The Roma were looked down on both by church leaders and politicians, and laws were passed to segregate or forcefully remove them. An example is the decree from 1637 stating that Roma males should be hanged without trial wherever in the country they were found, and women and children expelled (Arnstberg and Ehn 1976: 85–86). It proved impossible to exterminate the Roma and instead they were expelled to the eastern area of Sweden, i.e. to Finland. In spite of continual persecution there were for centuries Roma in Sweden left from the original wave of Roma immigration as proven by the continuously issued decrees against gypsies. A certain amount of movement back and forth across the borders went on but in 1809, the year when the frontier between Sweden and Finland was drawn up, the Roma's freedom of movement was seriously curtailed and a group of Roma remained in Finland and they were permanently separated from Roma in the other Nordic countries (Fraurud and Hyltenstam 1999). After passports were abolished in 1954 between the Nordic countries a few thousand 'Finnish' Roma have crossed over to Sweden. Further immigration of Roma has come during recent years with refugees from south and east European countries, mainly from former Yugoslavia.

Because of the harsh conditions under which the Roma live they have had to develop mechanisms for protecting their identity. One such group-identifying mechanism is the Romani language itself which, against the odds, has been admirably preserved over time. There is little contact with the majority population and the contacts are only superficial, which means that Swedish has been learnt only to the extent that it is sufficient for everyday contacts with the majority population. However, most Swedish Roma can be considered bilingual. On the other hand, it is difficult to establish how many in Sweden today speak some form of Romani variety. One reason is the fact that Swedish population statistics do not register ethnicity, and the numbers, which have been quoted, are based on fairly vague calculations. According to the latest available figures from 1996 there are between 15,000–20,000 Roma in Sweden (SIV-NZR 1996).

Groups of Jews arrived in Sweden mainly during three periods. The first group came from central Europe from the latter part of the eighteenth century and settled mainly in the Stockholm area. The second wave of Jewish immigration started about 1870 and this time the Jews came from eastern Europe, especially Poland, Lithuania and Russia. In this period, the number of Jews in Sweden quadrupled and in 1910 it was estimated at about 6,000 (Zitomersky 1988). The next period of Jewish immigration came before, during and after the Second World War when many fled Nazi persecution. During the war Sweden's policy towards refugees was very restrictive, especially towards Jews from Germany, and for this reason very few arrived (Boyd and Gadelii 1999). By the end of the war approximately 10,000–12,000 mainly Yiddish-speaking Jews arrived (Gordon and Grosin 1973) who were in the main survivors from the concentration camps. Many of them later moved on to Palestine and the US but about one-third stayed which meant a revitalization of Yiddish in Sweden. In more recent years Jews have arrived due to events in eastern Europe, from Hungary in 1956, Czechoslovakia in 1968, Poland in the late 1960s and, during the 1990s, Russian Jews also arrived in Sweden.

These languages, along with Finnish, have attained a certain position in Sweden because of their long existence in the country. For that reason the Swedish government in 2000 ratified, if somewhat late, the Council of Europe convention on protection of national minority languages and the

European legislation of regional and minority languages (SFS 1999: 1175–1176). The national minority languages in Sweden number five: Saami (all varieties), Finnish, Meänkieli (Tornedalsfinnish), Romani (all varieties) and Yiddish. Three of these; Saami, Finnish and Meänkieli, have historically strong geographical concentration in the north of the country which means that they are also protected by special regional rules, and speakers of these three languages have the right to use them in all official and legal matters.

The new language minorities

Beside the historical linguistic minorities small groups of immigrants have arrived in Sweden through the centuries which introduced other languages and cultures into the country. In the Middle Ages German merchants established the Hanseatic League on the Swedish island of Gotland and in coastal towns. During the sixteenth and seventeenth centuries a large number of Finns arrived to work in the forests in the inhospitable regions along the border between Sweden and Norway. During the first part of the seventeenth century a few thousand French-speaking Walloons from southern Belgium were recruited to work in the mines and during the seventeenth century immigrants from England, Holland and Scotland arrived in Gothenburg where they settled as merchants. A century later when interest in French culture was at its peak, many Frenchmen arrived to work for the nobility. But these numbers were small and probably never totalled more than 20,000 people (Samuelsson 1999). During the following century and in the early twentieth century Sweden became a country of emigrants when more than a million Swedes emigrated to America.

Larger numbers of immigrants only started arriving after the Second World War. Europe was in ruins and in neutral Sweden industry was doing well but needed a larger labour force than was available in the country and import of labour started (Samuelsson 1999). Workers were recruited from Italy, Hungary, Austria and Greece as well as from Germany and Belgium. Many accepted and moved with their families to Sweden where on the whole they were well received by the population at large. During the 1960s a new wave of workers came from Yugoslavia and Turkey among other countries. Workers also arrived from the other Scandinavian countries and in particular from Finland, especially after 1954 when Scandinavia became a common labour market.

In 1967 new immigration laws[2] were introduced to reflect the economic downturn and immigrants from outside Scandinavia found it more difficult to enter the country. From the mid 1970s this type of immigration ceased altogether and the period of 'regulated immigration' was introduced (Migrationsverkets Statistik 2002) on the grounds that immigrants who had permission to stay in the country should be guaranteed living conditions of the same standard as native Swedes. At this time Sweden also tried to introduce a conscious and coherent immigration policy which involved a number of different measures supposed to benefit those immigrants who had already been allowed into the country. A large number of laws were passed which entitled the immigrants to have Swedish language lessons and for their children to have mother tongue tuition and extra support for learning Swedish. In the municipalities special immigrant services bureaus were established and immigrants received financial support for establishing their own cultural societies and for publishing magazines in their own languages (Samuelsson 1999). In addition, a special minister for migration was appointed.

From the mid 1970s refugees started arriving in Sweden from troubled countries such as Lebanon, Iraq, Iran and countries in Latin America. For years immigrants and refugees from countries outside Europe dominated but during the 1990s immigration from within Europe started again, mostly because of the war in the former Yugoslavia. As an example, in 1992 a total of 84,000 people sought asylum in Sweden (Migrationsverkets Statistik 2002) of whom 69,000 came from the former Yugoslavia, more than 3,000 from Iraq (mostly Kurds) and about 2,700 from the civil war in Somalia. The latest figures are from 2002 when the number of asylum seekers decreased to 33,000, of whom 9,100 came from the former Yugoslavia and approximately 5,400 from Iraq. This large and varied immigration during the past 50 years has led to 13 per cent of a population of 9 million being of foreign extraction (SI 1994). This has meant that a number of languages such as Arabic, Spanish, Persian, Kurdish and Bosnian are in use in Sweden today along with Swedish and the five national minority languages. Thus Sweden has become a multilingual country even though it has taken the population at large and the authorities a while to realize the fact and, in some quarters, also to accept it.

The effects of immigration on education

The waves of immigrants of the past decades have had a deep influence on education in Sweden. In virtually every school class in the country there will be one or more pupils of foreign extraction with a different language as his/her mother tongue. In some suburban areas it is possible to find 80–90 per cent of the pupils being of foreign extraction, sometimes even more. There are about 150 mother tongues represented in Swedish schools and about 15 per cent of the pupils were either born abroad or have parents who were both born abroad (Sveriges Officiella Statistik 2003). The ten main mother tongues in comprehensive schools 2002/2003, apart from Swedish, were:

1	Arabic	21,073
2	Bosnian/Croatian/Serb	14,829
3	Finnish	11,384

4	Spanish	10,207
5	Albanian	7,704
6	Persian	6,574
7	English	6,335
8	Turkish	5,102
9	Kurdish	4,832
10	Polish	4,262

(Sveriges Officiella Statistik 2003)

The realization that pupils with other mother tongues needed different and additional tuition to develop their knowledge of their second language, Swedish, as well as of other subjects, came fairly early. Swedish as a second language was introduced as an auxiliary subject and the migrant pupils were also offered mother tongue tuition, or home language tuition as it was called at this time, from the end of the 1960s.

Swedish as a second language

The aims of the subject *Swedish as a second language* were officially put very high from the very beginning. People of foreign extraction living in Sweden need to master their second language Swedish to such an extent that they can assert themselves on the labour market as well as in everyday life. They must be able to have social contacts with Swedes, be able to take part in cultural events in Swedish and be able to manage all contacts with the authorities (Tingbjörn 1994). Migrant pupils must achieve competence in the Swedish language up to a level comparable with native pupils of the same age. Through second language research it was already known that developing a second language represents a special learning process in many important ways different from both first language and foreign language acquisition (Viberg 1996). Unlike pupils who learn a foreign language the second language learners must not only learn a new language at school, they must also use their second language as a means of learning other subjects at school as well as for their general cognitive development. These facts necessitate good and efficient tuition in Swedish and these were also the reasons for the new subject Swedish as a second language which was introduced in school from the end of the 1960s. From the start it became an auxiliary subject which should be adjusted to the very many different needs of the pupils. The state gave subsidies for the tuition and in the early 1970s teacher training in Swedish as a second language started at certain universities. However, the new subject was taught very differently in different parts of the country since there was no special syllabus for it. The quality of the teaching therefore was very much dependent on headteachers' understanding of the subject, if any, and the number of teachers at hand educated in Swedish as a second language. Furthermore there was a political and ideological discussion going on for a long time among decision-makers, surprisingly unaffected by available research in second language acquisition, about the use of tuition in Swedish as a second language. It was not until 1995, after many years of political wavering, that Swedish as a second language became a subject in its own right with its own curriculum for all educational levels (SFS 1997: 599). The intention was to replace Swedish language with Swedish as a second language for the pupils concerned. The school decides which pupils are entitled to the tuition and so it is an obligatory and not an optional subject. But in spite of the fact that there now exist clear and distinct regulations for the subject the knowledge about them has not spread everywhere and still there are many pupils entitled to the special tuition who do not get it. Statistics show that 64,125 pupils were taught Swedish as a second language in comprehensive schools in the school year 2002/2003 (Sveriges Officiella Statistik 2003), which is 6 per cent of all pupils in comprehensive school but only 47 per cent of those pupils who are entitled to being offered this subject.

Mother tongue tuition

From the late 1960s all pupils with immigrant background were given the opportunity to be taught their own languages even though it was not compulsory for schools to offer this until 1977. In that year 'the home language reform' came into force which meant that educational authorities were obliged to provide mother tongue tuition on all levels for those pupils who wanted this option. At this time 'home language classes' for pupils belonging to the more numerous language groups were also introduced at junior and intermediate level where the instruction from the beginning was mainly in the mother tongue and then later gradually switched over to Swedish. This was a part of the immigrant policy which aimed for freedom of choice and integration and a pluralistic society which consciously rejected a 'Guest-worker policy' with remigration as its goal (Hyltenstam and Tuomela 1996). The motives behind the 'home language reform' were basically of two different kinds: the first aimed to strengthen ethnic or cultural identity and the second to support a normal linguistic, academic and general cognitive development in migrant and minority pupils. Mother tongue tuition was until 1985 open to all those in whose homes the mother tongue was used. Since then the rules for mother tongue tuition have become more restricted and now the claim that the language of the parents is used on a daily basis is called for.

In the late 1980s a lively debate about the quality, organization and general benefit of mother tongue tuition started. The debate was initiated mainly by political parties, which expressed general discontent and even hostility towards foreigners. These parties had developed as a result of the economic downturn at that time which necessitated substantial savings to be made within the public sector. Mother tongue tuition was considered too inefficient and too expensive and it was argued that immigrants instead should concentrate on learning Swedish. On the other hand defenders of mother tongue tuition, including linguists and researchers within the field of minority children's language development, argued that mother tongue tuition can be of importance both for the development of the mother tongue and Swedish as a second language. They also pointed out that mother tongue tuition is of great importance for developing academic knowledge and is an essential support for developing a confident ethnic identity (Hyltenstam and Tuomela 1996). The outcome of the discussions came in 1991 when changes to the regulations were made (Proposition 1990/1991: 18) so that mother tongue tuition will now be offered only if there is a minimum of five pupils requiring it. Schools are free to offer it if there are fewer than five pupils, which in practice very rarely happens. The restriction also resulted in mother tongue tuition being offered mainly in the afternoons after the regular school day. Altogether these changes led to fewer immigrant pupils opting for home language tuition, or mother tongue tuition as the official term is now since the 1997/1998 academic year. The restrictions do not apply to children speaking Saami, Tornedalsfinnish or Romani who receive the tuition even with fewer than five pupils in a group because of these languages' status as national minority languages.

During the 2002/2003 academic year more than 66,400 comprehensive school pupils received mother tongue tuition which is 54 per cent of the 136,000 pupils who are entitled to it (Sveriges Officiella Statistik 2003).

Academic success for minority pupils

In spite of the schools offering Swedish as a second language and mother tongue tuition, many pupils of foreign extraction do not achieve academic results which equal those of pupils with Swedish as their first language. According to statistics that the National Agency for Education presented in 2002 (Skolverket 2002b) altogether 25.4 per cent of the pupils in comprehensive school (ninth grade) did not pass in the subjects necessary for entering a national programme in upper secondary school. The differences in academic achievements were considerable between pupils with Swedish and pupils with foreign backgrounds. Thirty nine per cent of immigrant pupils did not pass in one or more of the compulsory subjects and for newly arrived immigrant pupils this figure was 66.2 per cent (Skolverket 2002a). For obvious reasons this latter group of pupils will have limited prospects of passing in all subjects at the same time as they are learning a new language. The same tendency can be seen in upper secondary school. The statistics from the academic year 2001/2002 presented by the National Agency for Education (Skolverket 2003a) show that 75 per cent of the pupils with Swedish backgrounds did pass the exams within the normal four years. For pupils of foreign extraction born in Sweden the corresponding figure was 64 per cent and for pupils with both parents born abroad as low as 56 per cent.

Sweden was one of the 32 countries taking part in the extensive survey PISA[3]-2000, initiated by OECD, where reading comprehension and proficiency in mathematics and natural science were compared among a quarter of a million 15-year-olds (cf. Statens Skolverk 2001). The Swedish pupils did achieve better than average in all three subjects tested in the survey. The National Agency for Education has made an evaluation of the results and finds that the Swedish educational system shows a high degree of equality when compared to other OECD countries (Skolverket 2003b). The variation in results between individual pupils as well as between schools is insignificant in an international perspective and the socio-economic status of the pupils has not had as great influence on the pupils' results as in many other countries. The investigators argue that these are proof of Sweden having one of the most equal educational systems among the participant countries.

One discouraging result, however, is the fact that there is a considerable gap between the achievements of native pupils and pupils of foreign extraction. This difference may not be significantly bigger than in the other OECD countries but considering Sweden's ambition to have one of the most *equal* educations in the world these results are considered far from satisfactory (Skolverket 2003b). In order to let politicians and decision-makers know whether the results are due to a school system that is ill-suited to minority pupils or if there may be other possible explanations, the Swedish National Agency for Education has made a more thorough analysis of the results of the PISA-survey (Skolverket 2003b). They find that differences in achievements between countries and different groups of pupils are due to many more factors than just the quality of teaching that pupils get. One suggested explanation is the fact that the Scandinavian countries have a more complicated immigration and integration situation than other countries in the investigation. During the 1990s Sweden, Denmark and Norway have had the largest amount of refugees of all the participating countries of which Sweden has received the greatest amount per capita. The Scandinavian countries have had ambitious immigration policies which have made the task of integration more difficult to handle, especially since the Swedish school system has suffered from public sector savings during the 1990s which has meant less support for newly arrived pupils.

The analysis also suggests that measures and strategies for decreasing the gap between the achievements of native and minority pupils probably must tackle the problem from a much broader perspective where not only the individual pupil is in focus but where the integration process of the whole family must be considered (Skolverket 2003a, b). The results show that factors such as segregation and the family's integration into society at large do affect the possibilities for pupils of foreign extraction to develop good reading abilities in Swedish.

Today there is some research being carried out into the situation of minority pupils in the Swedish school system. In view of the country's growing multi-ethnicity, pedagogical researchers, in particular, have wanted to investigate to what extent the school reflects this new society and if all pupils irrespective of ethnic background have equal opportunities and are treated according to their particular needs. I especially want to focus on three recent dissertations which all establish that there are problems in the attitudes which schools show towards minority pupils and that their situation is therefore not as good as it could be. Attempting to establish a link between their ethnicity and the difficulties experienced at school by immigrant children, Pirjo Lahdenperä (1997) made a study of 'reform programmes' for immigrant pupils. She found that more than half of the teachers (55 per cent) perceived the immigrant background of pupils as problematic and as a reason for their difficulties at school. About 83 per cent of the teachers regarded the pupils' problems in school as of their own making and only 16 per cent looked for explanations of these problems within the school system itself. And regarding the teachers' attitudes towards the pupils' immigrant backgrounds Lahdenperä (1997) found that 70 per cent of the teachers saw some aspect of the pupils' backgrounds or ethnicity as negative for their achievements in school. None of the teachers showed an altogether positive attitude towards the pupils' immigrant backgrounds.

Ing-Marie Parszyk (1999), in her dissertation '*A school for others*',[4] has made qualitative studies of minority pupils in a comprehensive school in a multi-ethnic housing area. The aim of the dissertation was to shed light on how immigrant pupils perceived their time at school, as related in the pupils' own stories about the attitude of teachers, parents and friends towards them. What Parszyk (1999) finds is that in spite of the fact that these pupils have been at school during a time when the official 'motto' was *a school for all*, most of the minority pupils think that it is *a school for others*. They report that in the school's atmosphere and in the attitudes of the teachers they feel that the school is not for them and that they are not good enough as pupils. The results that Parszyk (1999) has found indicate very strongly that something must be changed in the way the Swedish school system takes care of minority pupils.

The ethnologist Ann Runfors deals in her dissertation '*Pluralism, contradictions and margins*' (2003)[5] with the question of how the school defines and categorizes 'immigrant children'. Her aim is to describe and analyse the attention the school gives to the category 'immigrant children' and also to focus on how this attention creates certain living conditions for these children. Runfors' (2003) research is based on field studies in three different multi-ethnic schools in the outskirts of Stockholm. She found that the fundamental criterion for who was defined as an 'immigrant child' was if the pupil had a mother tongue other than Swedish. Otherwise this very heterogeneous group of pupils only had two things in common. One was the experience of having moved from one country to another and therefore having experiences formed outside of Sweden; and secondly the fact that they were categorized, referred to and treated as 'immigrant children' by the teachers themselves. Runfors (2003) found the same kind of attitudes towards the minority pupils in all three schools. To sum up, Runfors' study (2003) shows that those pupils who were defined as immigrant children by the school were also ascribed difference by the school and that this decreased these pupils' space of activity to a great extent. They seem to be seen for what they were *not* but were made invisible as the individuals they were. This is an example, Runfors (2003) says, of how a well-intended society, through well-intended positive actions like education, can in fact contribute to social alienation.

In order to find more recent research aiming to improve minority pupils' situation in school and ways to academic success for them, one has, however, to look outside of Sweden and to the international research arena. Some of these researchers' theories and results have also been received with interest and have to a great extent influenced the Swedish school debate. The Canadian Jim Cummins, for example, who for a long time has focused his studies on the challenges educators face in adjusting to classrooms where cultural and linguistic diversity is the norm, claims that the reason why minority pupils all too often fail in school can be found in the historically recurrent patterns of imperative power relations between dominating and subordinate groups. Such examples are the situation for the Aborigines in Australia, the Maoris in New Zealand, the Saami in Scandinavia, the Tornedalians and Roma in Sweden. A proof of the importance of power relations between majority and minority is the fact that the same ethnic group can fail and succeed in different countries, e.g. Finns in Sweden and the US or Koreans in Japan and the US (see Ogbu 1991).

Cummins (1996, 2001) expresses a positive belief in the school and its teachers and that they can contribute to the positive development of the minority pupils, their language acquisition as well as to their academic and identity development. One important condition for a change which would favour these pupils in school, Cummins claims (1996, 2001), is that teachers must become more conscious of the power structure in society as reflected in school. The interaction between teacher and pupil must recognize the pupil's cultural, linguistic and personal identity. According to Cummins these are the prerequisites for the pupil wanting to invest his identity in the learning process. The pedagogy that Cummins (1986, 1996) advocates for these means he calls 'transforming'. It is a sort of pedagogy which is aiming more at mutual interaction than in traditional pedagogy. Pupils should be inspired to analyse and to try to understand the social relations in their own lives and society around them. The teachers should therefore try to develop a critical way of understanding knowledge which should lead to action and change in conditions for the pupils. The overall object of this transforming pedagogy is to genuinely empower pupils, as regards both their identity and academic success. The ultimate objective is for the minority pupils to take charge of their own lives, to be able to make their own choices and to fulfil their plans for the future without being restricted by the identity ascribed to them by school and society. In this way, according to Cummins, the multilingual and multi-ethnic pupils are given the possibility to choose and to create their own identities.

It is in the complex interplay between personal, social, political and educational factors that we find explanations why pupils fail or succeed in school, Sonia Nieto (2000) claims. Like Cummins she sees possibilities for the school to create a more advantageous situation for minority pupils. In her book *Affirming Diversity* (2000) she investigates the necessity and the advantages of multicultural education in 12 case studies. The case studies are based on interviews with 12 young people of various ethnic backgrounds about their experiences from home, school and society and how these have affected their academic achievements. Nieto (2000) defines multicultural education in a socio-political context as follows:

> Multicultural education is a process of comprehensive school reform and basic education for all students. It challenges and rejects racism and other forms of discrimination in schools and society and accepts and affirms the pluralism (ethnic, racial, linguistic, religious, economic, and gender, among others) that students, their communities, and teachers reflect. Multicultural education permeates the schools' curriculum and instructional strategies, as well as the interactions among teachers, students, and families, and the very way that schools conceptualize the nature of teaching and learning. Because it uses critical pedagogy as its underlying philosophy and focuses on knowledge, reflection, and action (*praxis*) as the basis for social change, multicultural education promotes democratic principles of social justice.
>
> (Nieto 2000: 305)

According to Nieto (2000), affirming the pupils' cultural diversity is essential for the success of multicultural education and the solution to many of its problems. When the multicultural approach permeates all school activities, it can change and enrich the schooling of young people. Multicultural education involves the cultures, languages and experiences of all pupils and highlights the fact that the languages and cultures that children bring to school are resources for them as individuals, their families and the entire society. It insists that these resources be valued and affirmed. Nieto (2000) concludes that multicultural education is simply about good pedagogy since all good pedagogy takes pupils seriously, uses their previous knowledge as a base for continued learning and helps them to become critical and genuinely empowered citizens (see also Cummins above).

Wayne Thomas and Virginia Collier (1997, 2002) have made a longitudinal study of bilingual pupils' academic success in the US. Between 1982 and 1996 they followed the schooling of more than 42,000 pupils with mother tongue other than English in five different school districts from preschool until year twelve in different teaching programmes. The study focuses on academic success in all subjects and not only on proficiency in English. Thomas and Collier (1997) claim that the aim of the school for both minority and majority pupils must be to have the same possibilities of academic success at the end of their schooling.

In their substantial data Thomas and Collier (1997) can distinguish two different types of programmes; 'enrichment programmes and supportive programmes'. The 'enrichment programmes' have an additive approach and build on what the pupils already know while the 'supportive programmes' deal with helping the pupils out with whatever current problems they may have. Thomas and Collier (1997) maintain that it is only in the 'enrichment programmes' that minority pupils can develop their academic skills properly. The researchers count only two kinds of programmes; 'two-way developmental bilingual education'[6] and 'one-way developmental bilingual education',[7] as 'enrichment programmes'. In these programmes, which only involve about 10 per cent of the pupils studied, the bilingual pupil has the possibility to develop his cognitive ability and to learn in his both languages. These pupils also achieve better results than the average native English-speaking pupils after 11 years of schooling.

Thomas and Collier (1997) state that bilingual pupils who, during their first five to six school years, have had the chance to develop thinking and learning in their first language parallel to the same development in their second language will reach the same level as monolingual English-speaking pupils both linguistically and academically when they finish school. The researchers come to the conclusion that the more solid a pupil's cognitive and academic development is in his or her first language the faster he or she will make progress in the second. The more the children develop their first language cognitively and academically at an age-adequate level, the more academic skills they will have at the end of schooling. Therefore, Thomas and Collier (1997) see the possibility to develop the mother tongue in formal education at school for some length of time (five to six years) as the most important background factor for academic success in all the school districts studied.

Considering the results of Thomas and Collier (1997) one can argue that Sweden's early introduction of mother tongue tuition to minority pupils in school was a positive step, especially the launch of home language classes during the 1970s and 1980s. However, there are not many of these classes left today as a result of the extensive savings in the public sector during the 1990s. The results of Thomas and Collier's (1997) research, as well as Cummins' (1986, 1996, 2001) theories of empowerment, have had a considerable impact on teachers working in multi-ethnic and multilingual areas and today a greater awareness of the importance of the first language and its use in everyday school activities can be noticed. Many schools do now, for example, offer subject teaching in various mother tongues, such as mathematics in Arabic, geography in Somali or biology in Kurdish. The official authorities also seem to have understood the importance of offering teaching in the various mother tongues which exist in Sweden today. As an example, a report (*Mål i mun*) was presented in the spring of 2002 by the Committee for the Swedish Language (Kulturdepartementet 2002), suggesting how to strengthen the position of the language vis-à-vis English as well as stressing everybody's right to a mother tongue. The report further stresses that the existence of minority languages enriches the cultural life of the country and the importance of supporting the minority and immigrated languages in Sweden. The committee suggests that steps be taken to strengthen the position of Swedish as a second language in school and that equal steps should be taken to strengthen home language training in preschool and home language instruction in comprehensive and secondary school.

During the spring of 2002 the National Agency for Education (Skolverket 2002c) presented another report, *More Languages – More Possibilities*, which stresses the importance of mother tongue tuition in Swedish schools for three reasons; its importance for immigrant children to develop their own identity, the mother tongue as one of immigrant children's languages and, third, as an instrument for learning.

Conclusion

One condition for a country to be multilingual is that it values multilingualism and that it facilitates development and maintenance of multilingual competence (see Romaine 1995), otherwise multilingualism can be a handicap. Altogether, the above examples show that Sweden accepts, at least officially, that the country is multilingual by supporting and stimulating the development and preservation of foreign languages within the country. The most obvious example of this is the fact that Sweden ratified the Council of Europe convention on protection of national minority languages and the European legislation for regional and minority languages which has given Saami, Finnish, Meänkieli, Romani and Yiddish status as national minority languages. I have in this article also shown how the country has always been a multilingual country through its historical minority languages, but also through an early, if limited, immigration from different parts of Europe.

After ever increasing immigration during two decades the Swedish government decided in the middle of the 1970s to launch an immigration policy whose pronounced aim was to integrate immigrants into the Swedish society as well as aiming at a multicultural society. An example of this are the official aims of the immigration policy which were unanimously passed in the Swedish Riksdag in 1975 (Samuelsson 1999) and again in 1986 and 1991. These aims were expressed as equality, freedom of choice and cooperation. The 'equality' motto expressed that immigrants should have the same rights, obligations and possibilities as the rest of the population. Freedom of choice means, among other things, that the linguistic minorities in Sweden should be able to choose to what extent they want to maintain and develop their original cultural and linguistic identity or if they would want to have a Swedish identity. And cooperation stands for cooperation between immigrants and the majority population in matters of common interest. Of these three aims, which stood firm until 1998, the aim of freedom of choice was to become the most problematic one. What has been mostly discussed is to what extent it should be possible for immigrants to keep their ways of life and their cultures in the new country. This discussion has also contained the question whether mother tongue tuition in school is a good thing or not.

Research about and evaluations of home language tuition have stated that there have been problems with its organization and content, as well as its quality (Hyltenstam and Tuomela 1996). That difficulties arise when the school introduces a new and very complex teaching subject such as home language tuition is to be expected. One can only note that remarkably few attempts to solve these problems have been made by the responsible authorities which suggests that Swedish society has shown very little real interest in this tuition and that the whole field in actual fact has had low priority. It would seem as if the mere *existence* of the new teaching subject mother tongue tuition has been more important than its quality and actual significance for immigrant and minority children. Thus one could find reasons to question the seriousness of the Swedish society and its commitment to the pluralistic ideology. Should the launching of mother tongue tuition in Swedish schools be seen more as a symbolic act, something that creates a positive image, than a conscious step towards a truly multilingual and multicultural society?

Statistics show that many minority pupils' achievements in school are not as good as those of native Swedish pupils. The reasons for this have been analysed by, for example, the National Agency for Education (Skolverket 2003a, b) and they find that the explanations can not only be found in the way the Swedish school takes care of and integrates pupils of foreign extraction. The problem must be tackled from a much broader perspective. The integration of the whole family into society at large must also be taken into consideration. In the last few years the noticeable tendency is that Swedish society is becoming more and more segregated. People with foreign backgrounds can very often find flats only in certain housing areas where there already are many immigrants. Unemployment is also high among immigrants. Therefore the chances of integration have become worse. Many more or less successful attempts at a local level to counteract this situation have been made and the government also invests money in different projects to help immigrants get jobs and to break the ethnic segregation (Proposition 1997/8). What effects on the minority pupils' academic achievements these projects will have still remains to be seen.

Swedish schools today have many committed and competent teachers who have a good knowledge about second language acquisition and bilingualism. The subject Swedish as a second language can be studied at universities and in teacher training institutions and many students also choose to study it.

In spite of these facts Swedish schools could do more for the minority pupils. More adequate means of developing their languages, academic skills and identities should be found. What school above all must improve upon is the capability of seeing the pupil as a *whole* individual, with all his or her experiences, skills and languages and to recognize all these parts as equally important.

Notes

1 The Viking Age (approx. AD 600–1000) linguistically marks the transition from a common Nordic language to an individual Swedish language (Bergman 1968).
2 All non-Scandinavians had to have a valid working permit before entering the country. The rights for relatives to immigrate were also restricted (Samuelsson 1999).
3 PISA: Programme for International Student Assessment.
4 My translation. The Swedish title is *En skola för alla.*
5 My translation. The Swedish title is *Mångfald, motsägelser och marginaliseringar.*
6 In a two-way Developmental BE-programme half of the pupils have English as their first language and the other half another first language, e.g. Spanish. The pupils are taught half of the time in English and half of the time in Spanish, which means that all children in the class learn both in a first and a second language.
7 In a one-way Developmental BE-programme the minority pupils will be taught half of the school day in English and the other half in their first language. The majority pupils do not learn a second language.

References

Arnstberg, K.-O. and Ehn, B. (1976) *Etniska minoriteter förr och nu*, Lund: Liber Läromedel.
Bergman, G. (1968) *Kortfattad svensk språkhistoria*, Stockholm: Bokförlaget Prisma.
Boyd, S. (2002) 'Språken i Sverige', in E. Ahlsén and J. Allwood (eds) *Språk i fokus*, Lund: Studentlitteratur: 89–115.
Boyd, S. and Gadelii, E. (1999) 'Vem tillhör talgemenskapen? Om jiddisch i Sverige', in K. Hyltenstam (ed.) *Sveriges sju inhemska språk*, Lund: Studentlitteratur: 299–328.

Cummins, J. (1986) 'Empowering minority students: a framework for intervention', *Harvard Educational Review* 56 (1): 18–36.

—— (1996) *Negotiating Identities: Education for Empowerment in a Diverse Society*, Los Angeles: California Association for Bilingual Education.

—— (2001) 'Second language teaching for academic success: a framework for school language policy development', in K. Nauclér (ed.) *Symposium 2000 – ett andraspråksperspektiv på lärande*, Stockholm: Sigma Förlag: 324–344.

Etzler, A. (1944) *Zigenarna och deras avkomlingar i Sverige: historia och språk*. Stockholm Studies in Scandinavian Philology, Uppsala: Almqvist and Wiksell.

Fraurud, K. and Hyltenstam, K. (1999) 'Språkkontakt och språkbevarande: romani i Sverige', in K. Hyltenstam (ed.) *Sveriges sju inhemska språk*, Lund: Studentlitteratur: 241–298.

Gordon, H. and Grosin, L. (1973) *Den dubbla identiteten: Judars anpassningsmönster i historisk och psykologisk belysning*, Stockholm: GEBE Grafiska.

Helander, E. (1984) *Om trespråkighet*, Umeå universitet, Stockholm: Almqvist and Wiksell International.

Hoffman, C. (1994) *An Introduction to Bilingualism*, London: Longman.

Hyltenstam, K. (1999) 'Begreppen språk och dialekt – om meänkielis utveckling till eget språk', in K. Hyltenstam (ed.) *Sveriges sju inhemska språk*, Lund: Studentlitteratur: 98–137.

Hyltenstam, K. and Tuomela, V. (1996) 'Hemspråksundervisningen', in K. Hyltenstam (ed.) *Tvåspråkighet med förhinder? Invandrar- och minoritetsundervisning i Sverige*, Lund: Studentlitteratur: 9–109.

Jaakkola, M. (1974) *Språkgränsen*, Stockholm: Aldus/Bonniers.

Kenttä, M. and Pohjanen, B. (1996) *Meänkielen kramatiikki*, Aapua: Kaamos.

Kenttä, M. and Wande, E. (eds) (1992) *Meänkielen sanakirja: Tornedalsfinsk ordbok*, Luleå: Kaamos.

Korhonen, O. (1997) 'Hur samiskan blev samiska', in E. Westergren and H. Åhl (eds) *Mer än ett språk*, Stockholm: Nordstedts förlag: 79–115.

Kulturdepartementet (2002) *Mål i mun. Förslag till handlingsprogram för svenska språket*. SOU 2002: 27, Stockholm.

Lahdenperä, P. (1997) *Invandrarbakgrund eller skolsvårigheter? En textanalytisk studie av åtgärdsprogram för elever med invandrarbakgrund*, Stockholm: HLS Förlag. Institutionen för pedagogik, Lärarhögskolan i Stockholm.

Migrationsverkets Statistik (2002) www.migrationsverket.se.

Nieto, S. (2000) *Affirming Diversity: The Sociopolitical Context of Multicultural Education*, New York: Longman.

Ogbu, J. (1991) 'Immigrant and involuntary minorities: a cultural-ecological theory of school performance with some implications for education', in M. Gibson and J. Ogbu (eds) *Minority Status and Schooling: A Comparative Study of Immigrant and Involuntary Minorities*, New York: Garland Publishing.

Parszyk, I.-M. (1999) *En skola för andra: Minoritetselevers upplevelser av arbets- och livsvillkor i grundskolan*, Stockholm: HLS Förlag. Institutionen för pedagogik, Lärarhögskolan i Stockholm.

Proposition (1990/1991) 18, *Om ansvaret för skolan*, Stockholm: Utbildningsdepartementet.

Proposition (1997/1998) 165, *Utveckling och rättvisa – en politik för storstaden på 2000-talet*, Stockholm: Kulturdepartementet.

Romaine, S. (1995) *Bilingualism*, Oxford: Blackwell.

Runfors, A. (2003) *Mångfald, motsägelser och marginaliseringar*, Stockholm: Prisma.

Samuelsson, W. (1999) *Det finns gränser*, Stockholm: Utbildningsradion.

SFS (1997) 599, *Förordning om ändring i grundskoleförordningen (1994: 1194)*. Stockholm: Utbildningsdepartementet.

SFS (1999) 1175–1176, *Lagar om rätt att använda samiska, finska och meänkieli hos förvaltningsmyndigheter och domstolar*. Stockholm: Kulturdepartementet 2000.

SI (1994) *Immigrants in Sweden*. FS 63. Stockholm: Svenska Institutet.

SIV-NZR (1996) *Romer i Sverige: Situationsbeskrivning*. Rapport från Arbetsgruppen SIV-Nordiska Zigenarrådet, Januari 1996. Statens invandrarverk and Nordiska Zigenarrådet.

Skolverket (2002a) Resultatuppföljning 16–12, Stockholm.

—— (2002b) Pressmeddelande 12–18, Stockholm.

—— (2002c) *Flera språk – fler möjligheter – utveckling av modersmålsstödet och modersmålsunder-visningen*, Stockholm.

—— (2003a) Resultatuppföljning 02-03, Stockholm.

—— (2003b) *Läsförståelse hos elever med utländsk bakgrund – En fördjupad analys av resultaten från PISA 2000 i 10 länder*, Skolverkets rapport nr 227. Stockholm.

Statens Skolverk (2001) *PISA 2000: Svenska femtonåringars läsförmåga och kunnande i matematik och naturvetenskap i ett internationellt perspektiv*. Skolverkets rapport 1103-2421: 209, Stockholm.

Sveriges Officiella Statistik (2003) www.skolverket.se/fakta/statistik/sos/sos032/index.shtml.

Thomas, W. and Collier, V. (1997) *School Effectiveness for Language Minority Students*, NCBE Resource Collection Series, No. 9. George Washington University.

—— (2002) *A National Study of School Effectiveness for Language Minority Students' Long-Term Academic Achievement*, Washington DC: Centre for Research on Education, Diversity and Excellence.

Tingbjörn, G. (1994) *Svenska som andraspråk: En introduktion. Lärarbok 1*, Stockholm: Natur och Kultur.

Viberg, Å. (1996) 'Svenska som andraspråk i skolan', in K. Hyltenstam (ed.) *Tvåspråkighet med förhinder? Invandrar- och minoritetsundervisning i Sverige*, Lund: Studentlitteratur: 110–147.

Wande, E. (1997) 'Anteckningar om tornedalsfinskans historia', in E. Westergren and H. Åhl (eds) *Mer än ett språk*, Stockholm: Nordstedts förlag: 116–129.

Zitomersky, J. (1988) 'The Jewish population in Sweden, 1780–1980: an ethno-demographic study', in G. Broberg, H. Runblom and M. Tydén (eds) *Judiskt liv i Norden. Studia Multietnica Upsaliensia 6*, Uppsala: Acta Universitatis Upsaliensia.

10 Australia

Educational changes and challenges in response to multiculturalism, globalization and transnationalism

Christine Inglis

At the beginning of the twenty-first century major social, political and economic changes have led to the redrawing of the international map of ethnic diversity. Long-established ethnic minorities have experienced major changes in their situation and circumstances in their countries of residence while the growth of diverse forms of international population movements have introduced new patterns of ethnic diversity, often in countries which have viewed themselves as ethnically homogeneous. The growth and diversity in international migration occurs within the framework of globalization which, since the middle of the 1970s, has been associated with the expansion and diversification of international trade and the growth of multinational enterprises. Politically, globalization has been seen as calling into question the ability of individual states to control developments within their own territory. Globalization, through the increasing technical and institutional ability to transmit cultural practices and content, is also implicated in undermining the cultural autonomy and distinctiveness of individual societies. Whereas globalization is an abstract process focusing internationally on political, economic and cultural institutions, transnationalism refers to the specific movements and relationships of people and groups which link individuals from common ethnic backgrounds across national borders. The impact of these changes in ethnic diversity and the relationships associated with globalization and transnationalism have been felt both in long established and homogeneous states and in countries which have traditionally been viewed as countries of immigration, open to the entry of ethnically diverse populations. Australia is one such country whose national development has long been predicated on extensive immigration which has been actively controlled and managed by the state. How the state, and society, have responded to the new circumstances and challenges is the focus of this chapter.

Before examining in detail how Australia's experiences of immigration and incorporation and educational responses to diversity have changed in recent decades it is important to identify the historical background and context for these developments. While often grouped together with the United States, Canada and New Zealand as a white settler colony with shared British institutional traditions, Australia's settlement and subsequent development as a country of immigration has certain characteristics which distinguish it from these countries and which are relevant to discussions of educational responses. These include its patterns of ethnic diversity and the role of the state in policy-making.

Compared to Canada and the United States, British migration to Australia has been relatively more important, especially in the first half of the twentieth century. As a result, prior to the commencement of the mass migration programme at the end of the Second World War, Australia was a remarkably homogeneous society. While immigration from the United Kingdom continues at a reduced level, immigration from other countries has changed over time as the early arrivals from eastern and northern Europe were followed by immigrants from southern Europe, the Middle East and then Asia. Many of these individuals are from non-English speaking backgrounds and 20 per cent of the population speak a language other than English at home. However, apart from those of Anglo-Celtic background, Australia has no sizeable ethnic minorities comparable to the French in Canada or the Spanish in the United States. The diverse, and changing origins of Australia's immigrant population and the absence of mono-ethnic residential concentrations, imposes on individual educational institutions the need to cater for students from many different national and linguistic backgrounds. The issue of how to address extensive diversity within a single school or other educational setting, often with only small numbers of students from a particular background, is an enduring feature of Australian educational debates about provisions for diversity.

During the nineteenth century, governments in each of the Australian colonies played an active role in many areas of economic development and social life, including education and migration. Following federation in 1901, the state governments of the six former colonies retained control of education, operating what are, by international standards, large and highly centralized, public education systems. This has implications for the ways in which extensive change is highly dependent on government initiatives. In recent decades, the Commonwealth government has played an increasingly important role in education through its control of funds to state governments which are often required to use them for specific educational programmes and initiatives identified by the Commonwealth. Through this use of its financial power the Commonwealth government can integrate educational policies with other national policies concerning migration, incorporating diversity and the economy.

Changing Australian patterns of migration

During the second half of the twentieth century Australia underwent a transformation from a predominantly Anglo-Celtic, British society to one characterized by increasing diversity. Australia's population has increased from 7.4 million people in 1947 to 20 million people in 2003. Of the 19 million people living in Australia at the time of the 2001 census, 22 per cent were immigrants born outside Australia while another 18 per cent born in Australia had at least one immigrant parent. Major foreign birthplaces were the United Kingdom (5.5 per cent), New Zealand (1.9 per cent), Italy (1.2 per cent) Vietnam and China (0.8 per cent), Greece and Germany (0.6 per cent) and the Philippines (0.5 per cent). Although English remained the dominant language with 79 per cent of the population speaking only English, the range of other languages spoken in the home is extremely diverse. The major language after English is now Chinese, spoken by 2.1 per cent of the population followed by Italian (1.9 per cent), Greek (1.4 per cent), Arabic (1.1 per cent) and Vietnamese (0.9 per cent). The prominence of non-European languages is a recent phenomenon which reflects the growing importance of Middle Eastern and Asian migration since the 1970s.

The initial origins of this population growth and ethnic diversity was the government's decision after the Second World War to institute a programme of mass migration to increase Australia's population by 1 per cent per year. This was to facilitate the post-war reconstruction of the economy, especially the development of manufacturing. Migration was to provide the workers and consumers underpinning the new economy. A larger population was also seen as making Australia less vulnerable to a military attack. The initial expectation was that migrants would come predominantly from the United Kingdom but, when sufficient numbers were not available, the government pragmatically turned to other sources beginning with eastern European refugees, followed by migrants from Germany and the Netherlands, then Italy, Greece and Yugoslavia in southern Europe and, eventually, Turkey and Lebanon in the Middle East. Over the same period there was also a gradual relaxation of the White Australia Policy which had restricted migration from Asia. The election of a Labour Party government in 1972 after two decades of conservative government was a major watershed. The preference for British immigrants, including preferential access to the rights of citizenship was abolished as, also, was the White Australia Policy. They were replaced by non-discriminatory immigration and citizenship policies which allowed migration and naturalization without reference to the individual's country of origin, race, ethnicity or religion. Underlying the changes was a redefinition of the national interest. The United Kingdom, the former colonial power, had signalled its own redirection by joining the European Economic Community. Also, in the post-colonial world, potential economic partners and diplomatic allies, such as the newly independent nations in Asia, resented discriminatory immigration policies based on ethnicity.

If the 1970s was the decade when Australia finally abandoned an immigration policy based on an individual's country of origin or their ethnicity, the major change in the 1980s was a shift in the preferred economic characteristics of migrants. Whereas in the post Second World War period the emphasis was on labour to work in factories and on major infrastructure projects, in the 1980s migration policy began to favour highly skilled professionals able to contribute to another major restructuring of the economy. This new restructuring was intended to reposition the Australian economy to better cope with the challenges posed by globalization and economic growth, especially in the neighbouring Asian region, where cheap labour costs threatened Australia's labour intensive manufacturing industries. The government's aim in restructuring was to develop the capacity of its service industries including tourism but, especially, the high level financial services and knowledge-based sectors, including education. An indication of the success of this strategy is that in terms of export earnings both tourism and the sale of educational services have now become major contributors to the Australian economy. With income from the training of overseas students in excess of $5 billion Australian dollars in 2002–2003, education is now Australia's third largest services export. Some of these educational services are provided in other countries but, in Australia, international students now constitute one-quarter of all university students. Far fewer international students attend school in Australia and enrolments are concentrated at the upper levels of secondary schooling as many students seek entry to Australian universities on the basis of their performance in the competitive Australian examinations held at the end of secondary school. In addition to these secondary and tertiary level students who are accommodated within the existing education system, many students also attend private English language teaching centres set up specifically to cater for international students.

Paralleling domestic initiatives to increase the educational skills of its existing population, the focus of immigration policies in the 1980s shifted from favouring migrants with family members resident in Australia. Increasingly since then preference has been given to individuals possessing tertiary education and professional experience, especially when they also are fluent in English, which is a necessity if they are to work at their appropriate professional level in Australia. The importance of Australian qualifications and experience for gaining appropriate employment led to an important recent change in entry policy. This allows graduates of Australian universities to apply for permanent residence in Australia without being required to return to their countries of origin. Now, more than half of all applications for permanent residence on the basis of economic skills come from this group of former students. The effect of these changes in immigration policy is a significant change in the class and educational background of Australian immigrants. Whereas in the 1950s and 1960s substantial numbers of immigrants had only primary or lower secondary levels of education, now the norm has shifted to individuals with middle class backgrounds and tertiary qualifications who often have different experiences and expectations of what constitutes appropriate education for their children (Inglis and Wu 1992; Inglis 1999).

By the 1990s another significant shift in immigration policy, again reflecting changes in the economic environment and globalization, was the decision to allow the temporary migration of highly skilled individuals and their families for initial periods of up to four years. Australia has had a long history of resisting temporary migrants who are seen as potential threats to the wages and working conditions of local workers. The change was a response to lobbying by local employers claiming that they were unable to recruit sufficient highly skilled workers locally and, also, by multinational companies wanting to introduce existing employees to manage their Australian branches. One effect of this change is that these new arrivals are also highly skilled, with middle class backgrounds. Although initially limited to four years residence, the temporary entrance visas are renewable and individuals can also apply for permanent residence status if they meet the criteria for selection. The importance of this new entry route is evident from the way in which long term temporary migrants have, since 1999–2000, outnumbered arrivals of new immigrants with permanent residence visas. By allowing long term temporary migration of skilled workers, Australian government policy may be seen as responding to the needs of local employers. It is particularly significant as it marks a major shift from earlier policies based on the assumption that all immigrants would settle permanently in Australia. While the government has long been aware that large numbers of postwar immigrants did not settle permanently, the new policy recognizes that, with increasing population mobility linked to globalization and transnational linkages, there is a need to rethink expectations about the inevitability of permanent settlement.

Changing policies on immigrant settlement and incorporation

Accompanying the major changes in Australian immigration policy over the last three decades there has also been a transformation of policies and institutions relating to immigrant settlement. This change is not just a reflection of the extent of ethnic diversity in the population. In the latter half of the nineteenth century Australia had a population as ethnically diverse as today's. However, the commitment to assimilation by the dominant society, based as it was on an emerging nationalism confident in the superiority of the new society combined with an expectation of permanent settlement, ensured that immigrants had little ability to change existing social relations and institutions. What has altered and allowed the contemporary metamorphosis is a significant change in the expectations surrounding the incorporation of migrants. This has resulted from the interplay of changing patterns of immigration with domestic and, more recently, international objectives. The immediate impetus for abandoning the policy of assimilation and its replacement, after a short-lived policy of integration, by multiculturalism, was the acknowledgement that for many immigrants assimilation was neither an achievable, nor equitable and necessary, goal. By the end of the 1960s, immigrant lobby groups had increased power as a growing number of recent migrants became Australian citizens. They were joined by professionals and community workers from the wider society who were increasingly aware of the difficulties associated with the existing policy and argued that not only was assimilation ineffective as a policy but that it was also often counter-productive. This was because it failed to overcome substantial social disadvantage which in turn created resistance which was harmful to the social consensus and cohesion it was meant to deliver.

In developing multiculturalism as an official policy, rather than a term simply describing the ethnic diversity of a society, Australia has followed an unusual route. Not surprisingly, multiculturalism has often been misunderstood, especially by non-Australians, to refer to more familiar differentialist or pluralist policies where the focus is on setting up parallel institutions catering for specific social groups with the potential for them to operate in an exclusive and exclusionary fashion. The criticism of such pluralist policies is that, while they may be seen as ensuring harmony through separate development, they tend to instability because of difficulties in achieving equality for those participating in minority institutions. They also fail to provide an overarching basis for unifying the diverse groups in society. In contrast to such policies multiculturalism, as developed in Australia, has had at its core an attempt to restructure existing institutions, especially those delivering government services, to cater for diverse cultural practices in a manner which provides equality of access and participation in society. Over nearly three decades as official policy, there have been changes in the emphasis and focus of multiculturalism in response to new circumstances and debates about the level of support which should be given to supporting specific ethnic cultural practices and social organizations.

Among the major milestones was the 1978 Galbally report on programmes for migrant arrivals which proposed that the Commonwealth government should provide funding to support the work of ethnic organizations to assist in migrant settlement (Australia 1978). The 1989 National Agenda for a Multicultural Australia, which was the basic statement of the principles of multiculturalism, made it explicit that multiculturalism was to be a policy not just for immigrants but for all Australians, including the indigenous population (Australia 1989). The Agenda

identified three main rights: social justice and equality, cultural maintenance and, most innovatively, the ability to contribute talents and skills to
national development. Alongside these rights were a series of responsibilities which include a commitment to Australian democracy and
parliamentary structures, accepting the role of English as the national language, respect for the rights of others to maintain their cultures, and
acknowledgement of the equality of women. In highlighting that multiculturalism is beneficial for all Australians, the Agenda also refers to the contribution which multiculturalism can make to the restructuring of the
Australian economy through using the skills, cultural knowledge and
social links of immigrants to facilitate international trade. This contribution of multiculturalism, relabeled as 'productive diversity' has been
actively promoted by the government as a means of involving business and
commerce in the policy. It also reflects the influence of globalization on
policy-makers seeking ways to identify the benefits of multiculturalism not
only for migrants but, also, for the whole economy.

Since the middle of the 1990s official support for multiculturalism has
been muted. In part this reflects a trend among Australian governments
from all political parties to replace free social welfare programmes by
shifting the delivery of services to the private sector and, also, asking those
using the restricted range of government services to pay for them. This
general reduction in government funding and service delivery has
inevitably affected multicultural services. At the same time, key politicians
have been less supportive of multiculturalism. The election of a coalition
government in 1996 brought to power a prime minister, John Howard,
who was distrustful of multiculturalism. One of his first actions was to
close the Office of Multicultural Affairs which had been located in his
department. The council advising the Commonwealth government on
multicultural affairs was also restructured and, in response to a 1999
report entitled *A New Agenda for Multicultural Australia* the government set
up a new body, the Council for Multicultural Australia. Most recently the
government issued a new report *Multicultural Australia: United in Diversity-
Updating the 1999 New Agenda for Multicultural Australia: Strategic Directions
for 2003–2006* (Australia 2003). Despite these initiatives, they have
received little publicity. They also highlight a shift away from an agenda
emphasizing equality of outcomes to an emphasis on harmony within a
more nationalistic framework of Australian multiculturalism; allegedly
inserted to gain the support of the Prime Minister.

A similar lack of support is evident at the state level in New South
Wales, the state with the largest and most diverse population, including
Sydney which is the major destination of immigrants to Australia.
Although the Labor Party premier, Bob Carr, is committed to the development of Sydney as a major global city, he is strongly opposed to the con-
tinuation of large scale settlement by migrants in Sydney because of the
perceived costs and impact on the city's infrastructure and physical

environment. His opposition to migration also is reflected in his approach to incorporation. He thus renamed the Ethnic Affairs Commission as the Community Relations Commission as part of a policy to remove the word 'ethnic' from state government usage. This was because he viewed it as discriminatory and marginalizing individuals labeled as 'ethnic'. However, as critics point out, the police continue to make extensive use of the term 'ethnic' when reporting on criminal activities associated with particular minority groups.

Australian educational responses to migration and ethnic diversity

A common focus of debates about educational responses to diversity is the role of languages in the curriculum and, in particular, the opportunities for language maintenance. This focus reflects the important instrumental and symbolic role of languages which provide access to the wider society and, also, to one's immediate social group. They are also important as a means of transmitting cultural beliefs and practices and may assume a particular symbolic significance when linked to specific ethnic minorities. This importance has been widely recognized historically in efforts to proscribe the use of ethnic minority languages such as Polish and Kurdish. Certainly, in the Australian case, changes in the role of languages in the curriculum constitute a litmus test indicating key changes in the way the educational challenges and issues are perceived and responded to. However, the Australian educational responses to multiculturalism, globalization and transnationalism go beyond language maintenance to other areas of the curriculum: its content, methods of pedagogy and assessment. They also have extended outside the classroom and formal curriculum to include activities involving parents and the local community. Indeed, one of the distinctive features of Australian educational responses is the extent to which they have emphasized the need to adopt what is often referred to as a 'whole school' approach to ethnic diversity. In doing so, they are highlighting the need to overcome inequality in educational attainment among children from minority backgrounds while at the same time supporting cultural maintenance and the ability to participate in the wider society. By including responses involving the whole student population and not just those from minority backgrounds, they also are acknowledging that the majority population play a critical role in any change.

Although educational policy is a matter for each of the six individual Australian states and two territories, the Commonwealth government through its allocation of educational funding is able to play a significant part in influencing educational policy and practice. There is also substantial cooperation between the states and the Commonwealth on curriculum matters, including the development of national curriculum and resource materials for Italian, Greek, Turkish and other languages. For this reason, although specific examples in this chapter will often be drawn from developments in New South Wales, the state with the largest and most diverse school population, broad similarities characterize the situation in other states.

In tracing the steps which led to the adoption of a policy of multiculturalism in Australia, Jean Martin has shown how the dominance of an ideology of immigrant assimilation carried within it the denial that any specific programmes or assistance were needed to cater for them in the education system (Martin 1978). By the end of the 1960s teachers were aware of a very different reality in their classrooms which were receiving an increasing number of children with no, or limited, English. The results were difficulties for the teachers, as well as for the students. Calls for action to overcome the communication problems led to the setting up of a pilot programme in English (the Child Migrant Education Programme). Its success led to its expansion in 1971 throughout Australia with funding being provided by the national government (Martin 1978). Initially it was thought that English as a Second Language (ESL) would only be needed for a short period until there was a change in the mix of the immigrant population. Experience soon showed that this was unrealistic and that there was also a need for specialist teaching for Australian born children described as second and third phase learners. While the ESL programmes may be viewed as 'assimilationist', competency in English is the foundation for educational and social attainment and mobility in Australian society. This explains the support they received from ethnic community groups as well as educators in 1986 when the Commonwealth government was planning to end their funding as part of an extensive range of reductions in government spending. As a result, ESL remains a cornerstone of all educational responses to student diversity to this day. Over time, the delivery of ESL programmes has become increasingly sophisticated with the development of curriculum and resources and the training of specialist teachers; a far cry from the first years when school broom cupboards and English language baby's books were used to teach students. The methods of delivery of ESL have also widened to include Intensive Language Centres where new arrivals of secondary school age attend special schools to learn English. Here they gain intensive exposure to English while also being introduced to the local curriculum and culture as a preparation for their subsequent transfer back to the regular schools where they can then be assisted by specialist ESL teachers.

The second major Australian response involved an expansion of the range of languages offered in the school curriculum. The driving force in this expansion of language teaching from the traditional languages offered in the curriculum: Latin, French, German, Indonesian, Italian and Japanese, came from ethnic community groups, linguists and language teachers. There were varying motivations at work amongst those lobbying for widening the language curriculum. Maintenance of cultural heritage and ability to communicate with family and friends were important among ethnic community lobbyists. Linguists and educators argued for the academic gains associated with access to the mother tongue and knowledge of a second language. Access to classes in the mother tongue were also seen as contributing to social justice and laying the basis for improving cultural understanding between diverse ethnic groups. There was also active lobbying by those concerned with maintaining and developing the nation's linguistic resources for economic and defence purposes. Throughout the 1980s, and culminating in the 1987 Lo Bianco Report (*National Policy on Languages*), those seeking to extend Commonwealth support for language teaching were divided about which languages should be given priority (Lo Bianco 1987). However, by the late 1970s in Sydney, students were already able to study an increased range of languages, if not in their own schools, at least in the Saturday School of Languages which was established to cater for students whose schools did not offer specific languages as examination subjects. At that time the government's Saturday School of Languages taught 25 languages ranging from Arabic and Armenian to Ukrainian and Vietnamese. Another response by the state government to the problems of providing language classes for all languages represented in often very diverse school populations was to fund after-hours language classes run by ethnic community groups. Practical issues associated with this expansion of opportunities to learn languages other than English included preparation of curriculum and resource materials relevant to the local, Australian setting and obtaining qualified teachers. Although exchanges were initiated with government school systems overseas, the exchanges were limited to individual curriculum consultants rather than classroom language teachers. Among the immigrant population there were often overseas trained teachers but little effort went into providing them with 'bridging' and upgrading courses to allow them to work effectively in the local schools where the school culture and teacher's role was often different from that with which they were familiar. In 1979 only 7 per cent of teachers had overseas training, the majority from English speaking countries and this figure increased only slightly by 1989 (Inglis and Philps 1995).

One common response to linguistic diversity which has been largely ignored in Australia is the provision of bilingual education. The major reason cited by educators for this omission are difficulties associated with developing bilingual programmes in schools with extremely diverse linguistic groups. In New South Wales, the most extensive effort has been the community language programme which began in 1981 with the appointment of 22 'specialist' teachers to primary schools. The outcome of active lobbying by ethnic groups, the programme was hurriedly initiated over the two month summer holiday, although in some languages the new teachers were able to use materials which had been developed by a specialist multicultural education group in the state's Department of Education. The programme still continues and provides, in some cases, a transitional bilingual programme.

In addition to the ESL and Languages other than English (LOTE) programmes which primarily target children from non-English-speaking backgrounds, teachers and schools also developed other responses to ethnic diversity involving non-language areas of the curriculum. All Australian schools operate in a system where external examinations at the end of secondary school determine entry to university. In primary schools there is also a growing number of 'achievement' tests to assess literacy, numeracy and, most recently, computer skills. A common concern is that the existence of external examinations and tests tied to a common curriculum severely restricts the ability of teachers to be innovative. In Australia, the organization of primary schools with a single classroom teacher has made the adoption of cross-curriculum perspectives, which are a significant element in multicultural education, far easier to achieve than in secondary schools. Among the initiatives being undertaken by individual primary teachers and schools since the 1970s were activities tracing family history and origins and discussing family celebrations and rituals. These were intended to make students aware of the diverse backgrounds of their classmates and were part of a wider effort to promote skills in intercultural contact and communication. While often criticized as simplifying and essentializing culture by focusing on folk traditions such as singing, dancing and food, this 'polka, pasta and pavlova' approach, as it has sometimes been labelled, remains popular with both teachers and families who became active participants in school functions such as ethnic food fairs and international concerts.

At the secondary level where the curriculum is more constrained by external examinations, there have been innovations to include material reflecting non-Anglo-Celtic traditions and regions in subject areas including English literature, geography, history, music and art. New examination subjects such as comparative religion have been introduced which allow students to study different religious traditions. This is particularly popular in the private schools often operated by Catholic and other religious denominations. In Australia, government schools are officially free, compulsory and secular which means that religious instruction is not provided by teachers. However, a period is set aside one morning a week when outside instructors can come in to the school to provide religious instruction for children whose parents have agreed to this. The fact that Australia is still predominantly a Christian society means that the Christian religious calendar guides the rhythm of the school year and is reflected in end of year nativity plays and carols which from time to time annoy non-religious or non-Christian parents. However, the debates over the wearing of the head scarf by Muslim girls, so common in France and other countries, has not become a major issue in Australian schools. In part this is because schools require students to wear a school uniform and principals can specify the type of head scarf which is part of the uniform for students wishing to wear one. This response reflects how, in Australia, the secular status of the school depends on its organization and actions rather than on imposing secularism on students and requiring that they do not display religious symbols such as crosses, scarves, skull caps and turbans. It also indicates how concerns about arranged marriages, especially involving girls from Islamic backgrounds, is less of a social issue. Hence the wearing of a head scarf does not immediately raise concerns among feminists aware that many Muslim women have argued for positive advantages associated with wearing a veil.

In addition to curriculum changes, schools have adopted a range of strategies, including the use of interpreters and translating schools' messages and documents into the languages of the local community, to improve communication with parents. In doing so, they are seeking to overcome barriers associated with the way contemporary Australian schools often have very different teaching methods, homework and disciplinary policies to those familiar to many immigrant parents. Without adequate communication schools are aware there can be major misunderstandings about the nature of the school and the role of its teachers.

'Migrant education' was the term initially used in the early 1970s to describe the educational responses involving ESL and mother tongue languages teaching. However, as the range of responses increased and targeted children from the mainstream population as well as immigrants, it was replaced in the 1980s with the more encompassing term 'multicultural' education. By then, New South Wales and other states had adopted multicultural education policies which included these wide-ranging strategies (New South Wales Department of Education 1983). These policies had been formulated in a period when there was increasing diversity in the origins of the immigrant population and they were very much focusing on ensuring that the process of settlement, based on permanent settlement in Australia, would be harmonious and not cause inequality or social conflict.

By the 1990s, there had been few changes in the range of educational responses developed 20 years earlier despite significant changes in Australia's patterns of immigration. The major innovation in the early 1990s were policies to address racism in schools and their communities. The absence of such responses from earlier policies reflected a belief that an emphasis on improving intercultural communication and educational equity would be adequate. However, as acknowledged in the 1995 NSW Whole School Antiracism Project, there was a growing recognition that racism was not confined to the school but also existed in the wider society thus requiring the development of new school responses to address it (New South Wales Department of Education 1995). Anti-racism responses continue to be very important given the support received by the populist Pauline Hanson One Nation Party for its anti-immigration, anti-Asian and anti-Indigenous policies in the late 1990s. More recently, since 11 September 2001 and the declaration by the US and its allies of the war on terrorism, Australian Muslims have also become targets for racism in the schools and elsewhere. While this racism initially had few direct links to globalization and transnationalism, many supporters of Pauline Hanson were from rural communities and outer suburban areas adversely affected by the restructuring of the Australian economy and changing government welfare policies frequently promoted as necessary to more effectively meet the challenges of globalization. The focus of their concerns related to the costs believed to be incurred in programmes catering for the indigenous and immigrant population whom they also saw as not sharing common cultural values and practices linked to Australian identity. Since the events of 11 September the emphasis on international terrorist networks and government responses to terrorism have, however, highlighted how globalization and transnationalism can amplify what had hitherto been essentially domestically-based racist responses.

The issue of Australian identity and consequent entitlement to full social citizenship is at the heart of the debate about the characteristics of an 'Australian'. When assimilation was the ideological model guiding migrant incorporation the characteristics of an 'Australian' may have seemed obvious even if, in practice, the depiction of a rugged bushman, loyal to his mates and friends, was atypical of the majority of the population, including women, who lived in large cities. With the shift to multiculturalism the characteristics of an 'Australian' became even more problematic. While this issue was not directly addressed within the context of multicultural education, the celebration of the bicentenary of European settlement in 1988 and the 2001 celebration of the formation of the Commonwealth of Australia through the federation of the six former British colonies led to educators' involvement in the public debate about the nature of Australian society and identity. The immediate educational response was the development of resource materials to use in teaching about citizenship and civics education. Much of this material focused on transmitting information about Australian political structures and the duties of a good citizen to participate in elections and other activities linked to being an 'active' citizen. It thus sidestepped the issue of whether individuals from ethnic minority backgrounds were included and, if so, how they were represented within discussions of Australianness. In these discussions more attention has been paid to the place of the Indigenous population than to those of immigrant backgrounds reflecting the unsettled political and social issues surrounding their dispossession following European settlement.

The nature of Australian identity has also been addressed in history curriculum where there have been moves to introduce Indigenous perspectives to the curriculum based on reinterpretations of the history of European settlement. National identity has also been addressed where, as in New South Wales, history syllabi emphasize the participation of Australian and New Zealand Army Corps (ANZAC) soldiers in the unsuccessful British-led Gallipoli campaign in World War One. This military campaign, which is the basis of what is called the ANZAC tradition, has gained increasing prominence among historians arguing that it constituted a defining moment in the development of an independent Australian national identity. An interesting feature in the promotion of this tradition is that it involves a positive treatment of the opposing Turkish forces under Kemal Ataturk who defeated those led by British commanders who are depicted negatively by their former colonial subjects. The unintended consequence of this depiction of the ANZAC tradition is that it provides a valued place for Turkish Australians, and by extension others from non-British background, in the development of contemporary Australia.

Apart from the important emphasis on anti-racism since the 1990s, much of the focus on multicultural education has been concerned with the actual delivery of material rather than on the development of new approaches. The use of the internet and other new technologies to reach and involve students growing up with television and the internet is obviously important. An example which highlights the value of the new technology is the nationally developed Racism No Way programme (www.racismnoway.com).

Despite the importance of these initiatives, by the 1990s, many stakeholders with an interest in multicultural education were concerned that it had largely disappeared off the policy-making agenda. Certainly there were new areas related to computerization, emerging technologies, physical and health education which were attracting funding and support when spending on education and the availability of educational resources were, in general, declining. However, at the same time there was also a sense of malaise surrounding multicultural education. This was not simply an outcome of the effective institutionalization of multicultural education programmes but involved the sense that multicultural education has lost its ability to be innovative and to respond to new developments. Certainly an evaluation of multicultural education in the middle of the 1990s concluded that there was a need to revisit multicultural education policy and redefine it to include a variety of new developments such as:

- the impact of the changing links between permanent and temporary migration;
- the insights to be gained from culturally inclusive and cultural learning approaches;
- a more global perspective to deflect racist and ethnonationalist undertones;

- imagining the nation as a pluralistic entity and the impetus for civics education;
- the Aboriginal component of Australian history (Cahill 1996).

Many of these developments are closely linked to globalization and, indeed, Cahill was arguing that there was a need to promote a more global perspective within Australian multicultural education (Cahill 1996). This concern to restructure multicultural education involves extending its focus from the domestic situation of ethnic minorities to an external, international focus which can better respond to the circumstances of Australian students while at the same time preparing them with skills which would allow them to live and work in other countries. This shift, in addition to recognizing the potential value of many of the areas of domestic multicultural education, including knowledge of languages other than English and, also, the ability to participate effectively in intercultural communication, also notes the potential change in the future educational and occupational paths of students which would take them overseas.

Indeed, soon afterwards, Victoria and New South Wales, the two states with the largest and most diverse immigrant populations, moved towards changing their multicultural education policies in terms which specifically acknowledged the need to take account of globalization in reformulating their multicultural educational policies. The revised 1997 Victorian multicultural policy thus spoke of the need to develop 'an awareness of the reality of the global village and national interdependence in areas of trade, finance, labour, politics and communications, and that the development of international understanding and cooperation is essential' (Victoria Department of Education 1997). The 1998 draft revision of the New South Wales multicultural policy statement made even more explicit the links between multicultural education and globalization.

> Multicultural education ... seeks to equip all students with the knowledge, skills and values needed to live, learn and work successfully as citizens in a culturally diverse world. Globalization, brought about by a rapidly increasing economic interdependence among all nations, has broadened the context and scope of education and training to include international perspectives and an increased emphasis on the skills and understandings necessary to function in diverse social and cultural environments.
>
> (NSW Department of Education and Training 1998: 4)[1]

Despite both policies addressing issues related to globalization, there is a somewhat surprising lack of prominence given to language maintenance. Indeed, since the 1990s one of the most striking features of responses to immigration and ethnic diversity in Australia has been the waning emphasis on language maintenance programmes and the teaching of languages other than English. This is despite the 1987 adoption of *The National Languages Policy*, and moves to ensure that all Australian children would study a language other than English for the major part of their schooling. However, in the early 1990s, the publication of the Commonwealth's white paper entitled *A National Language Policy* affirmed the Commonwealth government's focus on ensuring literacy in English. Since then, there has been little innovation or advance in access to learning languages other than English. In the Northern Territory, which has a substantial Indigenous population, funding was removed from bilingual programmes for teaching Indigenous languages. Most recently, the Commonwealth government has cut funding to support the teaching of Asian languages. While many language lobbyists linked to ethnic communities were concerned about what they viewed as the privileged status given to Asian languages such as Japanese because of their economic significance, languages such as Chinese and Vietnamese are also spoken by substantial sections of Australia's population. At the tertiary level, cuts to university funding have adversely affected many language departments which are amongst the most expensive non-science departments to operate. As a result, there have been many closures and amalgamations which negatively effect training opportunities for future teachers. Yet, at the same time, in Sydney, which has the most diverse language school population of any Australian city (Chinese and Arabic are the two most frequently languages spoken in the home after English), it is extremely difficult to find sufficient schools with language programmes able to supervise and offer practice teaching opportunities to trainee teachers in non-English language curriculum areas. A potential explanation for this lack of language classes in schools is that principals are discouraging student enrolments in languages, perhaps with the idea that students can always study languages at the Saturday School of Languages. However, this is too simple an explanation as it fails to take account of changing demand for language maintenance by those from non-English-speaking backgrounds.

In 2001, 24.4 per cent of all enrolments in NSW government schools were of students who were identified on the basis of their home language as being from non-English speaking backgrounds. This was an increase from the previous year when 23.7 per cent of all students were from non-English-speaking backgrounds. The major languages represented in the school population were Chinese (16.9 per cent), Arabic (14.8 per cent) and Vietnamese (6.1 per cent). Languages with a longer established population such as Greek (4.7 per cent) and Italian (4.2 per cent) were less represented indicating that in many of these families English had replaced the 'mother' tongue in the home. If parents were to emphasize the importance of language maintenance for their children it would be expected that this would be reflected in an increasing number of candidates sitting for languages at the end of school examinations. However, this has not been the case, with steadily falling numbers of candidates for the end of school examinations in languages other than English. This pattern suggests that immigrant parents may be placing less emphasis on their children studying their 'mother' tongue in the mainstream school system. Certainly an evaluation of multicultural education programmes in the mid-1990s found that students from non-English-speaking backgrounds showed little interest in studying their mother tongue unless there were instrumental advantages related to occupational objectives or good marks in the end of school examinations (Cahill 1996).

Consistent with this explanation for falling enrolments in languages other than English is that, in contrast to the 1970s, ethnic community groups have not been actively lobbying government for more resources to be put into the learning of languages other than English or, indeed, into other areas including ESL and across-the-curriculum multicultural educa-tion. This is somewhat surprising given that language learning has in the past been considered a key factor in long term cultural maintenance. At the same time language learning opportunities and resources remain scarce for more recently arrived or smaller language groups. However, in the 2001 national elections, when a group of prominent language scholars and educators organized the Australian Alliance for Languages to lobby politicians their initial documents cited only the following, not always most influential ethnic community groups, among their supporters:

- Applied Linguistics Association of Australia;
- Australian Council for Adult Literacy;
- Australian Linguistics Society;
- Ethnic Communities Council of Victoria;
- Federation Internationale des Professeurs de Langues Vivantes;
- Federation of Aboriginal and Torres Strait Islander Languages;
- Institute for Slovenian Studies of Victoria;
- National Ethnic and Multicultural Broadcasters' Council;
- Maltese Language School of Adelaide.

What was also noteworthy in the documents of this group is that they con-tinued with the distinction between 'community' languages (which refer to languages of immigrant groups whose members are the targeted group of learners) and 'foreign' languages, with priority given to community lan-guages. However, much of the emphasis in their documents was on the need to revive and support the teaching in schools of a range of indigen-ous languages as well as better provision for the teaching of Auslan – the Australian Sign Language for the Deaf. Significantly, a decade earlier, the same group of stakeholders had worked closely with the major, ethnic community associations to develop the National Languages Policy which argued strongly for more educational resources to be devoted to a number of other languages – from Asia and Europe. The absence of such a strong statement in 2001 suggests that the agenda for ethnic communities and recent immigrants concerning the role of languages other than English in the curriculum may have changed significantly since the 1970s.

For many immigrants to Australia the opportunity for their children to learn their mother tongue in the regular school is no longer seen as a major priority. The major reason for this diminished demand for mother tongue languages relates to changes within the ethnic communities. On the one hand there has been the emergence in the longer established groups of an Australian born second generation. Among the more recent immigrant groups there is also a high proportion of well-educated, English-speaking immigrants who may view a command of English and a 'solid' education in key subjects such as sciences as a more important educational objective for ensuring their children's future. For these families, cultural capital is very important but is defined in different ways to earlier generations of often less educated immigrants. In this they may be influenced by how much their own careers have been based upon the need to be fluent in English, not least because of its status as an international language. At the same time they are aware that to gain access to elite Australian and international universities the main criterion is a high mark in the end of school examinations rather than knowledge of a mother tongue. They and their children often place greater emphasis on subjects which are viewed as more 'relevant' for future careers or success in the end of school examinations (Cahill 1996). This is not to say they view languages as unimportant but, rather, that they see other ways than the public education system for their children to learn their mother tongue or other languages. These may include private instruction and home usage of the language, attendance at out of school classes or visits and study trips overseas. Such views are instrumental and less concerned with the significance of the mother tongue for identity and cultural maintenance. Indeed their emphasis may be on other areas of cultural and social life as embodying their own and their children's ties with their own family and an ethnic identity.

Conclusion

During the 1970s Australian education underwent a major transformation in the way it catered for children from immigrant non-English-speaking backgrounds. While lobby groups played an important role in this transformation, it was also facilitated by more extensive changes in educational ideology relating to giving greater priority to the needs of individual children and overcoming educational disadvantage. Many of the educational changes which Australian schools began to implement from the 1970s to cater for immigrant children from non-English-speaking backgrounds are found in other educational systems. What is more unusual about the Australian responses is that they have also specifically identified the need to use education as a means of changing the way the entire school population responds to ethnic diversity. While there has been a reasonable level of success in achieving this objective, educators are still working out how best to respond to the changing patterns of immigration in the 1980s and 1990s which have involved increasing numbers of well-educated middle class permanent and temporary migrants. One example is the way the apparently lower priority given by these parents to their children learning their mother tongue in the schools is calling into question many of the educators' long-held assumptions about what constitute appropriate educational responses to assist in cultural maintenance, especially in a society with a commitment to cultural diversity. There is also the practical challenge of how to respond to the needs of these newer types of immigrants while maintaining programmes addressing the needs of the continuing immigration of individuals, often from refugee backgrounds, who can benefit from existing programmes for support and incorporation. All of these are issues concerning the way Australian education can promote equitable and harmonious domestic incorporation of immigrants. However, one of the key challenges posed by globalization is how to prepare students to live as international citizens. In some educational systems, education for cultural diversity (sometimes referred to as 'global multiculturalism') has been understood to refer primarily to this international dimension while ignoring the need to focus on internal diversity within their own population (Braslavsky 2003). A continuing challenge for Australian educators will be to develop ways in which the programmes already developed for addressing internal cultural diversity can be extended to international cultural diversity without jeopardising their achievements in the context of domestic diversity.

Note

1 This revision of the NSW policy, although widely circulated, has never actually been adopted despite expectations that it would be announced by the state government in time for the 1999 state election which it subsequently won. The reasons for this failure to update the existing 1983 policy are unclear but suggest that the government, if not educators, lacks interest in revising multicultural education to take account of recent changes in Australian society.

References

Australia (1978) *Review of Post Arrival Programs and Services to Migrants (Galbally Report)*, Canberra: AGPS.

Australia (1989) *National Agenda for a Multicultural Australia*, Canberra: AGPS.

Australia (2003) *Multicultural Australia: United in Diversity-Updating the 1999 New Agenda for Multicultural Australia: Strategic Directions for 2003–2006*, Canberra: AGPS.

Braslavsky, C. (2003) *Payload and Accessories: The Context of Education*, Policy Forum on Planning for Diversity: Education in Multiethnic and Multicultural Societies, Paris: International Institute for Educational Planning.

Cahill, D. (1996) *Immigration and Schooling in the 1990s*, Canberra: Department of Immigration and Multicultural Affairs.

Inglis, C. (1999) 'Middle class migration: new considerations in research and policy', in G. Hage and R. Couch (eds) *Future of Australian Multiculturalism: Reflections on the Twentieth Anniversary of Jean Martin's 'The Migrant Presence'*, Sydney: RIHSS, University of Sydney: 45–63.

Inglis, C. and Philps. R. (1995) *Teachers in the Sun: The Impact of Immigrant Teachers in the Workforce*, Canberra: AGPS.

Inglis, C. and Wu, C.-T. (1992) 'The "new" migration of Asian skills and capital to Australia', in C. Inglis, G. Gunasekaran, G. Sullivan and C.-T. Wu (eds) *Asians in Australia: The Dynamics of Migration and Settlement*, Singapore: Institute of Southeast Asian Studies: 193–230.

Lo Bianco, J. (1987) *National Policy on Languages*, Canberra: AGPS.

Martin, J. I. (1978) *The Migrant Presence: Australian Responses 1947–1977*, Hornsby, Australia: George Allen & Unwin.

New South Wales Department of Education (1983) *Multicultural Education Policy Statement*, Sydney: NSW Department of Education.

New South Wales Department of Education (1995) *Whole School Anti-Racism Project*, Sydney: NSW Department of Education.

New South Wales Department of Education and Training (1998) *Learning in a Culturally Diverse Society: The Multicultural Education and Training Policy for New South Wales (draft)*, Sydney: Multicultural Programs Unit, NSW Department of Education and Training

Racism No Way, (www.racismnoway.com, 2002.

Victoria Department of Education (1997) *Multicultural Policy for Victorian Schools*, Melbourne: Department of Education, MACLOTE & ESL.

Index

A page number followed by a '*t*' indicates a reference to a table; a page number followed by an '*n*' indicates a reference to a footnote.